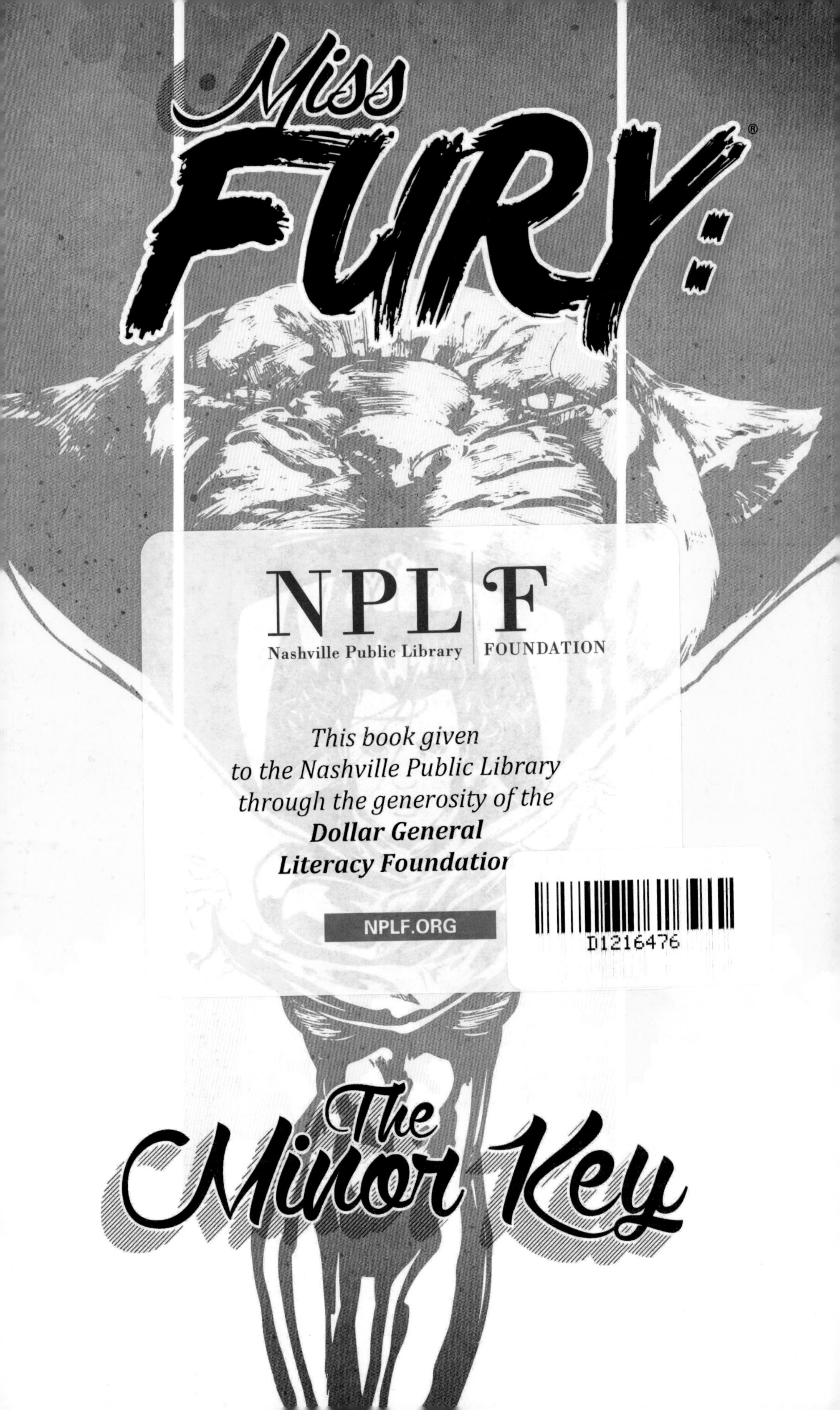
Miss
FURY®:
The
Minor Key

Miss FURY: The Minor Key

WRITTEN BY
CORINNA BECHKO

ILLUSTRATED BY
JONATHAN LAU

COLORED BY
VINICIUS ANDRADE

LETTERED BY
SIMON BOWLAND

COVERS BY
TULA LOTAY & JONATHAN LAU with IVAN NUNES

COLLECTION DESIGN BY
CATHLEEN HEARD

DYNAMITE 🅕 📷 🇹 🐦 YouTube

Online at www.DYNAMITE.com
On Facebook /Dynamitecomics
On Instagram /Dynamitecomics
On Tumblr dynamitecomics.tumblr.com
On Twitter @dynamitecomics
On YouTube /Dynamitecomics

Nick Barrucci, CEO / Publisher
Juan Collado, President / COO

Joe Rybandt, Executive Editor
Matt Idelson, Senior Editor
Anthony Marques, Assistant Editor
Kevin Ketner, Editorial Assistant

Jason Ullmeyer, Art Director
Geoff Harkins, Senior Graphic Designer
Cathleen Heard, Graphic Designer
Alexis Persson, Production Artist

Chris Caniano, Digital Associate
Rachel Kilbury, Digital Assistant

Brandon Dante Primavera, V.P. of IT and Operations
Rich Young, Director of Business Development

Alan Payne, V.P. of Sales and Marketing
Keith Davidsen, Marketing Director
Pat O'Connell, Sales Manager

For information regarding press, media rights, foreign rights, licensi
promotions, and advertising e-mail: marketing@dynamite.com

ISBN-10: 1-5241-0216-4
ISBN-13: 978-1-5241-0216-6

First Printing
10 9 8 7 6 5 4 3 2 1

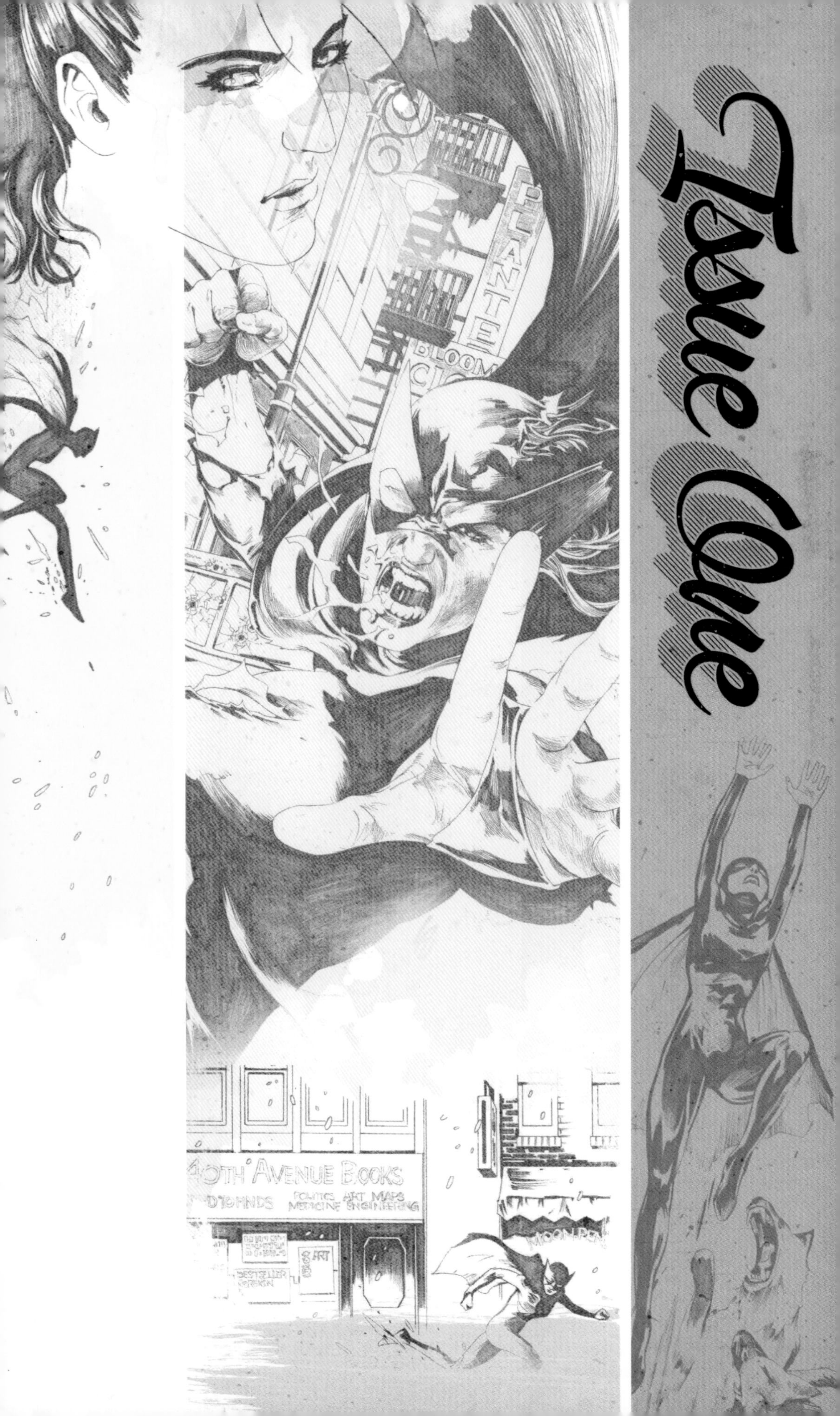
Issue One
PLANTE
BLOOM
40TH AVENUE BOOKS
POLITICS ART MAPS
MEDICINE ENGINEERING
BESTSELLER
ART

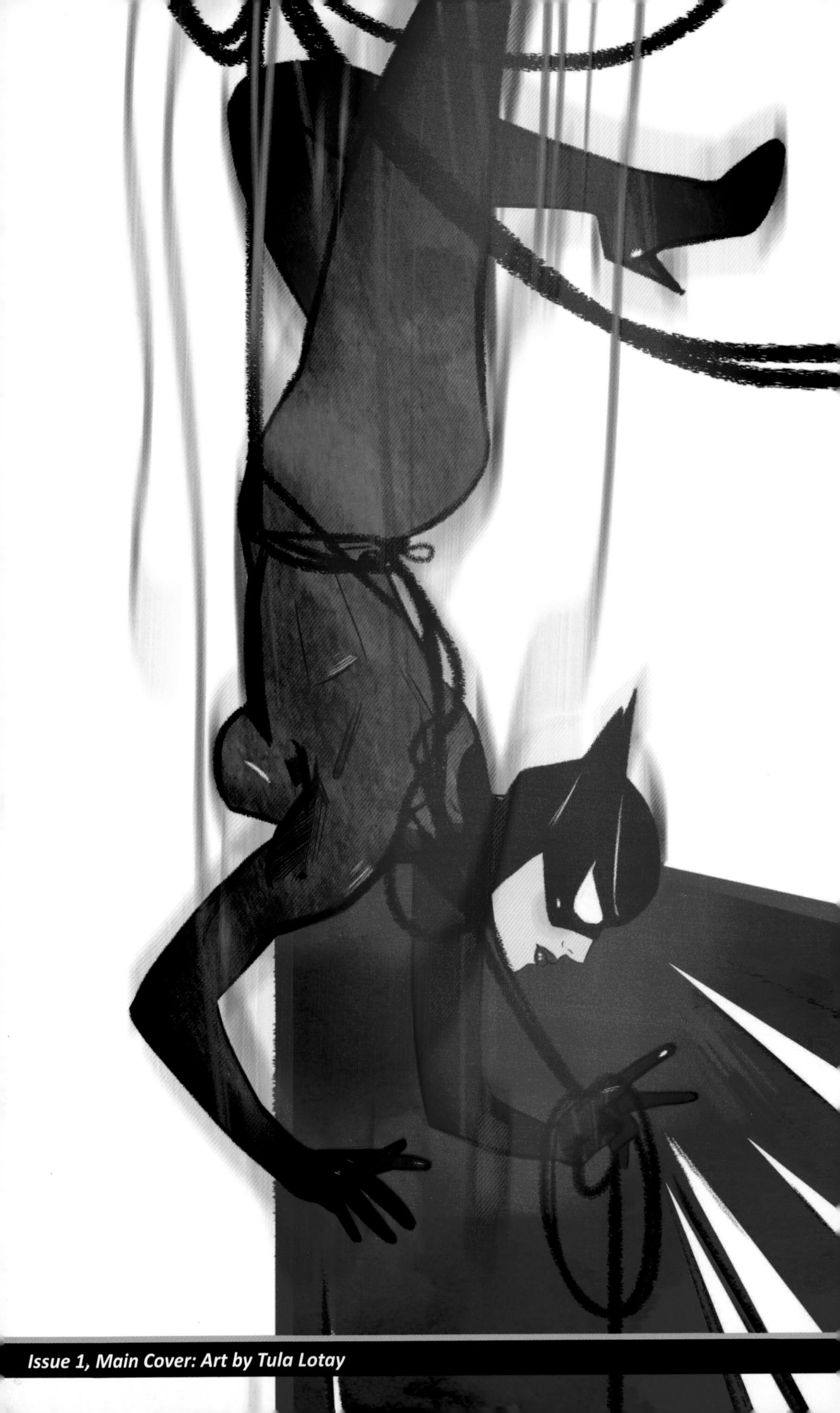

Issue 1, Main Cover: Art by Tula Lotay

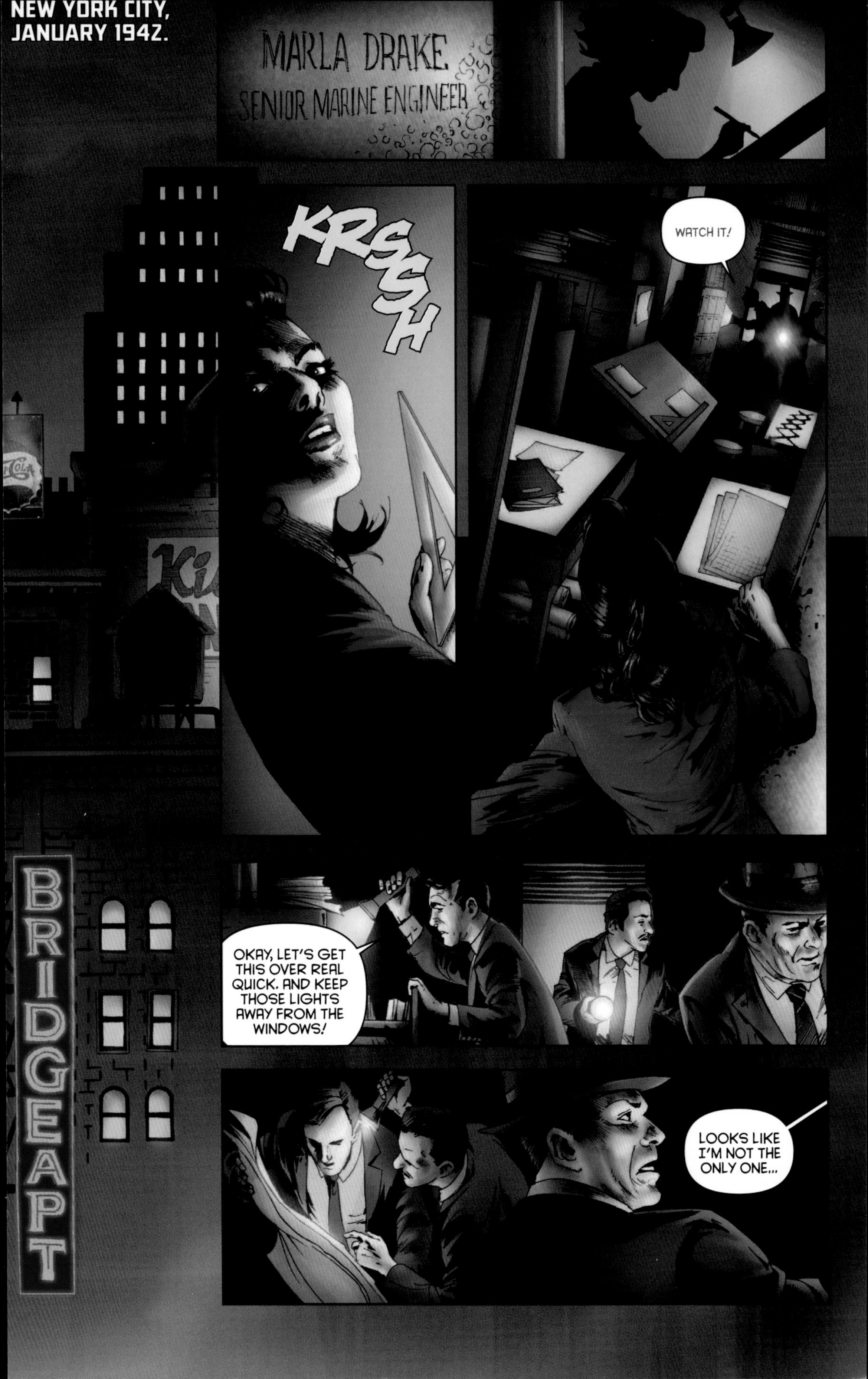
NEW YORK CITY, JANUARY 1942.
MARLA DRAKE
SENIOR MARINE ENGINEER
KRSSH
WATCH IT!
BRIDGEAPT
OKAY, LET'S GET THIS OVER REAL QUICK. AND KEEP THOSE LIGHTS AWAY FROM THE WINDOWS!
LOOKS LIKE I'M NOT THE ONLY ONE...

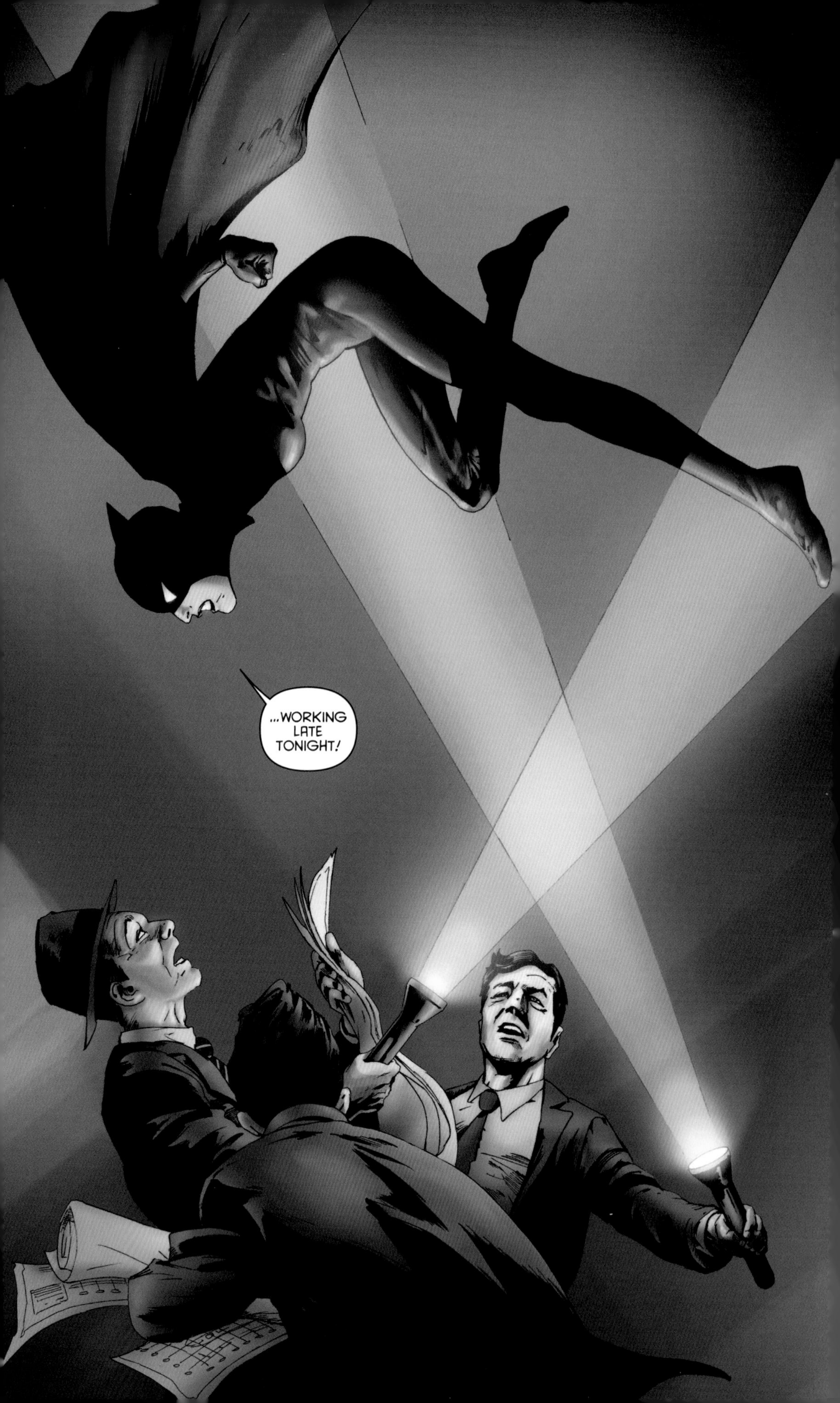
...WORKING LATE TONIGHT!

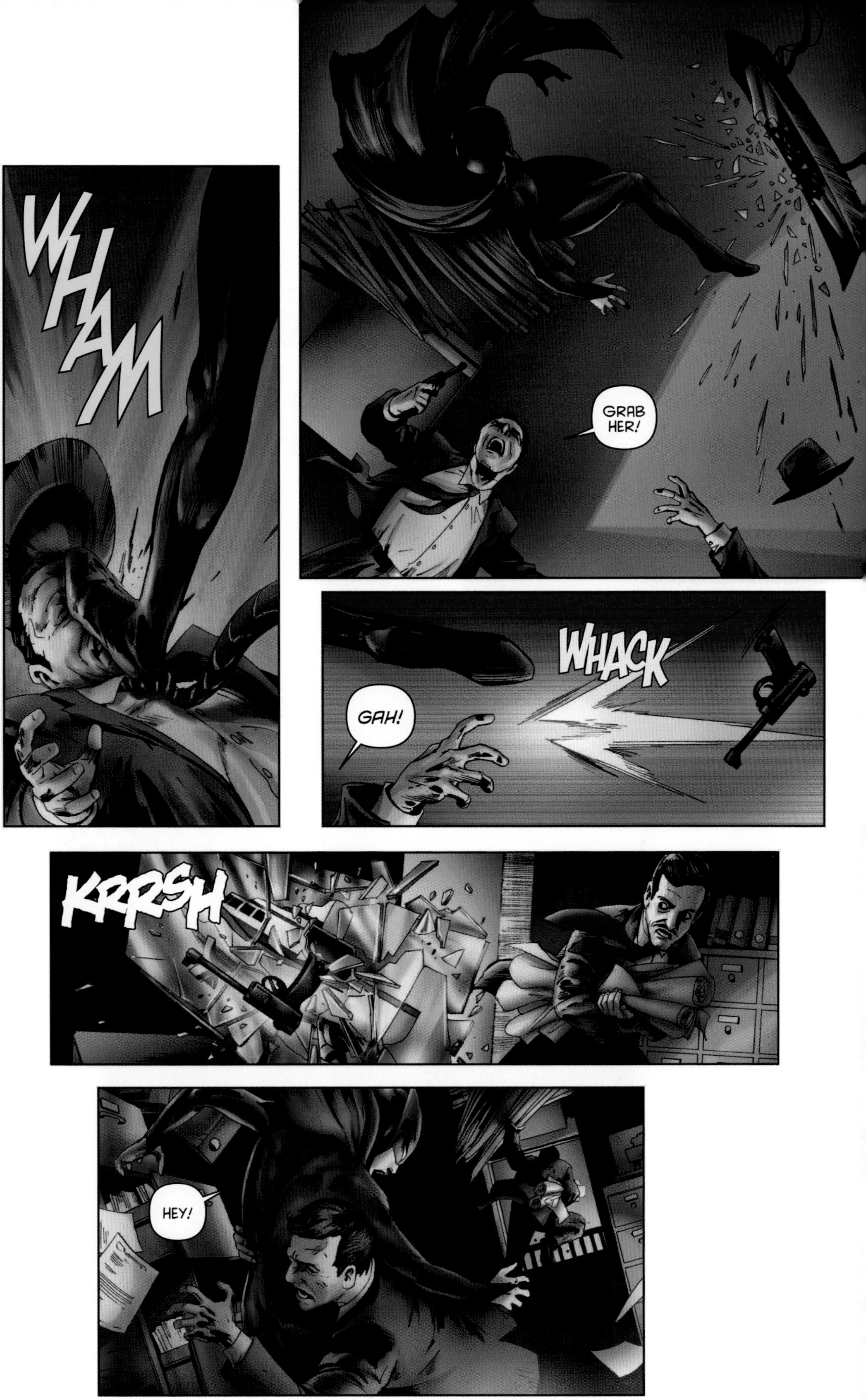
WHAM
GRAB HER!
WHACK
GAH!
KRRSH
HEY!

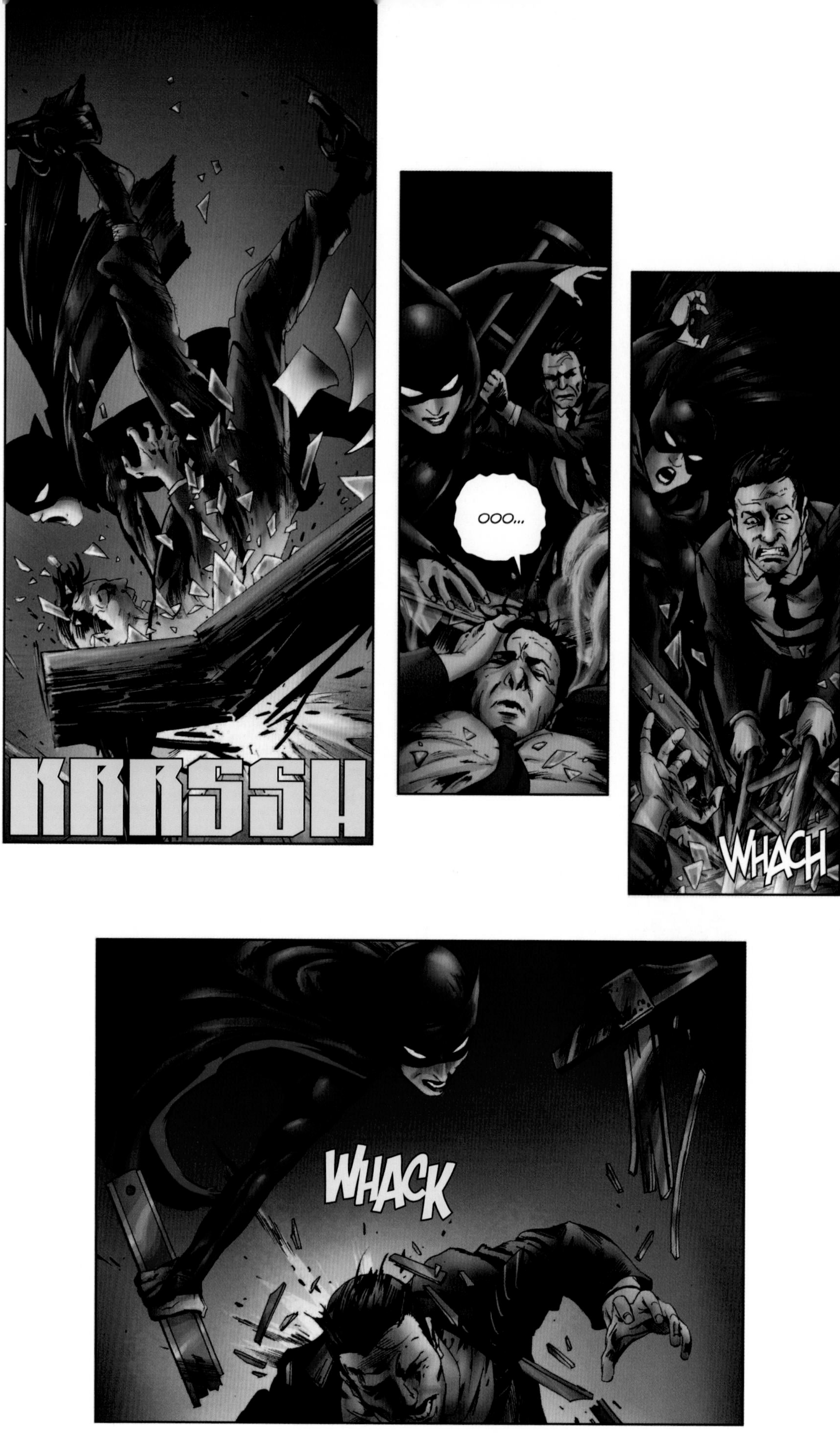
KRRSSH
OOO...
WHACH
WHACK

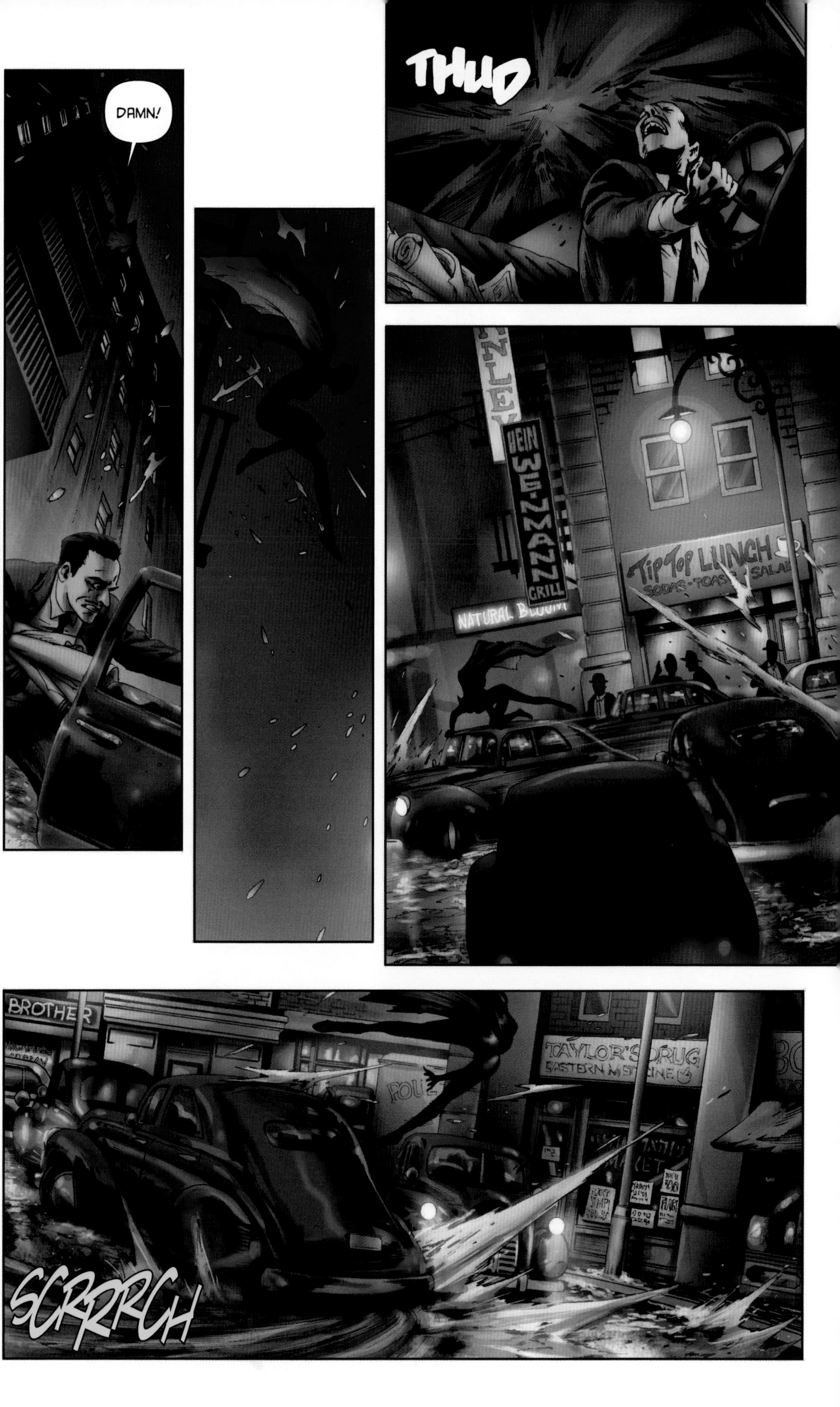
DAMN!
THUD
GRILL
TIP TOP LUNCH
NATURAL BLOOM
BROTHER
TAYLOR'S DRUG
SCRRRCH

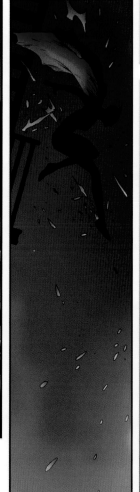

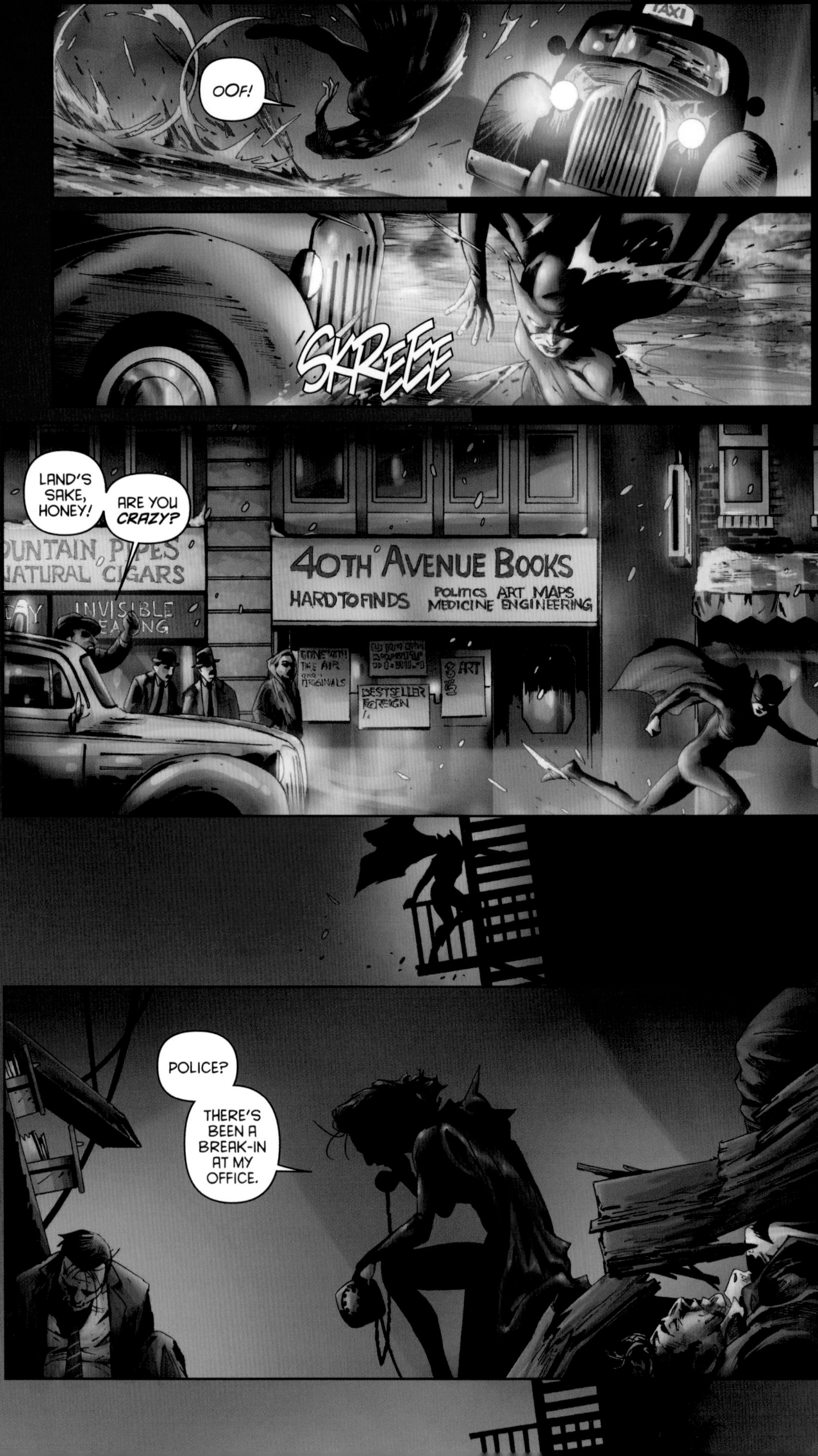
TAXI
OOF!
SKREEEE
LAND'S SAKE, HONEY!
ARE YOU CRAZY?
40TH AVENUE BOOKS
HARD TO FINDS
POLITICS ART MAPS
MEDICINE ENGINEERING
POLICE?
THERE'S BEEN A BREAK-IN AT MY OFFICE.

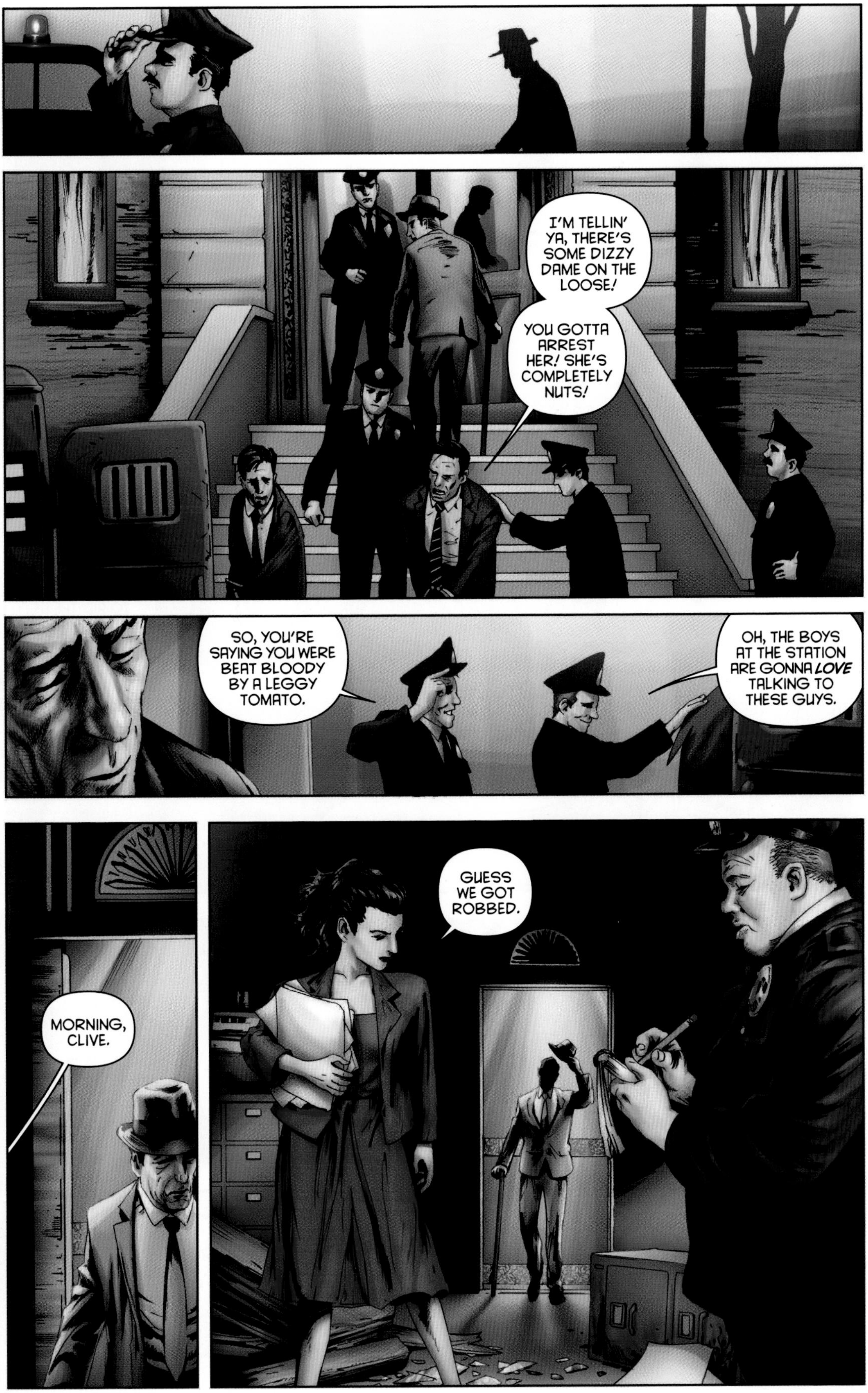
I'M TELLIN' YA, THERE'S SOME DIZZY DAME ON THE LOOSE!
YOU GOTTA ARREST HER! SHE'S COMPLETELY NUTS!
SO, YOU'RE SAYING YOU WERE BEAT BLOODY BY A LEGGY TOMATO.
OH, THE BOYS AT THE STATION ARE GONNA *LOVE* TALKING TO THESE GUYS.
MORNING, CLIVE.
GUESS WE GOT ROBBED.

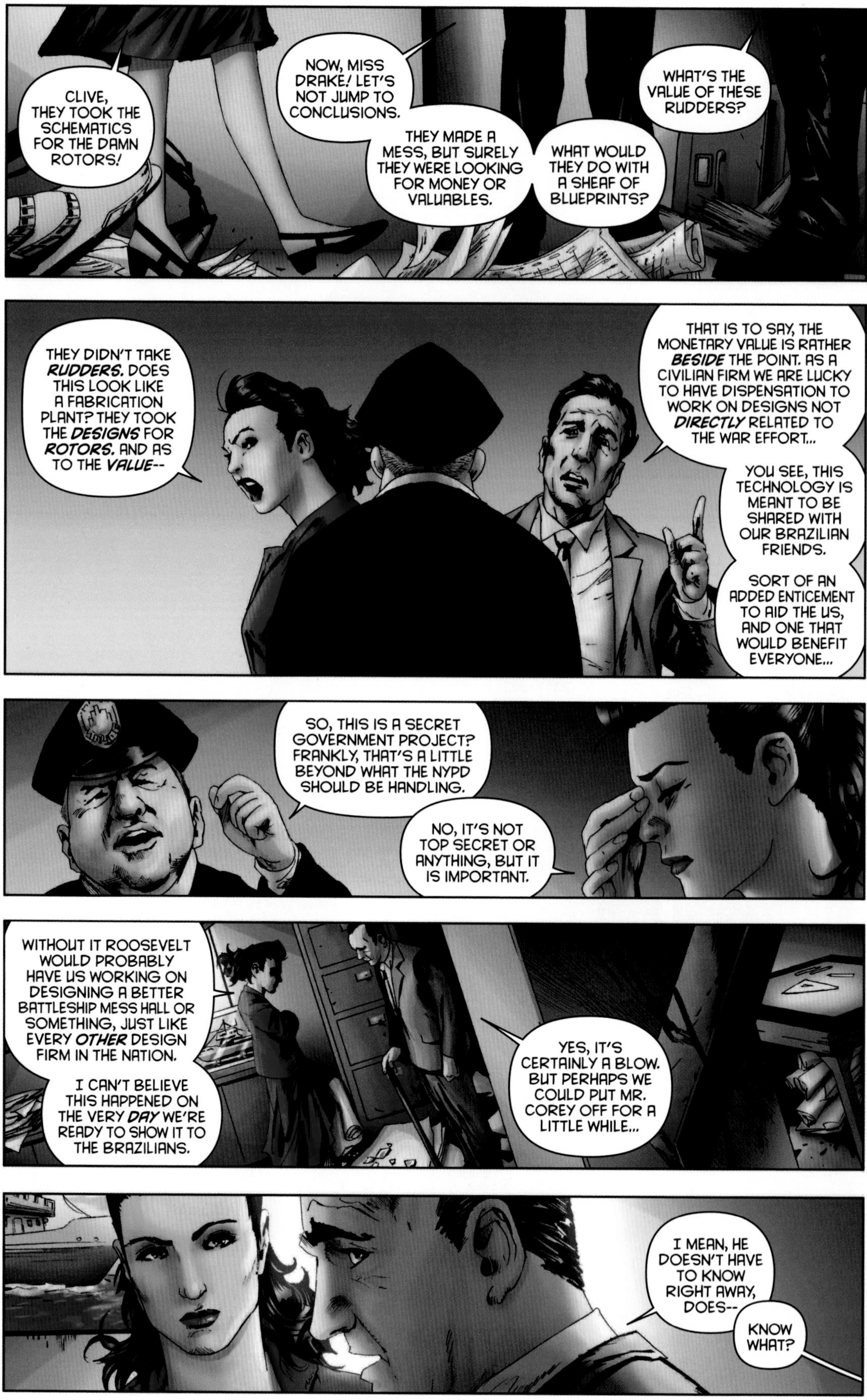
CLIVE, THEY TOOK THE SCHEMATICS FOR THE DAMN ROTORS!
NOW, MISS DRAKE! LET'S NOT JUMP TO CONCLUSIONS.
THEY MADE A MESS, BUT SURELY THEY WERE LOOKING FOR MONEY OR VALUABLES.
WHAT WOULD THEY DO WITH A SHEAF OF BLUEPRINTS?
WHAT'S THE VALUE OF THESE RUDDERS?
THEY DIDN'T TAKE *RUDDERS.* DOES THIS LOOK LIKE A FABRICATION PLANT? THEY TOOK THE *DESIGNS* FOR *ROTORS.* AND AS TO THE *VALUE*--
THAT IS TO SAY, THE MONETARY VALUE IS RATHER *BESIDE* THE POINT. AS A CIVILIAN FIRM WE ARE LUCKY TO HAVE DISPENSATION TO WORK ON DESIGNS NOT *DIRECTLY* RELATED TO THE WAR EFFORT...
YOU SEE, THIS TECHNOLOGY IS MEANT TO BE SHARED WITH OUR BRAZILIAN FRIENDS.
SORT OF AN ADDED ENTICEMENT TO AID THE US, AND ONE THAT WOULD BENEFIT EVERYONE...
SO, THIS IS A SECRET GOVERNMENT PROJECT? FRANKLY, THAT'S A LITTLE BEYOND WHAT THE NYPD SHOULD BE HANDLING.
NO, IT'S NOT TOP SECRET OR ANYTHING, BUT IT IS IMPORTANT.
WITHOUT IT ROOSEVELT WOULD PROBABLY HAVE US WORKING ON DESIGNING A BETTER BATTLESHIP MESS HALL OR SOMETHING, JUST LIKE EVERY *OTHER* DESIGN FIRM IN THE NATION.
I CAN'T BELIEVE THIS HAPPENED ON THE VERY *DAY* WE'RE READY TO SHOW IT TO THE BRAZILIANS.
YES, IT'S CERTAINLY A BLOW. BUT PERHAPS WE COULD PUT MR. COREY OFF FOR A LITTLE WHILE...
I MEAN, HE DOESN'T HAVE TO KNOW RIGHT AWAY, DOES--
KNOW WHAT?

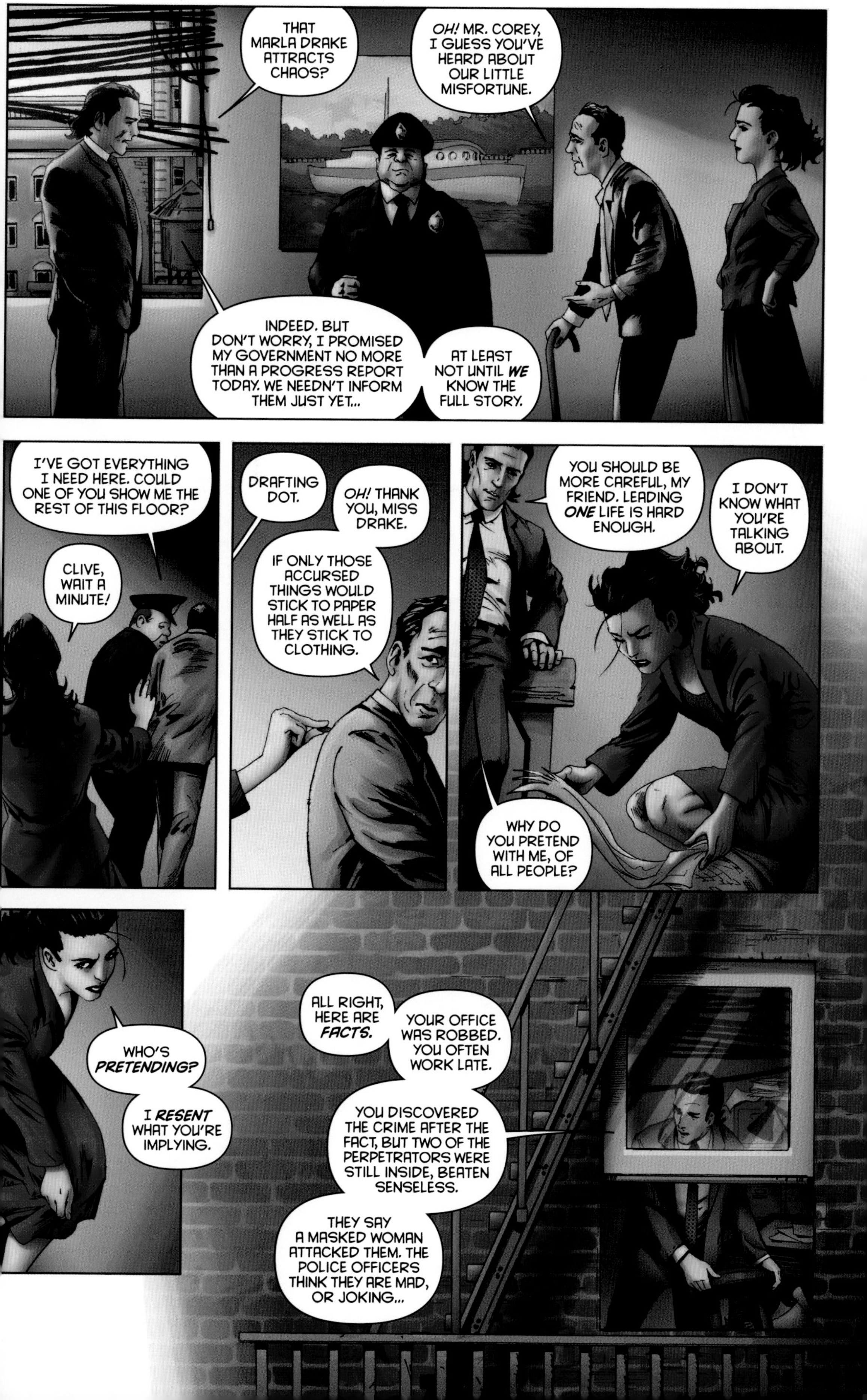
THAT MARLA DRAKE ATTRACTS CHAOS?
OH! MR. COREY, I GUESS YOU'VE HEARD ABOUT OUR LITTLE MISFORTUNE.
INDEED. BUT DON'T WORRY, I PROMISED MY GOVERNMENT NO MORE THAN A PROGRESS REPORT TODAY. WE NEEDN'T INFORM THEM JUST YET...
AT LEAST NOT UNTIL WE KNOW THE FULL STORY.
I'VE GOT EVERYTHING I NEED HERE. COULD ONE OF YOU SHOW ME THE REST OF THIS FLOOR?
CLIVE, WAIT A MINUTE!
DRAFTING DOT.
OH! THANK YOU, MISS DRAKE.
IF ONLY THOSE ACCURSED THINGS WOULD STICK TO PAPER HALF AS WELL AS THEY STICK TO CLOTHING.
YOU SHOULD BE MORE CAREFUL, MY FRIEND. LEADING ONE LIFE IS HARD ENOUGH.
I DON'T KNOW WHAT YOU'RE TALKING ABOUT.
WHY DO YOU PRETEND WITH ME, OF ALL PEOPLE?
WHO'S PRETENDING?
I RESENT WHAT YOU'RE IMPLYING.
ALL RIGHT, HERE ARE FACTS.
YOUR OFFICE WAS ROBBED. YOU OFTEN WORK LATE.
YOU DISCOVERED THE CRIME AFTER THE FACT, BUT TWO OF THE PERPETRATORS WERE STILL INSIDE, BEATEN SENSELESS.
THEY SAY A MASKED WOMAN ATTACKED THEM. THE POLICE OFFICERS THINK THEY ARE MAD, OR JOKING...

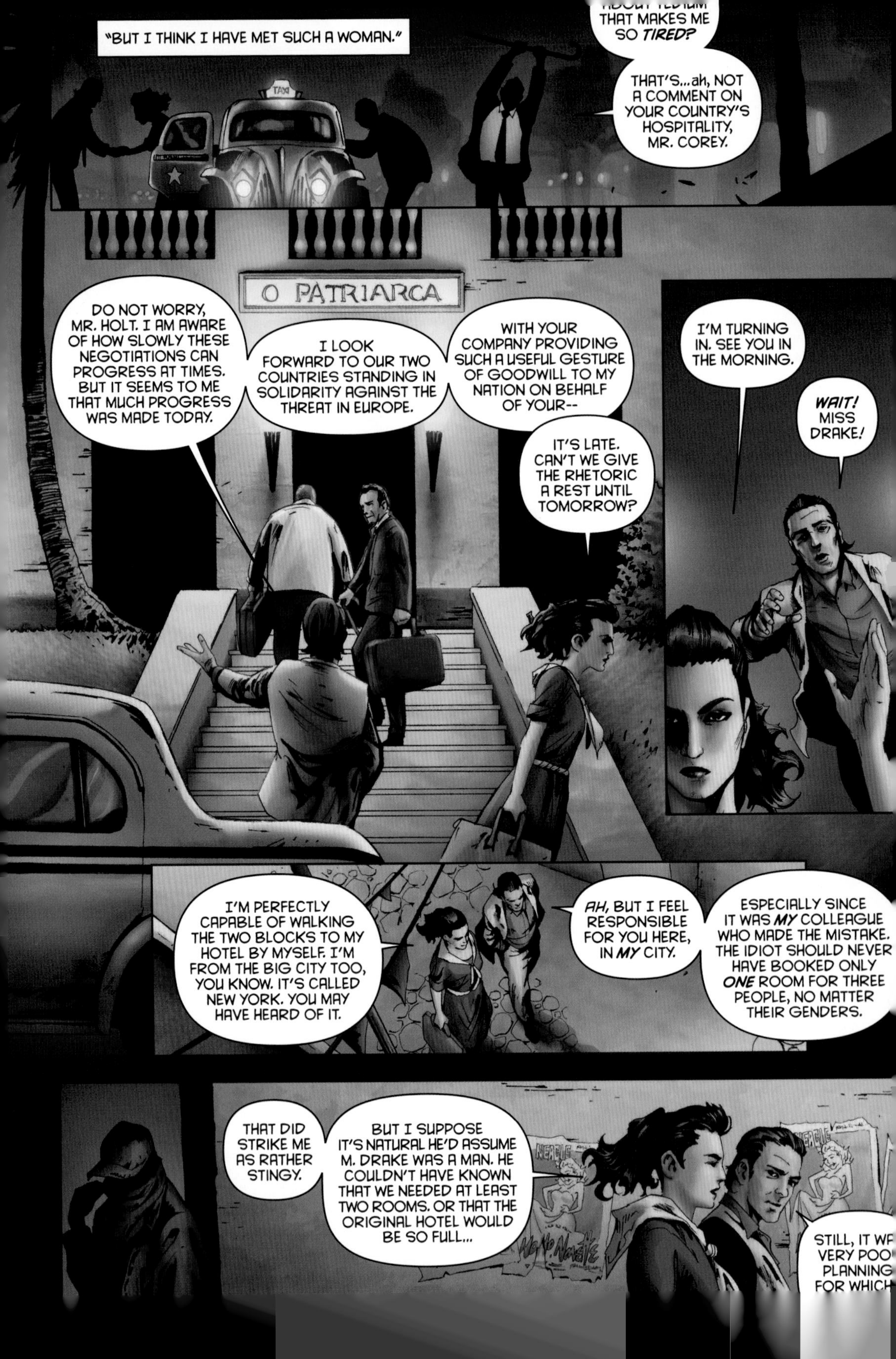
"BUT I THINK I HAVE MET SUCH A WOMAN."
THAT MAKES ME SO *TIRED?*
THAT'S...ah, NOT A COMMENT ON YOUR COUNTRY'S HOSPITALITY, MR. COREY.
O PATRIARCA
DO NOT WORRY, MR. HOLT. I AM AWARE OF HOW SLOWLY THESE NEGOTIATIONS CAN PROGRESS AT TIMES. BUT IT SEEMS TO ME THAT MUCH PROGRESS WAS MADE TODAY.
I LOOK FORWARD TO OUR TWO COUNTRIES STANDING IN SOLIDARITY AGAINST THE THREAT IN EUROPE.
WITH YOUR COMPANY PROVIDING SUCH A USEFUL GESTURE OF GOODWILL TO MY NATION ON BEHALF OF YOUR--
IT'S LATE. CAN'T WE GIVE THE RHETORIC A REST UNTIL TOMORROW?
I'M TURNING IN. SEE YOU IN THE MORNING.
WAIT! MISS DRAKE!
I'M PERFECTLY CAPABLE OF WALKING THE TWO BLOCKS TO MY HOTEL BY MYSELF. I'M FROM THE BIG CITY TOO, YOU KNOW. IT'S CALLED NEW YORK. YOU MAY HAVE HEARD OF IT.
AH, BUT I FEEL RESPONSIBLE FOR YOU HERE, IN *MY* CITY.
ESPECIALLY SINCE IT WAS *MY* COLLEAGUE WHO MADE THE MISTAKE. THE IDIOT SHOULD NEVER HAVE BOOKED ONLY *ONE* ROOM FOR THREE PEOPLE, NO MATTER THEIR GENDERS.
THAT DID STRIKE ME AS RATHER STINGY.
BUT I SUPPOSE IT'S NATURAL HE'D ASSUME M. DRAKE WAS A MAN. HE COULDN'T HAVE KNOWN THAT WE NEEDED AT LEAST TWO ROOMS. OR THAT THE ORIGINAL HOTEL WOULD BE SO FULL...
STILL, IT WA VERY POO PLANNING FOR WHICH

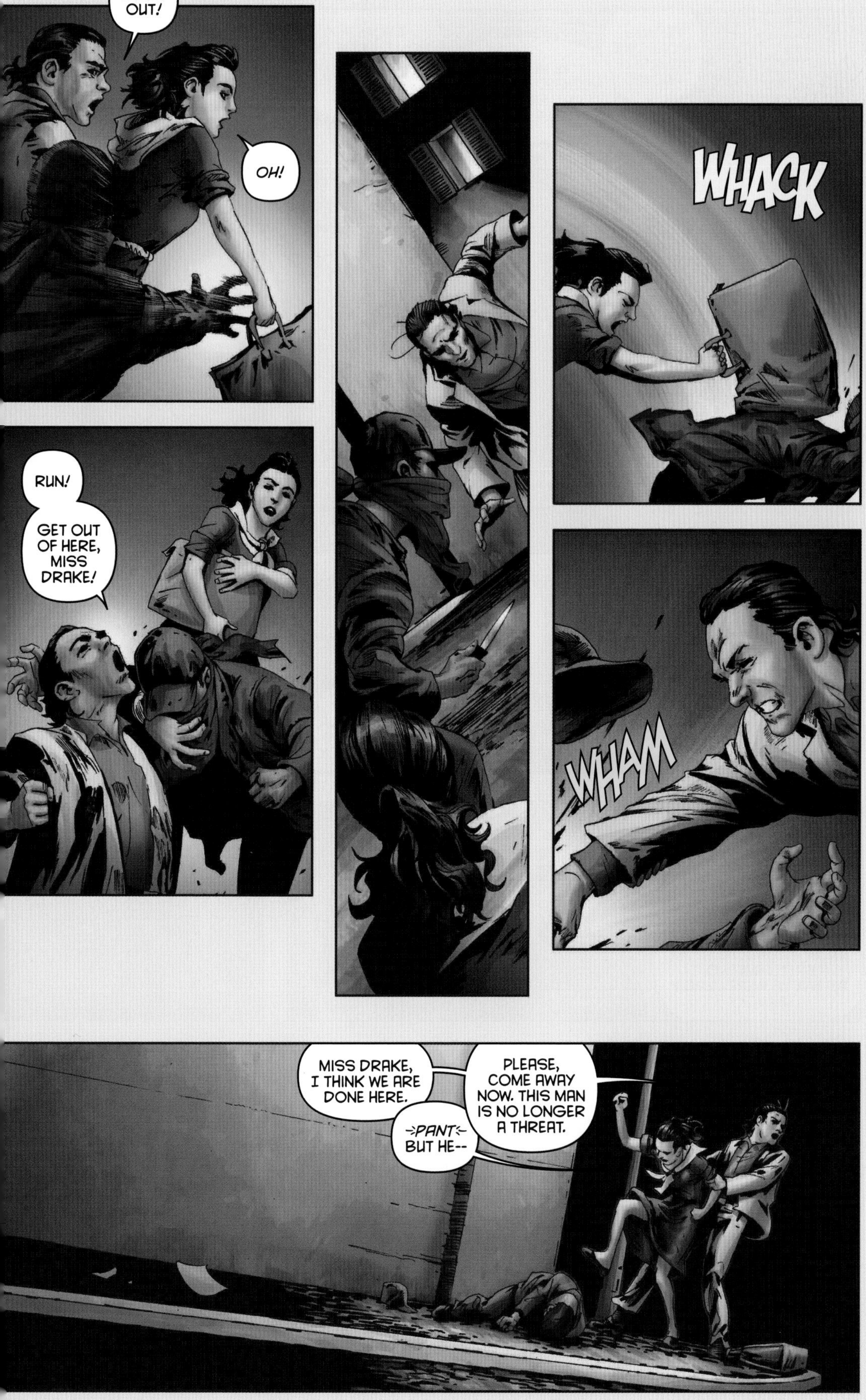
LOOK OUT!
OH!
RUN!
GET OUT OF HERE, MISS DRAKE!
WHACK
WHAM
MISS DRAKE, I THINK WE ARE DONE HERE.
PLEASE, COME AWAY NOW. THIS MAN IS NO LONGER A THREAT.
PANT
BUT HE--

FEELING MORE LIKE YOURSELF NOW?

I'VE NEVER BEEN MUGGED BEFORE. IT... IT RATHER NARROWS YOUR FOCUS.

I HOPE YOU DON'T JUDGE OUR WHOLE COUNTRY ON THIS ONE INCIDENT.

THE BIGGER MYSTERY IS WHY YOU DIDN'T RUN WHEN I TOLD YOU TO.

HE HAD A KNIFE. WAS I SUPPOSED TO LET HIM STAB YOU?

THAT IS APPRECIATED, BUT I ENDED UP FEELING A BIT SORRY FOR OUR ASSAILANT.

La Conga NIGHTS

I HAVE A FEELING THIS *WASN'T* RANDOM. THAT GUY REALLY SEEMED TO BE AFTER MY BRIEFCASE.

IMPOSSIBLE. THE REASON FOR OUR NEGOTIATIONS HAVE NOT BEEN MADE PUBLIC.

ONLY A SMALL CIRCLE SUSPECT BRAZIL WOULD EVEN *CONSIDER* SUPPORTING THE U.S., EVEN IF THE U.S. *DID* ENTER THE WAR.

AND MOST OF *THOSE* PEOPLE WOULDN'T KNOW A ROWBOAT FROM A BATTLESHIP. NO, I BELIEVE WE WERE MERELY UNLUCKY.

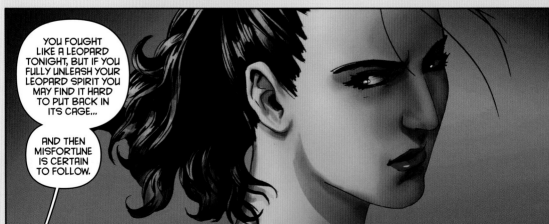

YOU FOUGHT LIKE A LEOPARD TONIGHT, BUT IF YOU FULLY UNLEASH YOUR LEOPARD SPIRIT YOU MAY FIND IT HARD TO PUT BACK IN ITS CAGE...

AND THEN MISFORTUNE IS CERTAIN TO FOLLOW.

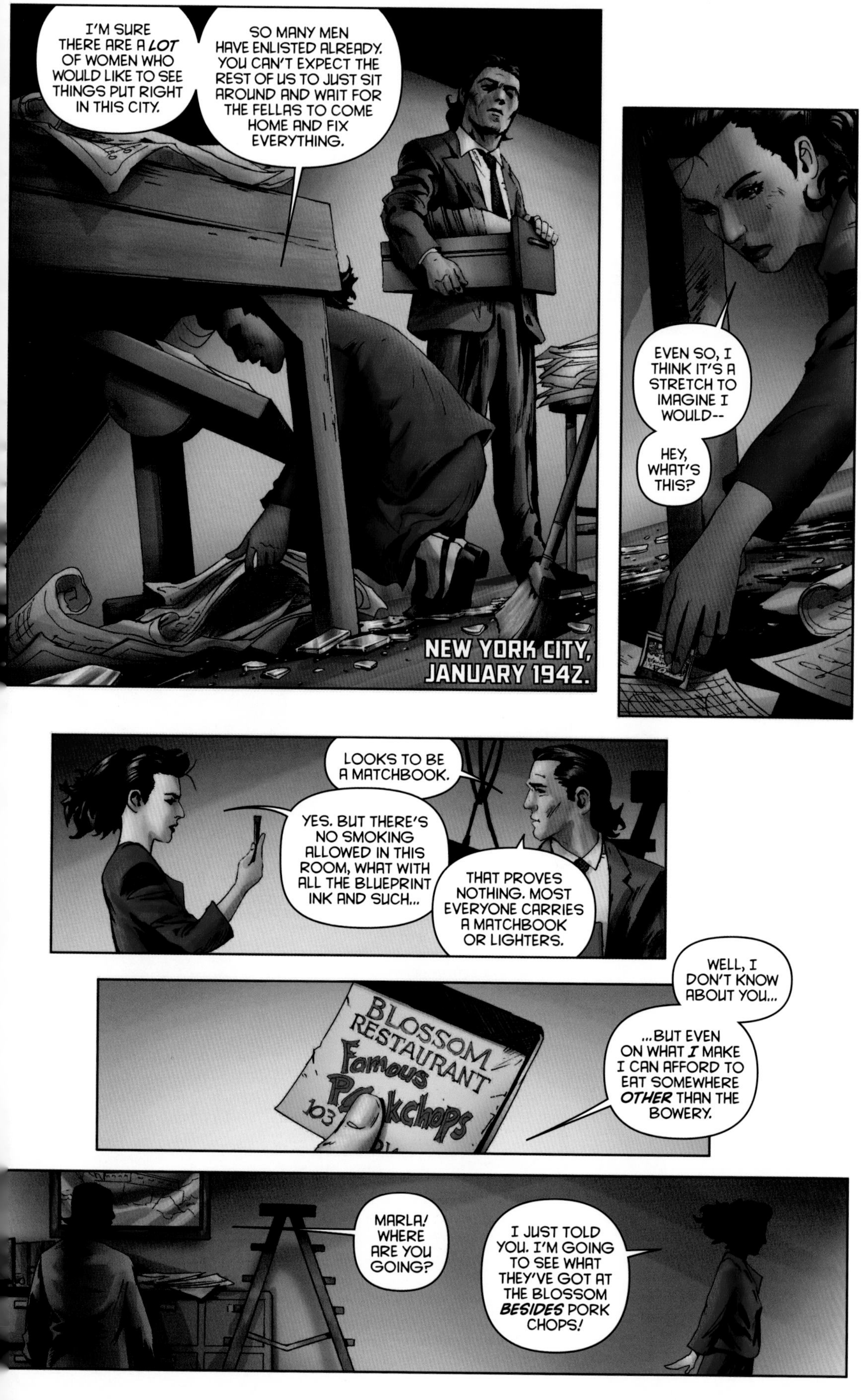
I'M SURE THERE ARE A *LOT* OF WOMEN WHO WOULD LIKE TO SEE THINGS PUT RIGHT IN THIS CITY.
SO MANY MEN HAVE ENLISTED ALREADY. YOU CAN'T EXPECT THE REST OF US TO JUST SIT AROUND AND WAIT FOR THE FELLAS TO COME HOME AND FIX EVERYTHING.
NEW YORK CITY, JANUARY 1942.
EVEN SO, I THINK IT'S A STRETCH TO IMAGINE I WOULD--
HEY, WHAT'S THIS?
LOOKS TO BE A MATCHBOOK.
YES. BUT THERE'S NO SMOKING ALLOWED IN THIS ROOM, WHAT WITH ALL THE BLUEPRINT INK AND SUCH...
THAT PROVES NOTHING. MOST EVERYONE CARRIES A MATCHBOOK OR LIGHTERS.
BLOSSOM RESTAURANT
Famous
P...kchops
103
WELL, I DON'T KNOW ABOUT YOU...
...BUT EVEN ON WHAT *I* MAKE I CAN AFFORD TO EAT SOMEWHERE *OTHER* THAN THE BOWERY.
MARLA! WHERE ARE YOU GOING?
I JUST TOLD YOU. I'M GOING TO SEE WHAT THEY'VE GOT AT THE BLOSSOM *BESIDES* PORK CHOPS!

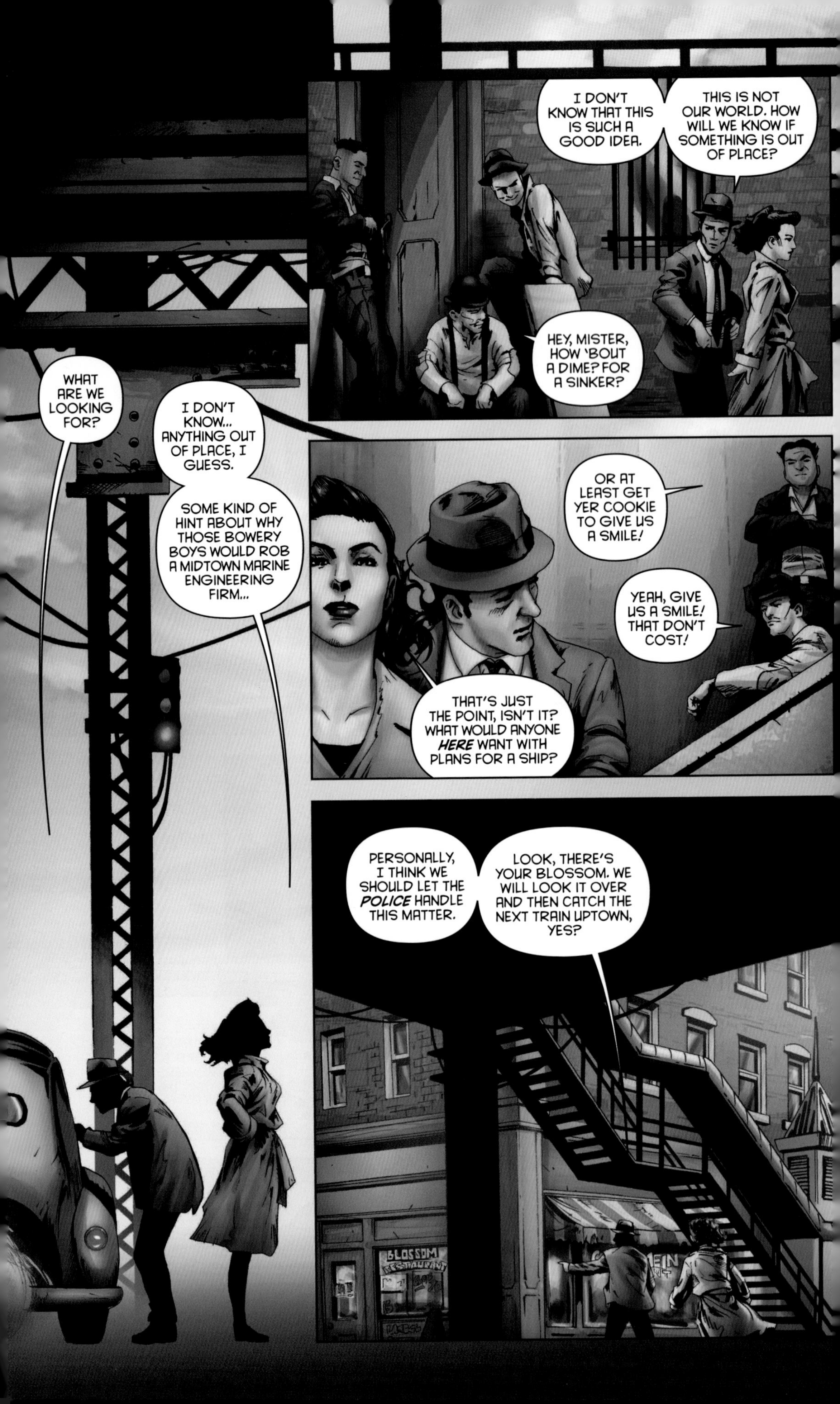
I DON'T KNOW THAT THIS IS SUCH A GOOD IDEA.
THIS IS NOT OUR WORLD. HOW WILL WE KNOW IF SOMETHING IS OUT OF PLACE?
HEY, MISTER, HOW 'BOUT A DIME? FOR A SINKER?
WHAT ARE WE LOOKING FOR?
I DON'T KNOW... ANYTHING OUT OF PLACE, I GUESS.
SOME KIND OF HINT ABOUT WHY THOSE BOWERY BOYS WOULD ROB A MIDTOWN MARINE ENGINEERING FIRM...
OR AT LEAST GET YER COOKIE TO GIVE US A SMILE!
YEAH, GIVE US A SMILE! THAT DON'T COST!
THAT'S JUST THE POINT, ISN'T IT? WHAT WOULD ANYONE *HERE* WANT WITH PLANS FOR A SHIP?
PERSONALLY, I THINK WE SHOULD LET THE *POLICE* HANDLE THIS MATTER.
LOOK, THERE'S YOUR BLOSSOM. WE WILL LOOK IT OVER AND THEN CATCH THE NEXT TRAIN UPTOWN, YES?
BLOSSOM RESTAURANT

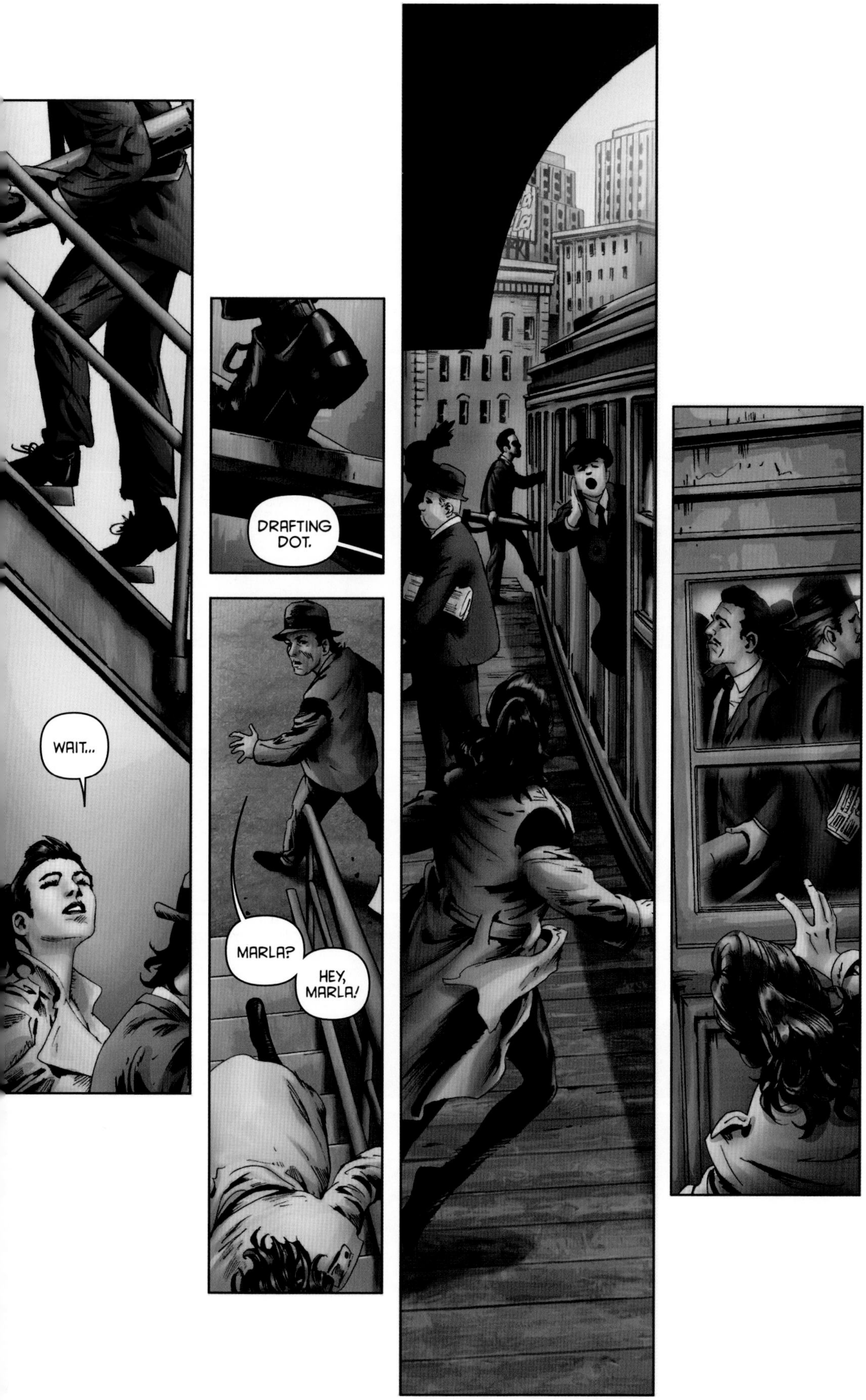
WAIT...
DRAFTING DOT.
MARLA?
HEY, MARLA!

CHK CHK CHK CHK CHK CHK CHK CHK CHK CHK CHK CHK

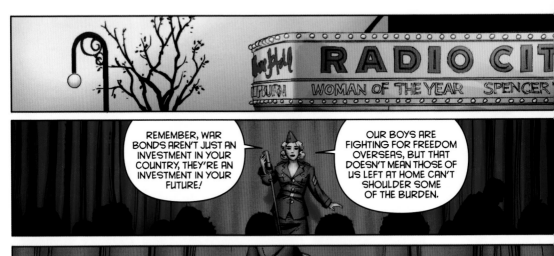

RADIO CIT
WOMAN OF THE YEAR   SPENCER

REMEMBER, WAR BONDS AREN'T JUST AN INVESTMENT IN YOUR COUNTRY, THEY'RE AN INVESTMENT IN YOUR FUTURE!

OUR BOYS ARE FIGHTING FOR FREEDOM OVERSEAS, BUT THAT DOESN'T MEAN THOSE OF US LEFT AT HOME CAN'T SHOULDER SOME OF THE BURDEN.

SO WON'T YOU JOIN ME, *LUANA GREY*, AND TOGETHER WE'LL *GET THIS SHIELD UP!*

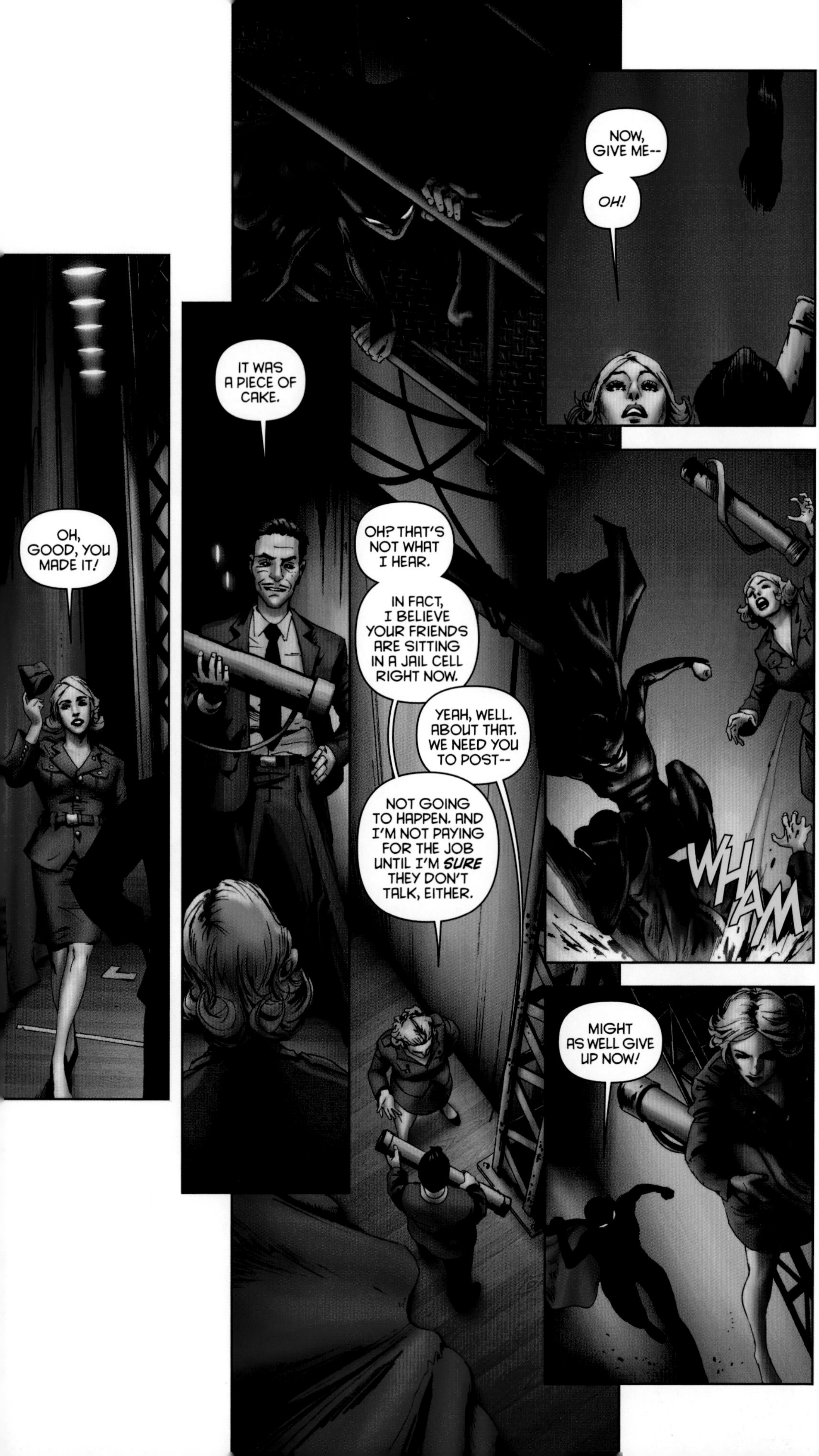
OH, GOOD, YOU MADE IT!
IT WAS A PIECE OF CAKE.
OH? THAT'S NOT WHAT I HEAR.
IN FACT, I BELIEVE YOUR FRIENDS ARE SITTING IN A JAIL CELL RIGHT NOW.
YEAH, WELL. ABOUT THAT. WE NEED YOU TO POST--
NOT GOING TO HAPPEN. AND I'M NOT PAYING FOR THE JOB UNTIL I'M *SURE* THEY DON'T TALK, EITHER.
NOW, GIVE ME--
OH!
WHAM
MIGHT AS WELL GIVE UP NOW!

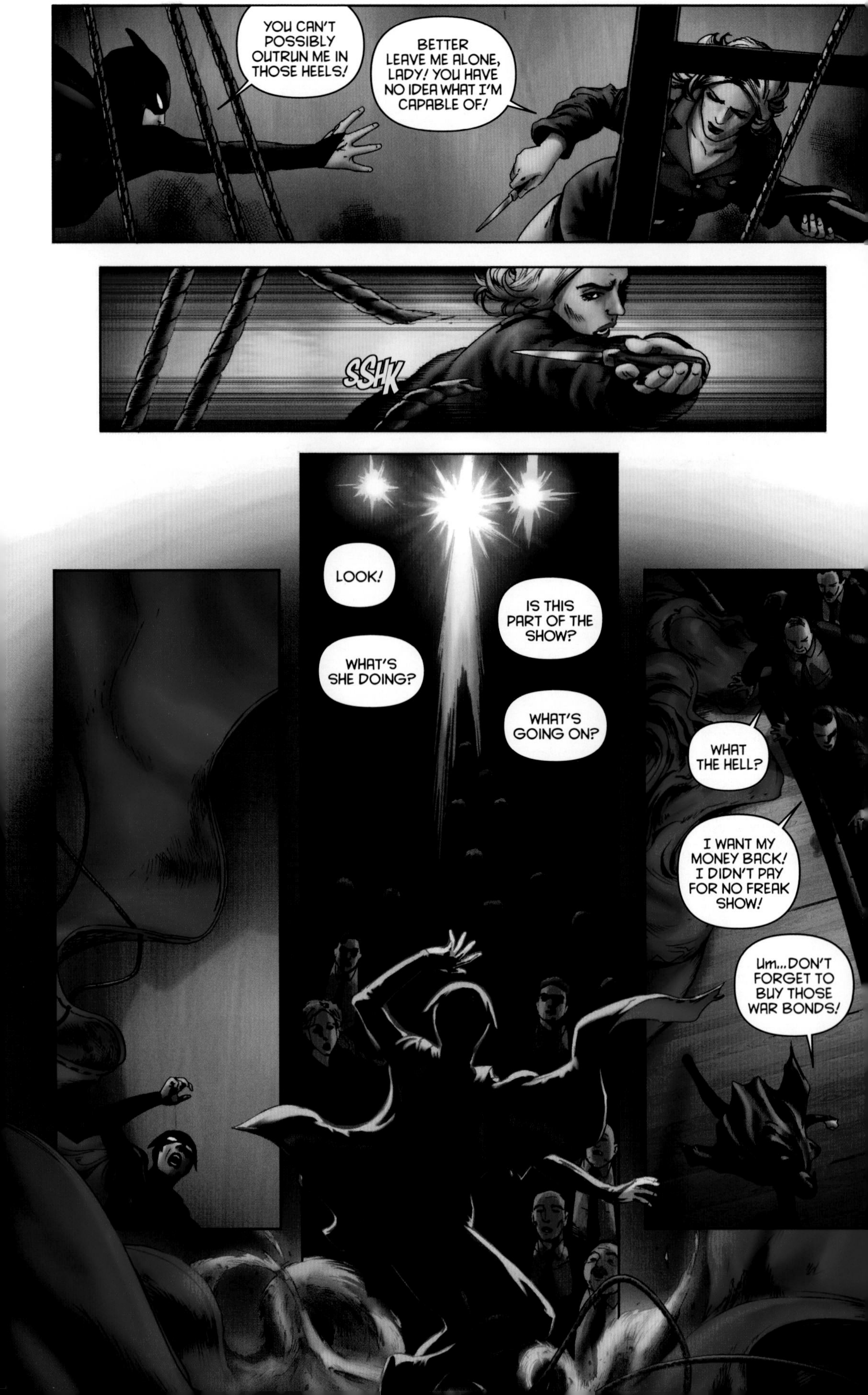
YOU CAN'T POSSIBLY OUTRUN ME IN THOSE HEELS!
BETTER LEAVE ME ALONE, LADY! YOU HAVE NO IDEA WHAT I'M CAPABLE OF!
SSHK
LOOK!
IS THIS PART OF THE SHOW?
WHAT'S SHE DOING?
WHAT'S GOING ON?
WHAT THE HELL?
I WANT MY MONEY BACK! I DIDN'T PAY FOR NO FREAK SHOW!
UM...DON'T FORGET TO BUY THOSE WAR BONDS!

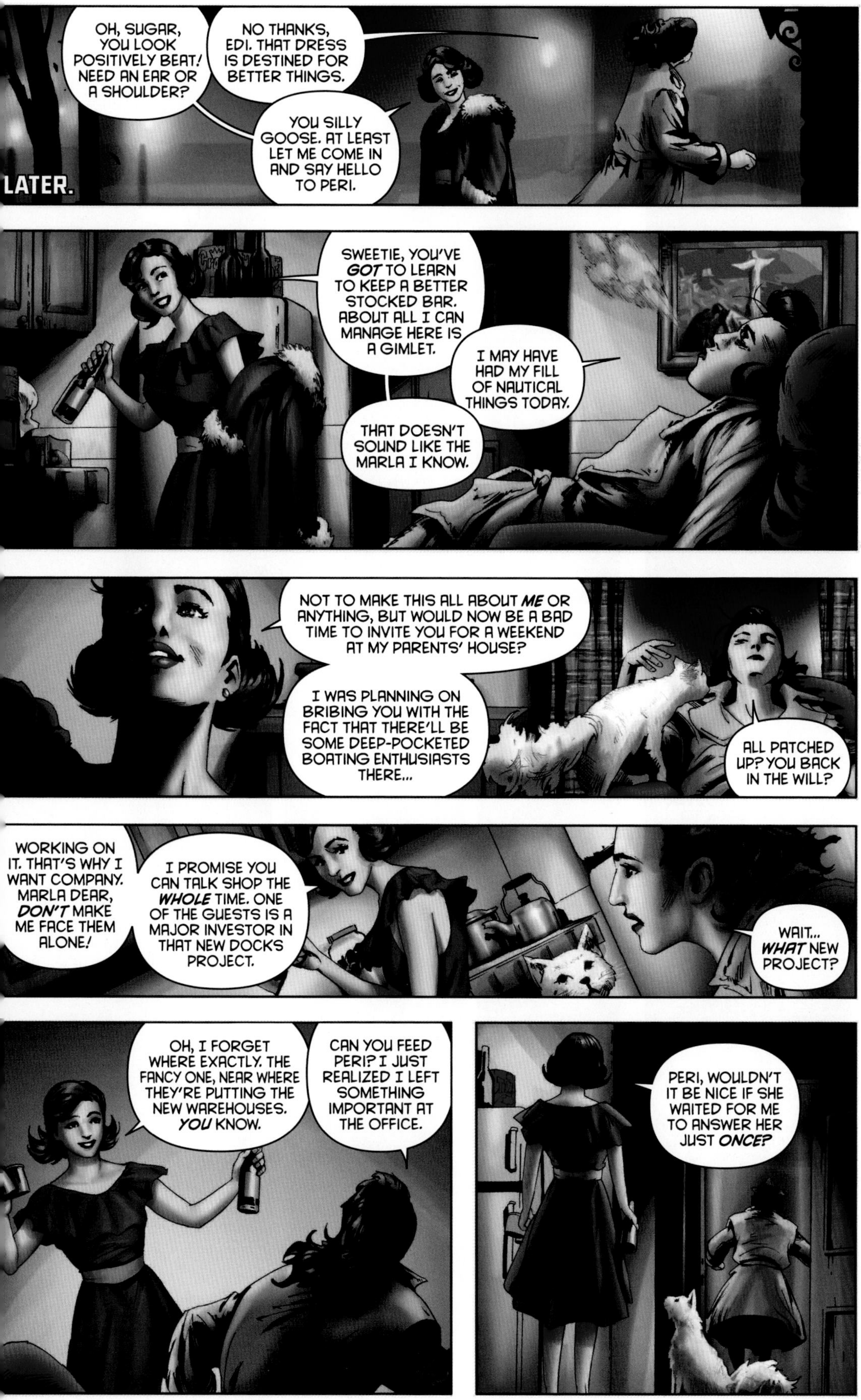
LATER.
OH, SUGAR, YOU LOOK POSITIVELY BEAT! NEED AN EAR OR A SHOULDER?
NO THANKS, EDI. THAT DRESS IS DESTINED FOR BETTER THINGS.
YOU SILLY GOOSE. AT LEAST LET ME COME IN AND SAY HELLO TO PERI.
SWEETIE, YOU'VE GOT TO LEARN TO KEEP A BETTER STOCKED BAR. ABOUT ALL I CAN MANAGE HERE IS A GIMLET.
I MAY HAVE HAD MY FILL OF NAUTICAL THINGS TODAY.
THAT DOESN'T SOUND LIKE THE MARLA I KNOW.
NOT TO MAKE THIS ALL ABOUT ME OR ANYTHING, BUT WOULD NOW BE A BAD TIME TO INVITE YOU FOR A WEEKEND AT MY PARENTS' HOUSE?
I WAS PLANNING ON BRIBING YOU WITH THE FACT THAT THERE'LL BE SOME DEEP-POCKETED BOATING ENTHUSIASTS THERE...
ALL PATCHED UP? YOU BACK IN THE WILL?
WORKING ON IT. THAT'S WHY I WANT COMPANY. MARLA DEAR, DON'T MAKE ME FACE THEM ALONE!
I PROMISE YOU CAN TALK SHOP THE WHOLE TIME. ONE OF THE GUESTS IS A MAJOR INVESTOR IN THAT NEW DOCKS PROJECT.
WAIT... WHAT NEW PROJECT?
OH, I FORGET WHERE EXACTLY. THE FANCY ONE, NEAR WHERE THEY'RE PUTTING THE NEW WAREHOUSES. YOU KNOW.
CAN YOU FEED PERI? I JUST REALIZED I LEFT SOMETHING IMPORTANT AT THE OFFICE.
PERI, WOULDN'T IT BE NICE IF SHE WAITED FOR ME TO ANSWER HER JUST ONCE?

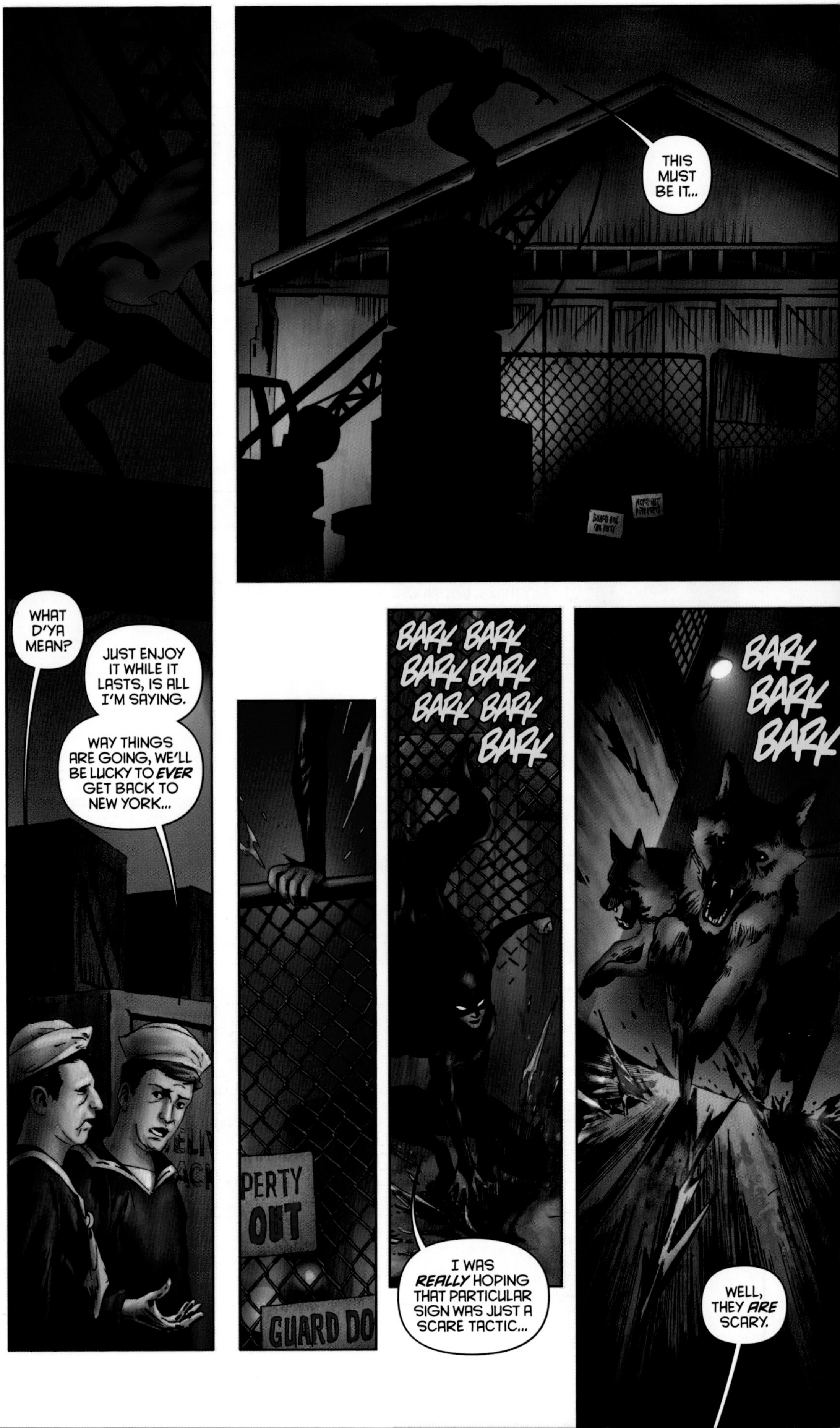
THIS MUST BE IT...
WHAT D'YA MEAN?
JUST ENJOY IT WHILE IT LASTS, IS ALL I'M SAYING.
WAY THINGS ARE GOING, WE'LL BE LUCKY TO *EVER* GET BACK TO NEW YORK...
PERTY
OUT
GUARD DO
BARK BARK BARK BARK BARK BARK BARK
I WAS *REALLY* HOPING THAT PARTICULAR SIGN WAS JUST A SCARE TACTIC...
BARK BARK BARK
WELL, THEY *ARE* SCARY.

BARK
BARK
BARK

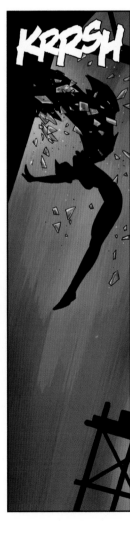

GOOD
DOGS!
DOWN!

BARK
BARK
BARK

KRRSH

NO...IT
CAN'T BE!

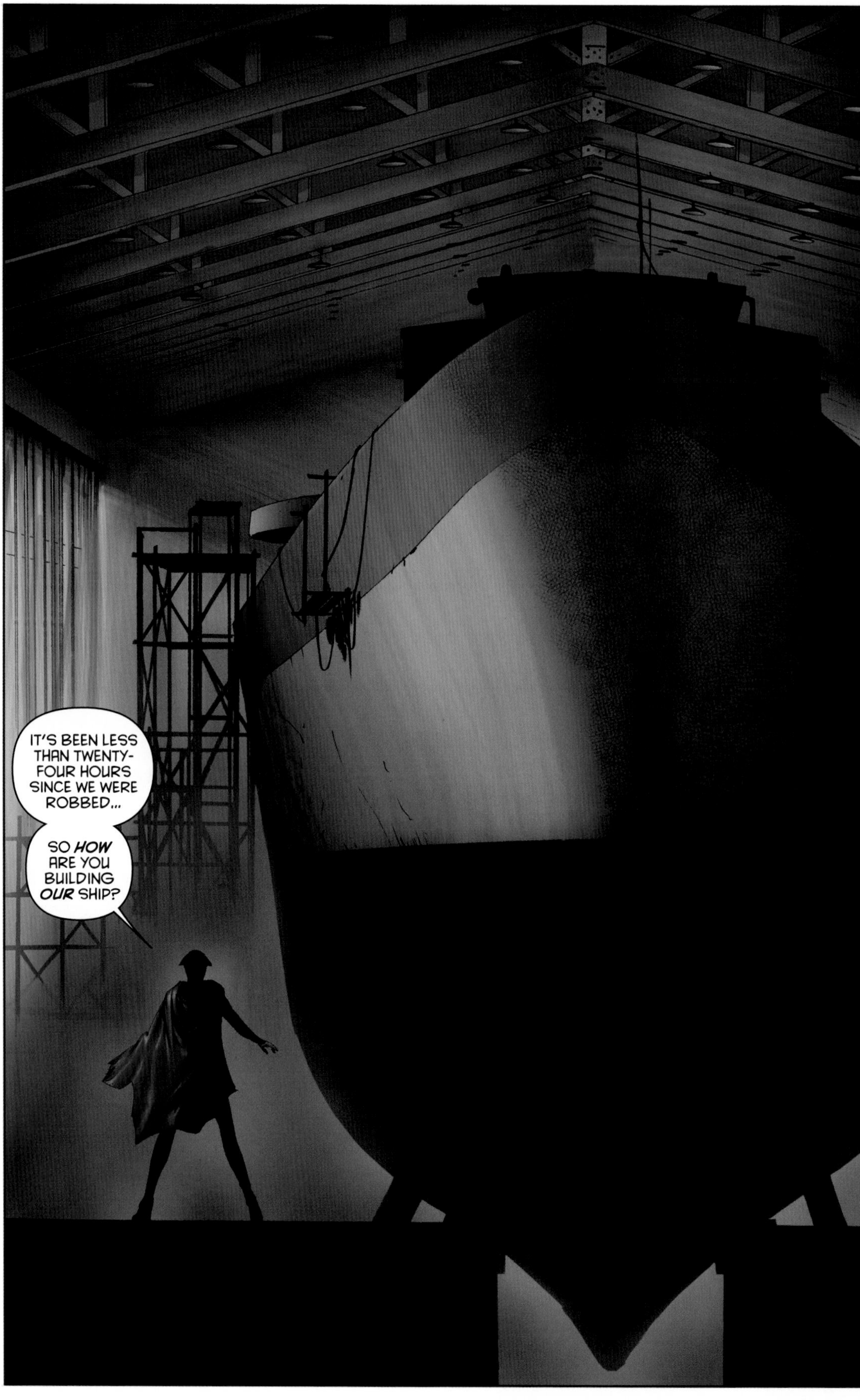
IT'S BEEN LESS THAN TWENTY-FOUR HOURS SINCE WE WERE ROBBED...
SO *HOW* ARE YOU BUILDING *OUR* SHIP?

Issue Two

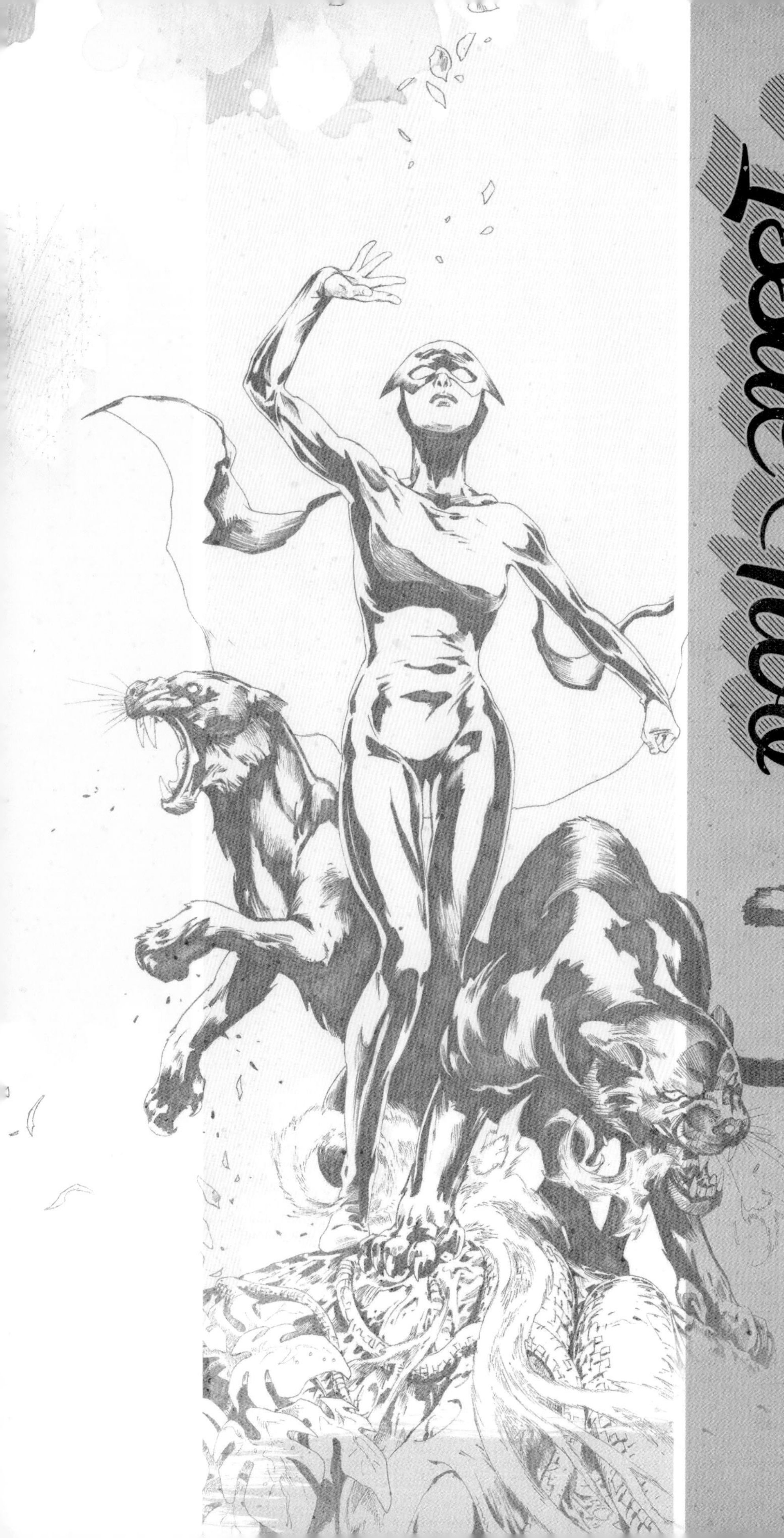

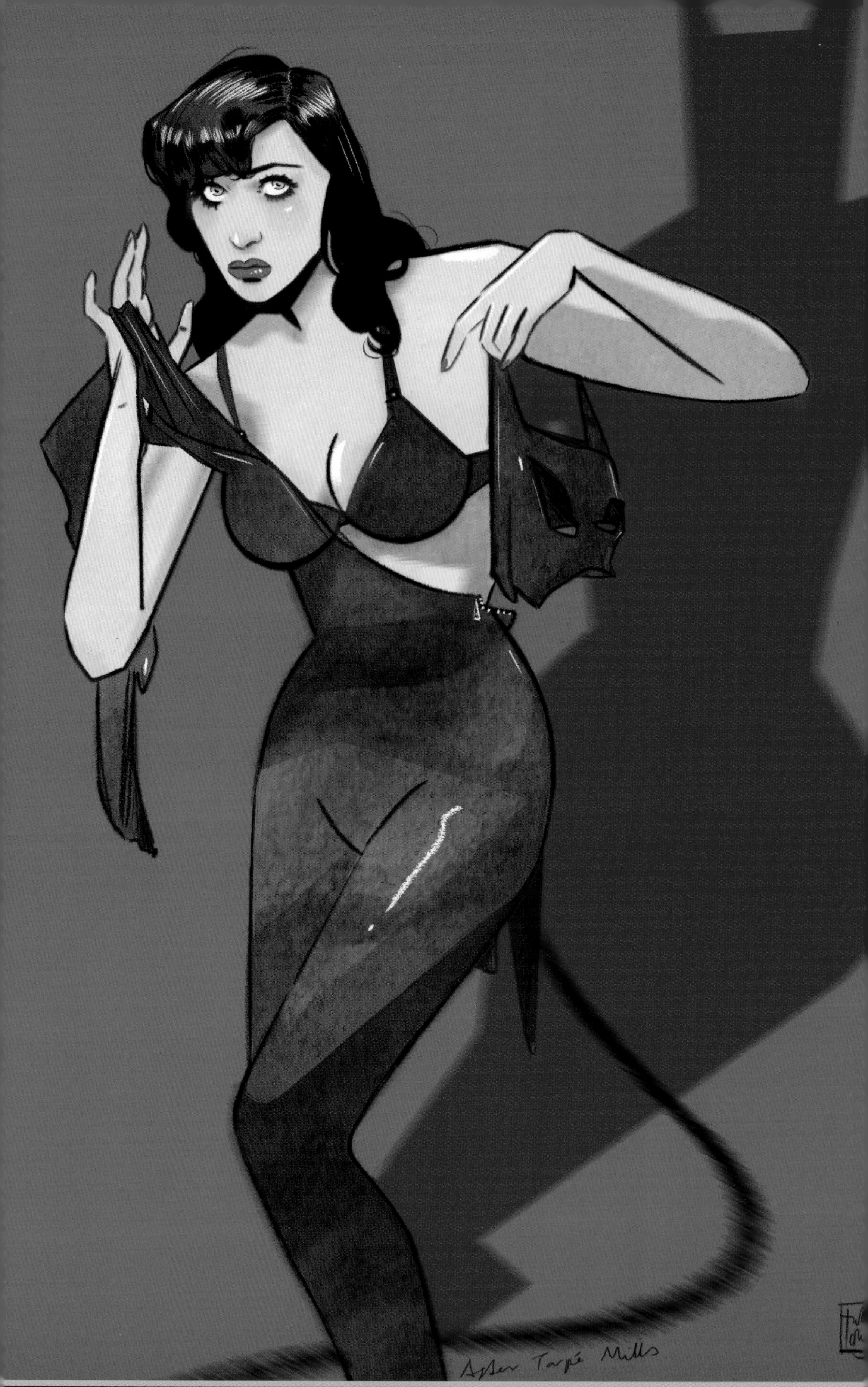
After Tarpé Mills

Issue 2, Main Cover: Art by Tula Lotay

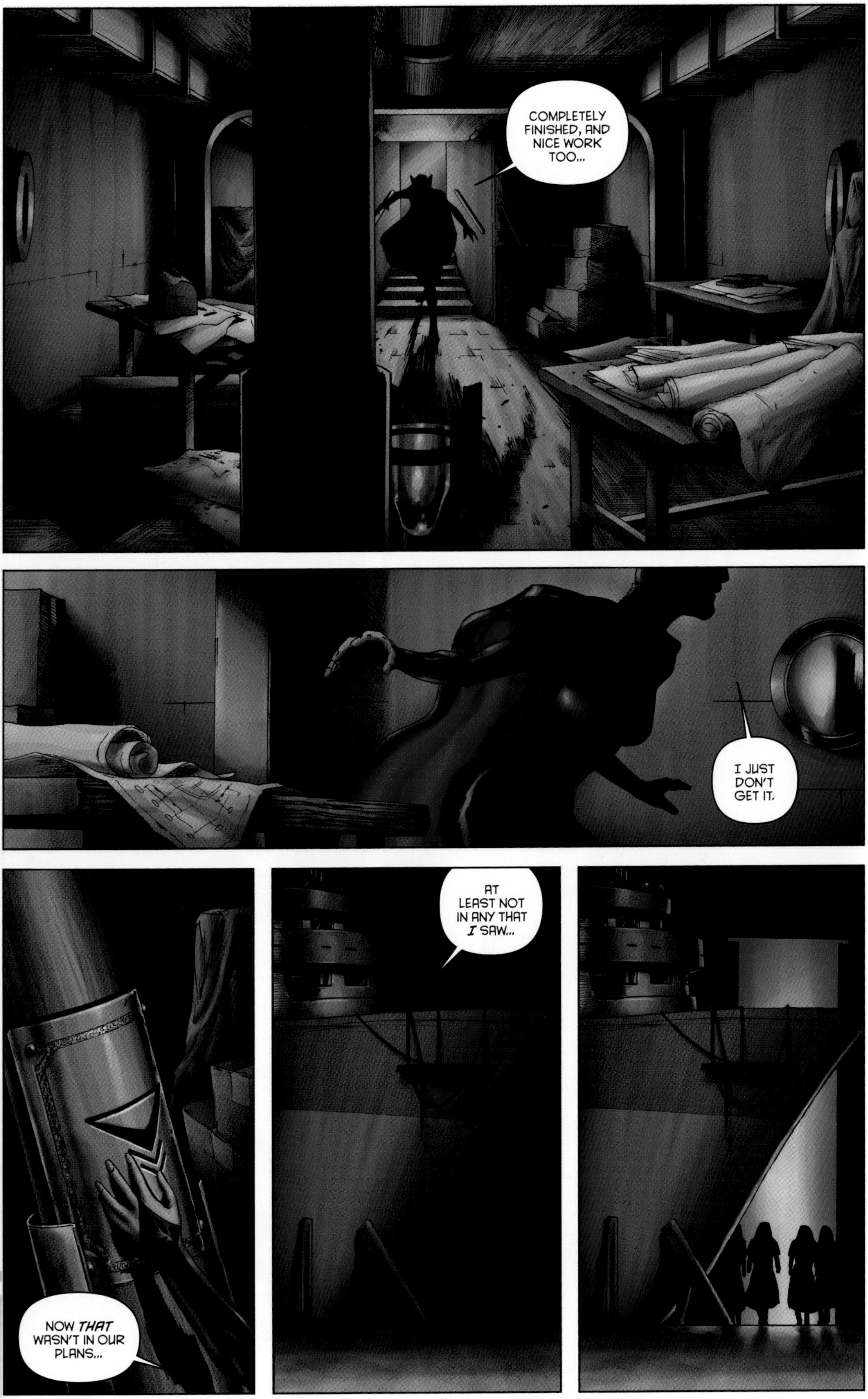
COMPLETELY FINISHED, AND NICE WORK TOO...
I JUST DON'T GET IT.
NOW *THAT* WASN'T IN OUR PLANS...
AT LEAST NOT IN ANY THAT *I* SAW...

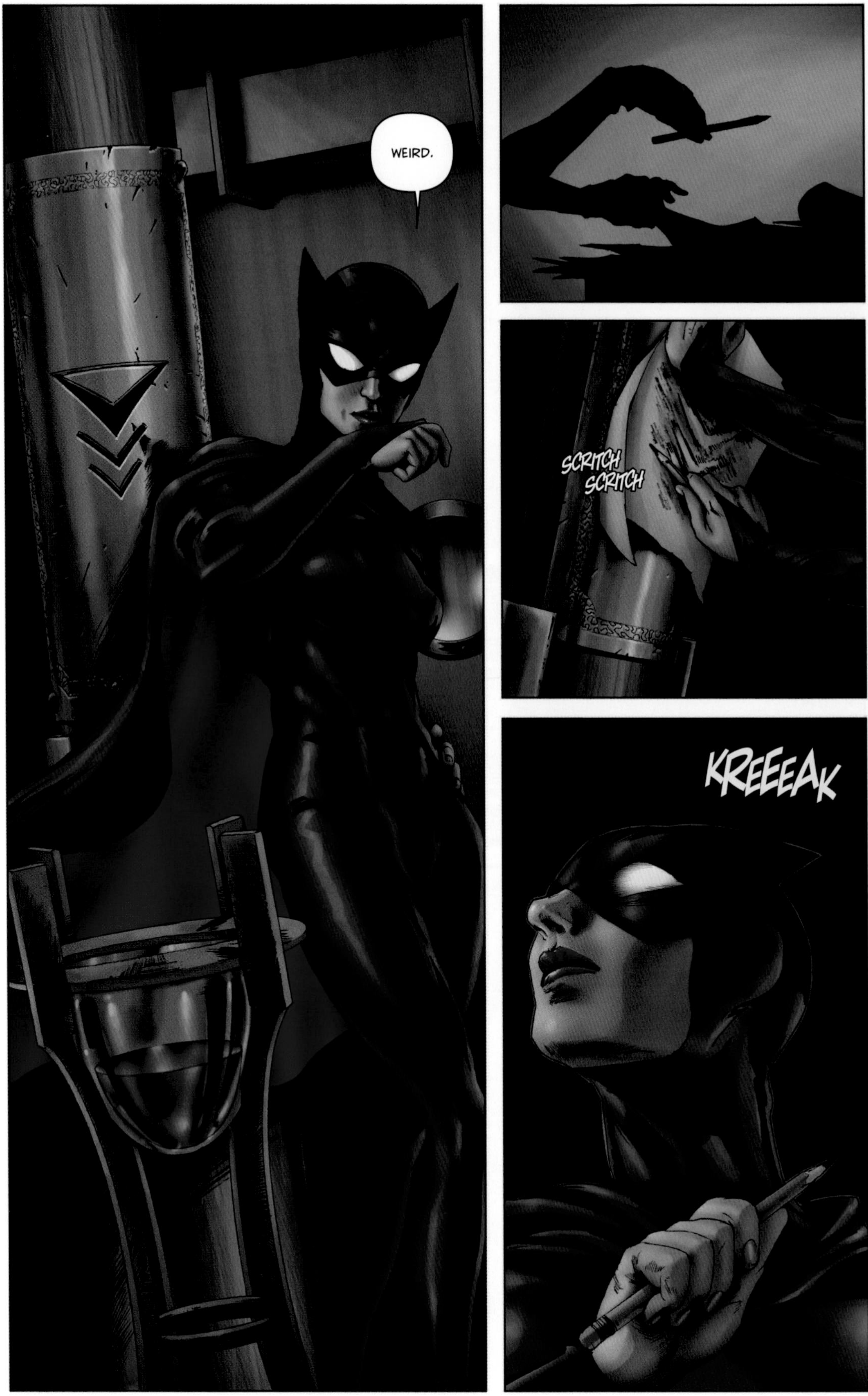
WEIRD.
SCRITCH
SCRITCH
KREEEAK

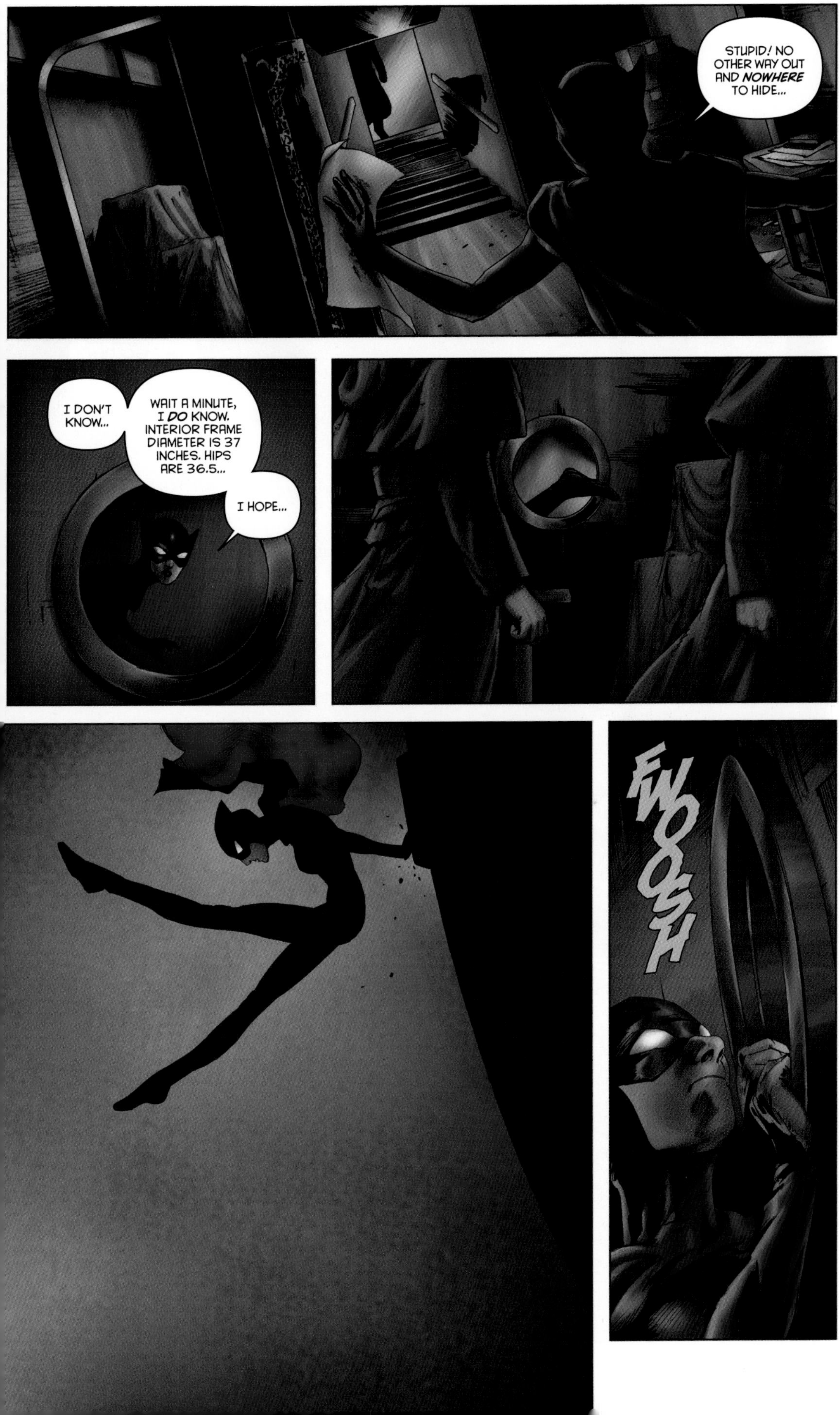

STUPID! NO OTHER WAY OUT AND NOWHERE TO HIDE...
I DON'T KNOW...
WAIT A MINUTE, I DO KNOW. INTERIOR FRAME DIAMETER IS 37 INCHES. HIPS ARE 36.5...
I HOPE...
FWOOSH

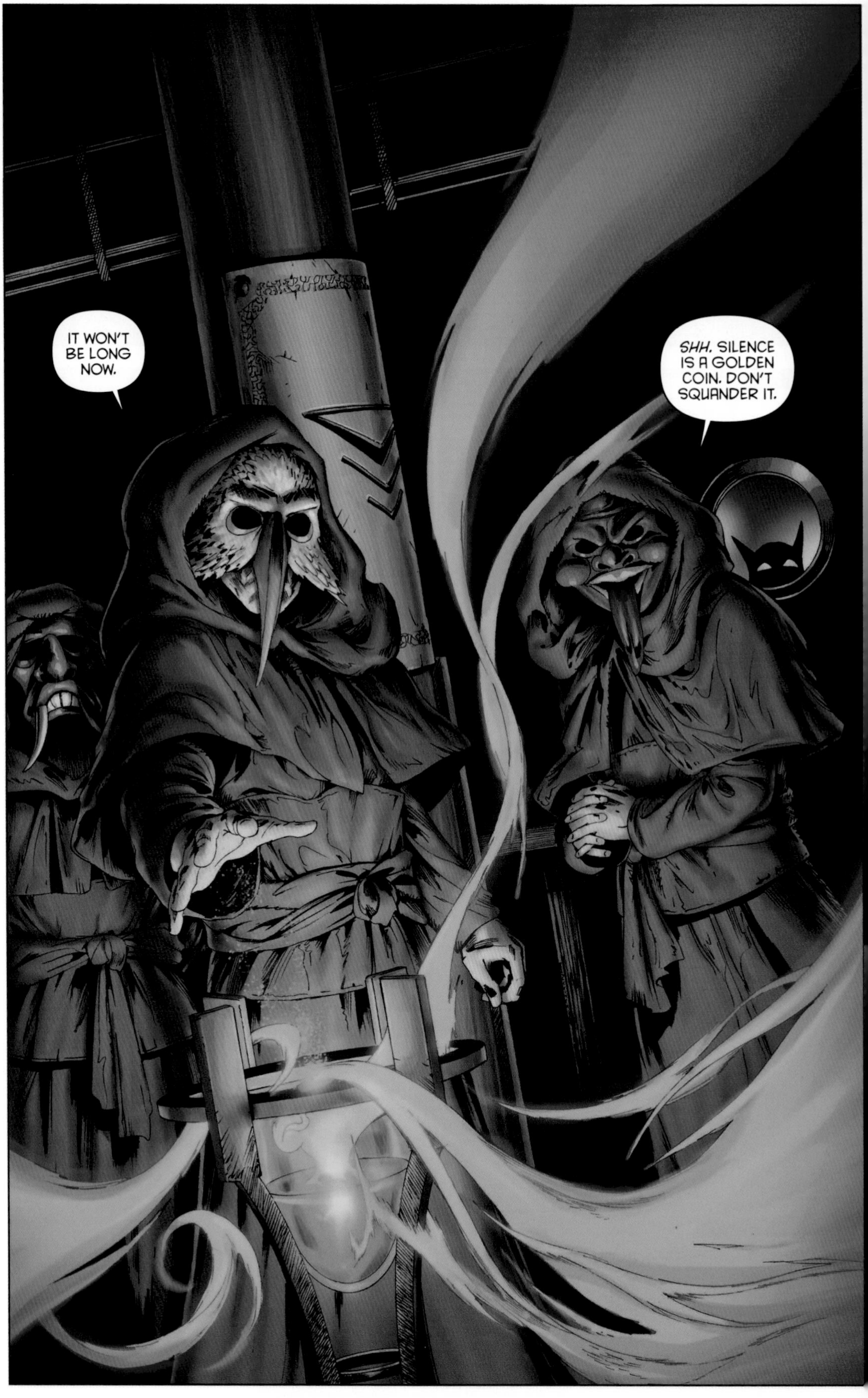
IT WON'T BE LONG NOW.
SHH. SILENCE IS A GOLDEN COIN. DON'T SQUANDER IT.

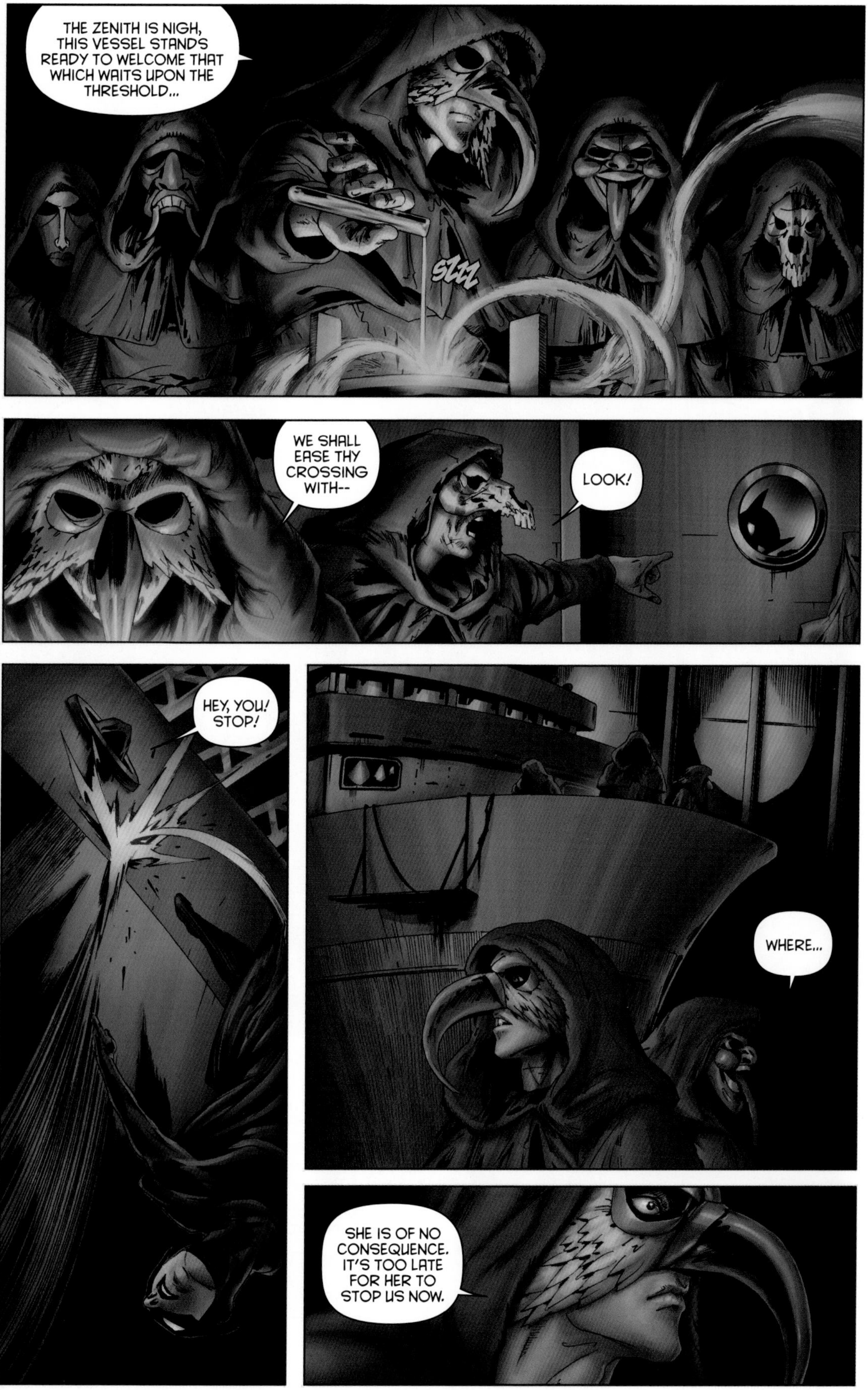
THE ZENITH IS NIGH, THIS VESSEL STAND'S READY TO WELCOME THAT WHICH WAITS UPON THE THRESHOLD...
SZZZ
WE SHALL EASE THY CROSSING WITH--
LOOK!
HEY, YOU! STOP!
WHERE...
SHE IS OF NO CONSEQUENCE. IT'S TOO LATE FOR HER TO STOP US NOW.

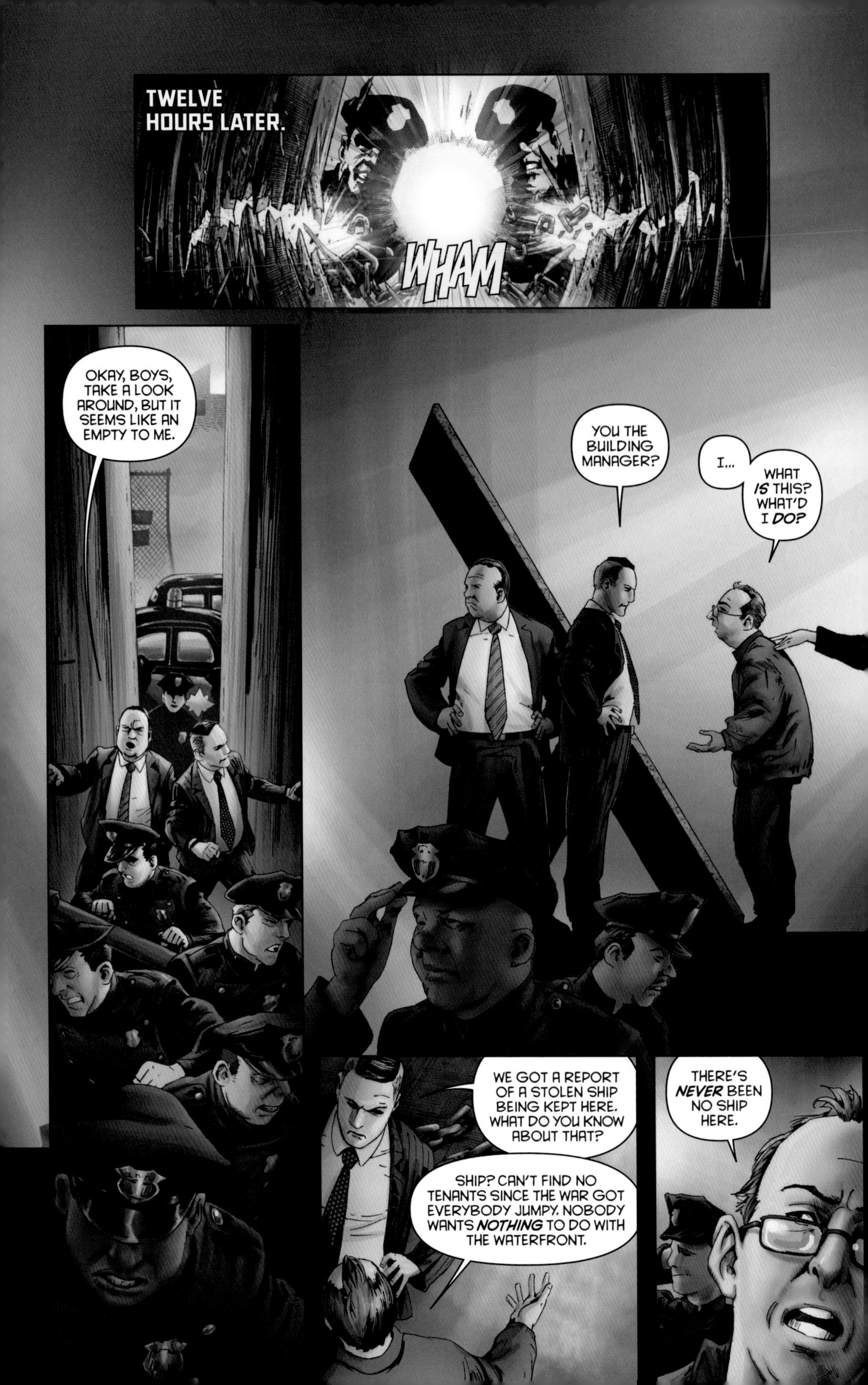
TWELVE HOURS LATER.
WHAM
OKAY, BOYS, TAKE A LOOK AROUND, BUT IT SEEMS LIKE AN EMPTY TO ME.
YOU THE BUILDING MANAGER?
I...
WHAT *IS* THIS? WHAT'D I *DO?*
WE GOT A REPORT OF A STOLEN SHIP BEING KEPT HERE. WHAT DO YOU KNOW ABOUT THAT?
SHIP? CAN'T FIND NO TENANTS SINCE THE WAR GOT EVERYBODY JUMPY. NOBODY WANTS *NOTHING* TO DO WITH THE WATERFRONT.
THERE'S *NEVER* BEEN NO SHIP HERE.

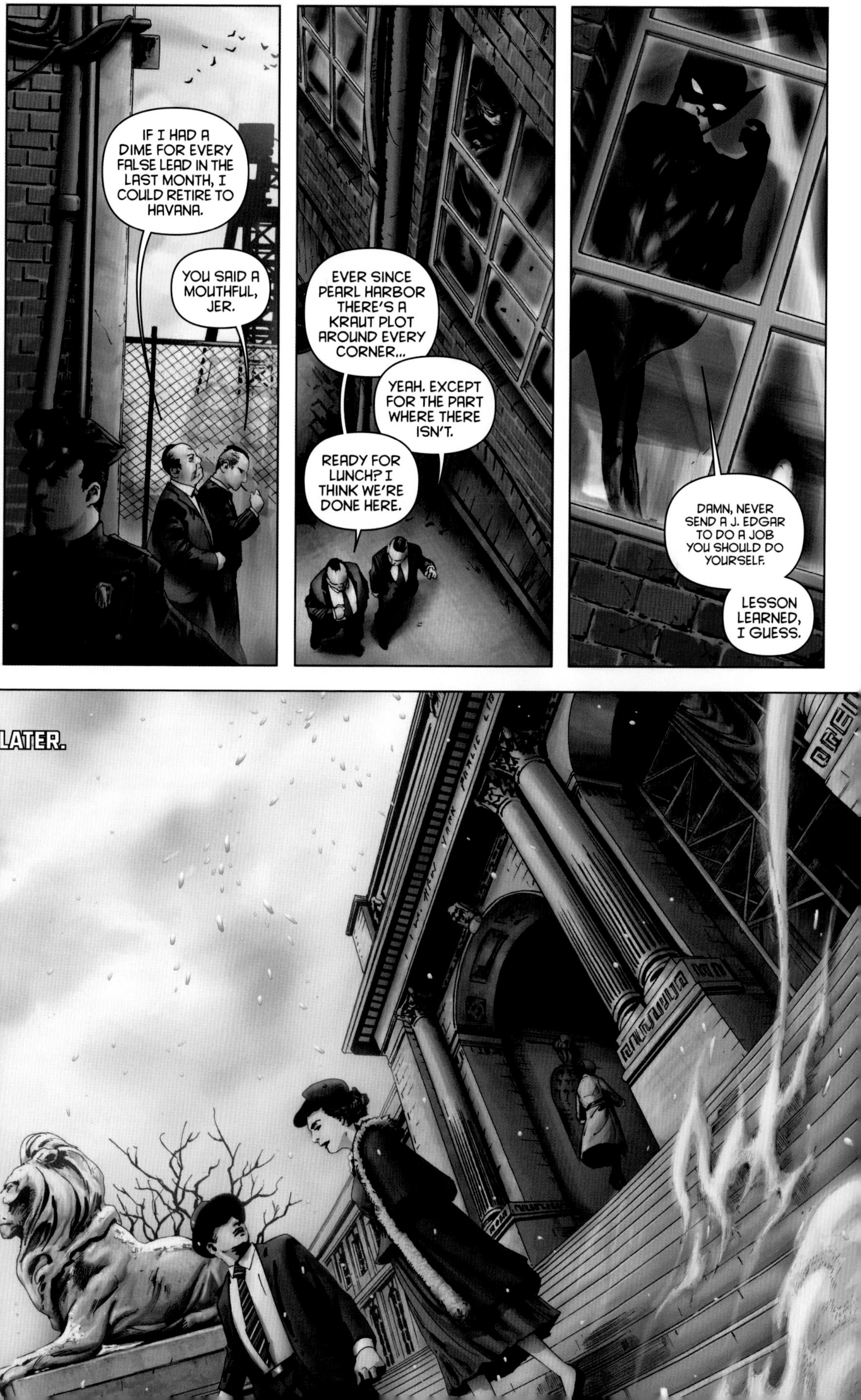
IF I HAD A DIME FOR EVERY FALSE LEAD IN THE LAST MONTH, I COULD RETIRE TO HAVANA.
YOU SAID A MOUTHFUL, JER.
EVER SINCE PEARL HARBOR THERE'S A KRAUT PLOT AROUND EVERY CORNER...
YEAH. EXCEPT FOR THE PART WHERE THERE ISN'T.
READY FOR LUNCH? I THINK WE'RE DONE HERE.
DAMN, NEVER SEND A J. EDGAR TO DO A JOB YOU SHOULD DO YOURSELF.
LESSON LEARNED, I GUESS.
LATER.

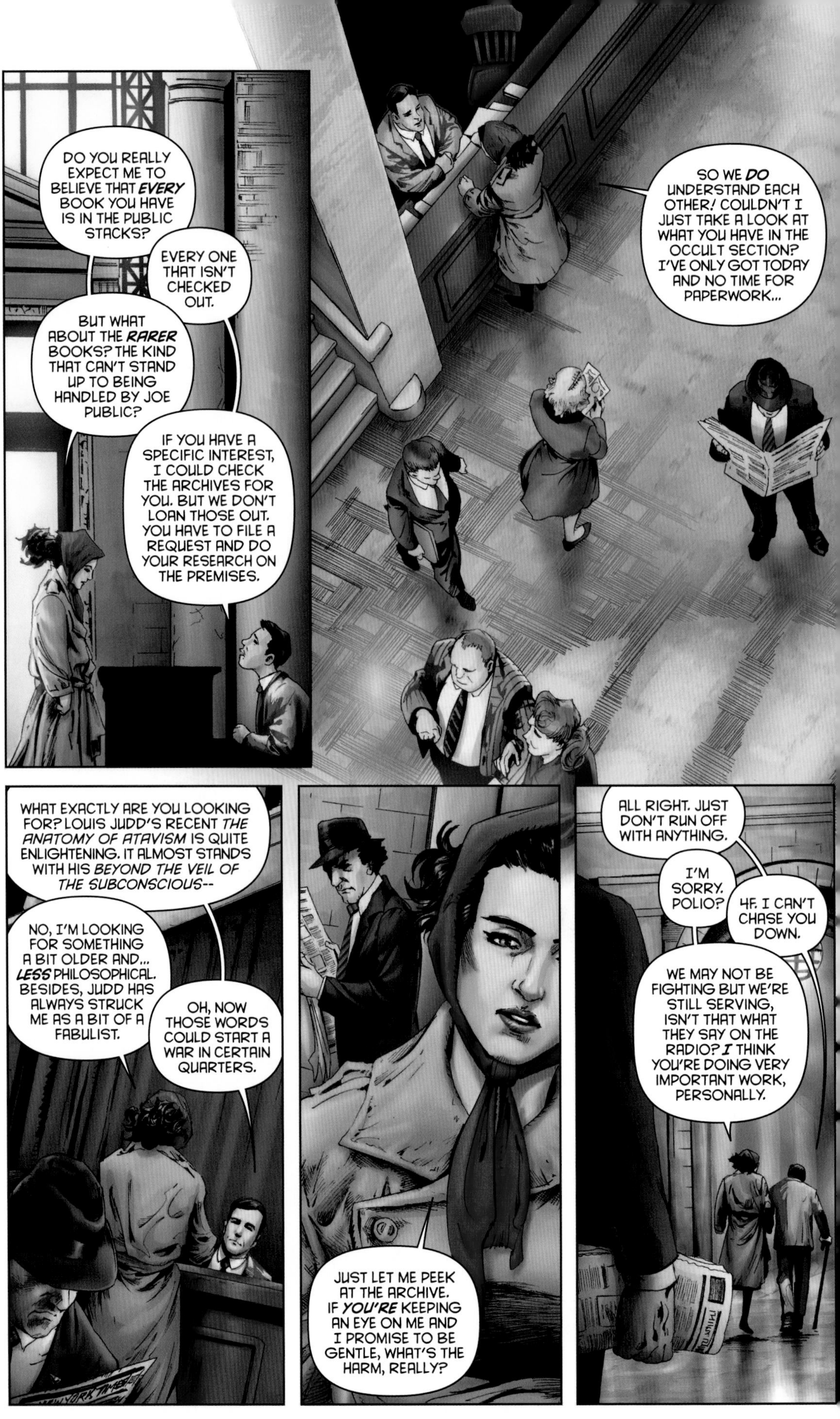
DO YOU REALLY EXPECT ME TO BELIEVE THAT EVERY BOOK YOU HAVE IS IN THE PUBLIC STACKS?
EVERY ONE THAT ISN'T CHECKED OUT.
BUT WHAT ABOUT THE RARER BOOKS? THE KIND THAT CAN'T STAND UP TO BEING HANDLED BY JOE PUBLIC?
IF YOU HAVE A SPECIFIC INTEREST, I COULD CHECK THE ARCHIVES FOR YOU. BUT WE DON'T LOAN THOSE OUT. YOU HAVE TO FILE A REQUEST AND DO YOUR RESEARCH ON THE PREMISES.
SO WE DO UNDERSTAND EACH OTHER! COULDN'T I JUST TAKE A LOOK AT WHAT YOU HAVE IN THE OCCULT SECTION? I'VE ONLY GOT TODAY AND NO TIME FOR PAPERWORK...
WHAT EXACTLY ARE YOU LOOKING FOR? LOUIS JUDD'S RECENT THE ANATOMY OF ATAVISM IS QUITE ENLIGHTENING. IT ALMOST STANDS WITH HIS BEYOND THE VEIL OF THE SUBCONSCIOUS--
NO, I'M LOOKING FOR SOMETHING A BIT OLDER AND... LESS PHILOSOPHICAL. BESIDES, JUDD HAS ALWAYS STRUCK ME AS A BIT OF A FABULIST.
OH, NOW THOSE WORDS COULD START A WAR IN CERTAIN QUARTERS.
JUST LET ME PEEK AT THE ARCHIVE. IF YOU'RE KEEPING AN EYE ON ME AND I PROMISE TO BE GENTLE, WHAT'S THE HARM, REALLY?
ALL RIGHT. JUST DON'T RUN OFF WITH ANYTHING.
I'M SORRY. POLIO?
4F. I CAN'T CHASE YOU DOWN.
WE MAY NOT BE FIGHTING BUT WE'RE STILL SERVING, ISN'T THAT WHAT THEY SAY ON THE RADIO? I THINK YOU'RE DOING VERY IMPORTANT WORK, PERSONALLY.

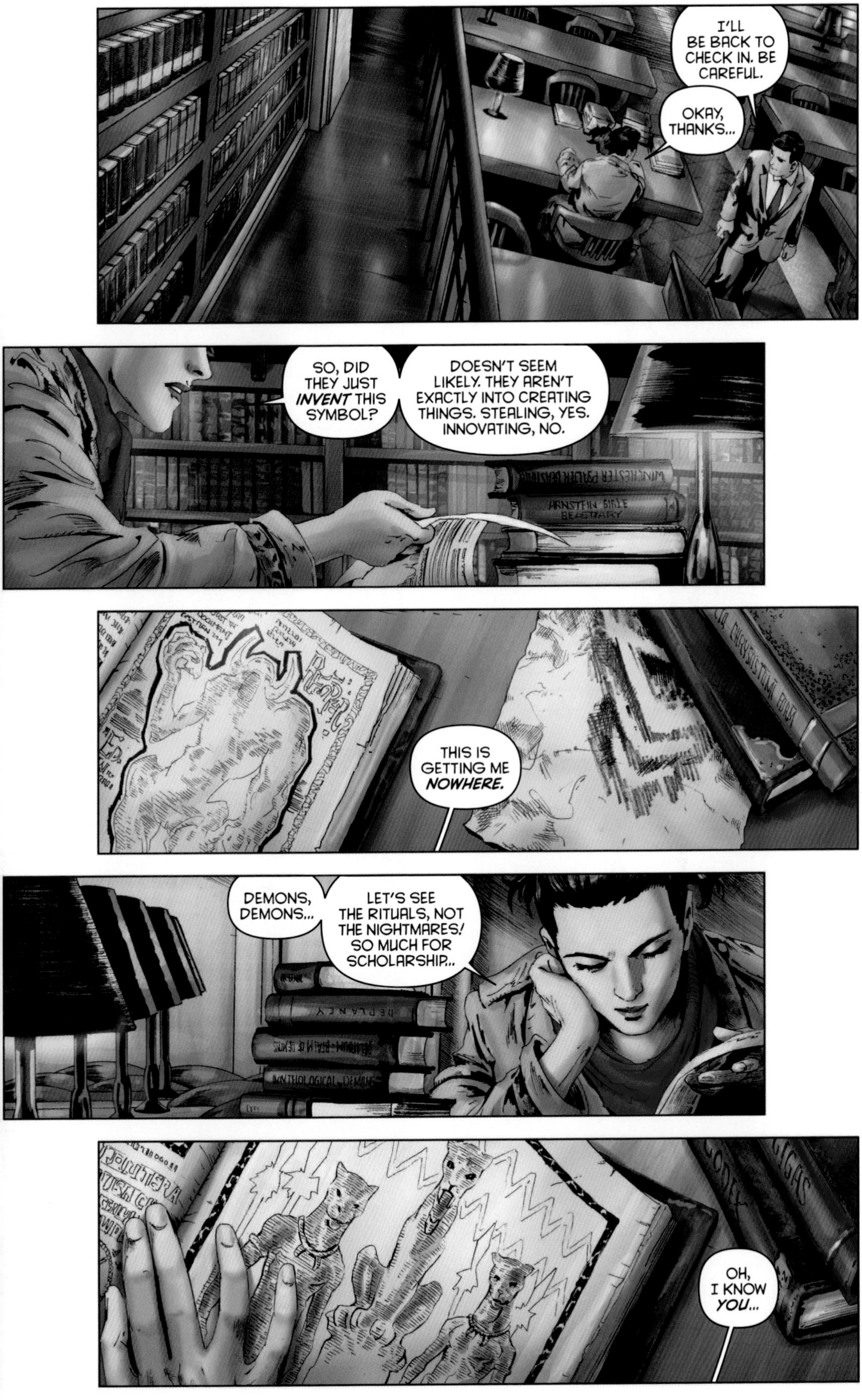

I'LL BE BACK TO CHECK IN. BE CAREFUL.
OKAY, THANKS...
SO, DID THEY JUST *INVENT* THIS SYMBOL?
DOESN'T SEEM LIKELY. THEY AREN'T EXACTLY INTO CREATING THINGS. STEALING, YES. INNOVATING, NO.
THIS IS GETTING ME *NOWHERE.*
DEMONS, DEMONS...
LET'S SEE THE RITUALS, NOT THE NIGHTMARES! SO MUCH FOR SCHOLARSHIP...
OH, I KNOW *YOU*...

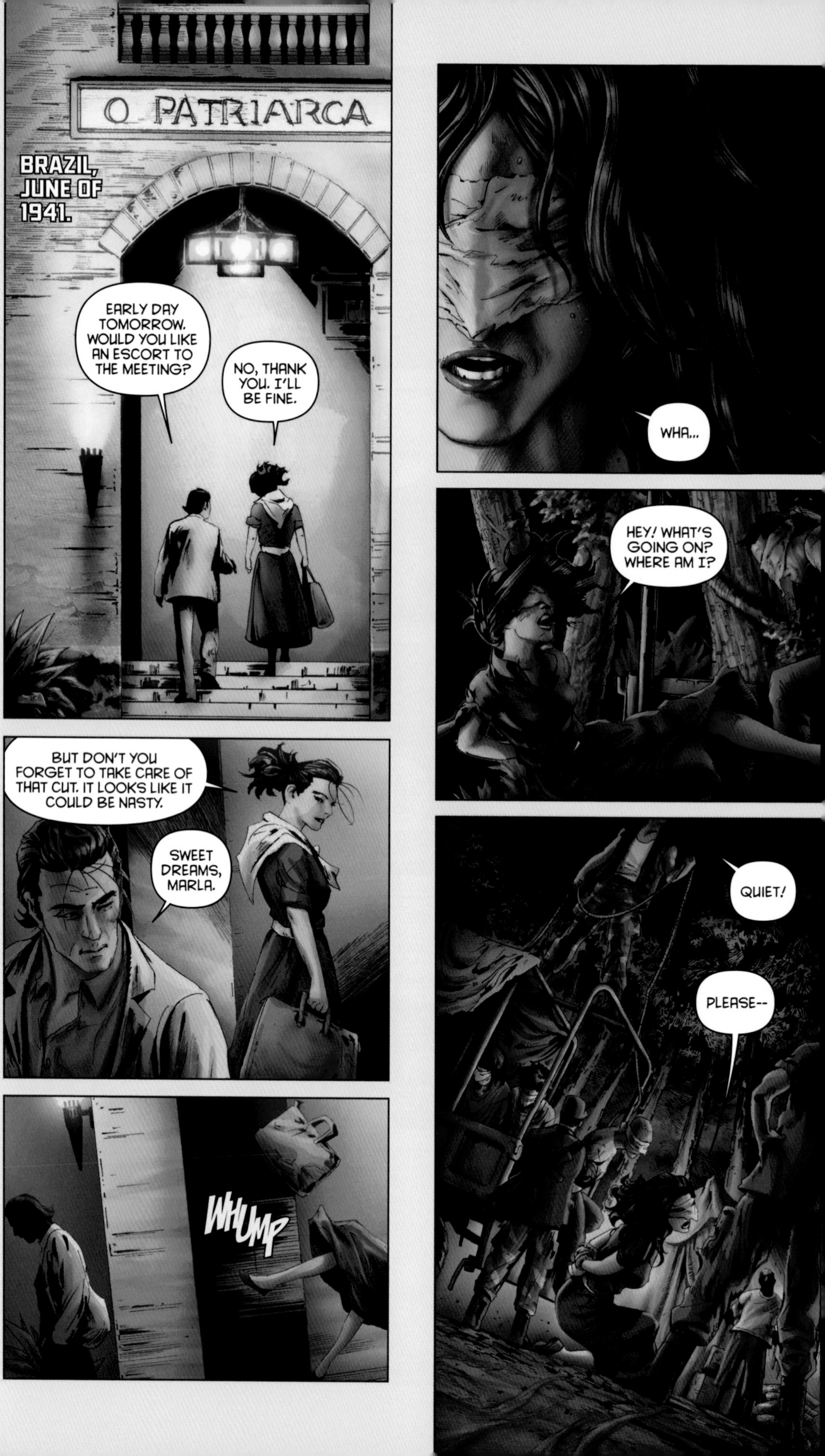
O PATRIARCA
BRAZIL, JUNE OF 1941.
EARLY DAY TOMORROW. WOULD YOU LIKE AN ESCORT TO THE MEETING?
NO, THANK YOU. I'LL BE FINE.
BUT DON'T YOU FORGET TO TAKE CARE OF THAT CUT. IT LOOKS LIKE IT COULD BE NASTY.
SWEET DREAMS, MARLA.
WHUMP
WHA...
HEY! WHAT'S GOING ON? WHERE AM I?
QUIET!
PLEASE--

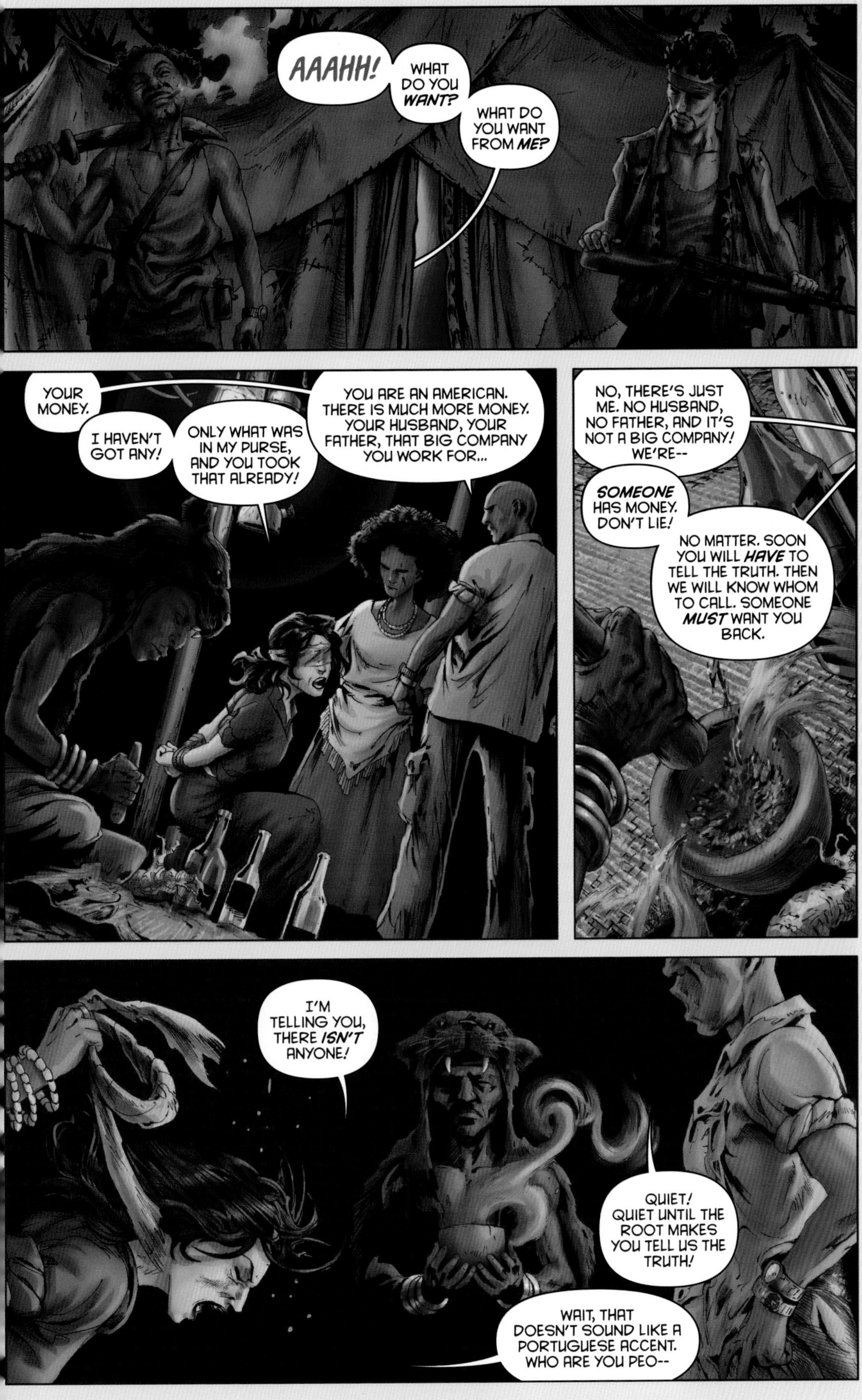
AAAHH!
WHAT DO YOU WANT?
WHAT DO YOU WANT FROM ME?
YOUR MONEY.
I HAVEN'T GOT ANY!
ONLY WHAT WAS IN MY PURSE, AND YOU TOOK THAT ALREADY!
YOU ARE AN AMERICAN. THERE IS MUCH MORE MONEY. YOUR HUSBAND, YOUR FATHER, THAT BIG COMPANY YOU WORK FOR...
NO, THERE'S JUST ME. NO HUSBAND, NO FATHER, AND IT'S NOT A BIG COMPANY! WE'RE--
SOMEONE HAS MONEY. DON'T LIE!
NO MATTER. SOON YOU WILL HAVE TO TELL THE TRUTH. THEN WE WILL KNOW WHOM TO CALL. SOMEONE MUST WANT YOU BACK.
I'M TELLING YOU, THERE ISN'T ANYONE!
QUIET! QUIET UNTIL THE ROOT MAKES YOU TELL US THE TRUTH!
WAIT, THAT DOESN'T SOUND LIKE A PORTUGUESE ACCENT. WHO ARE YOU PEO--

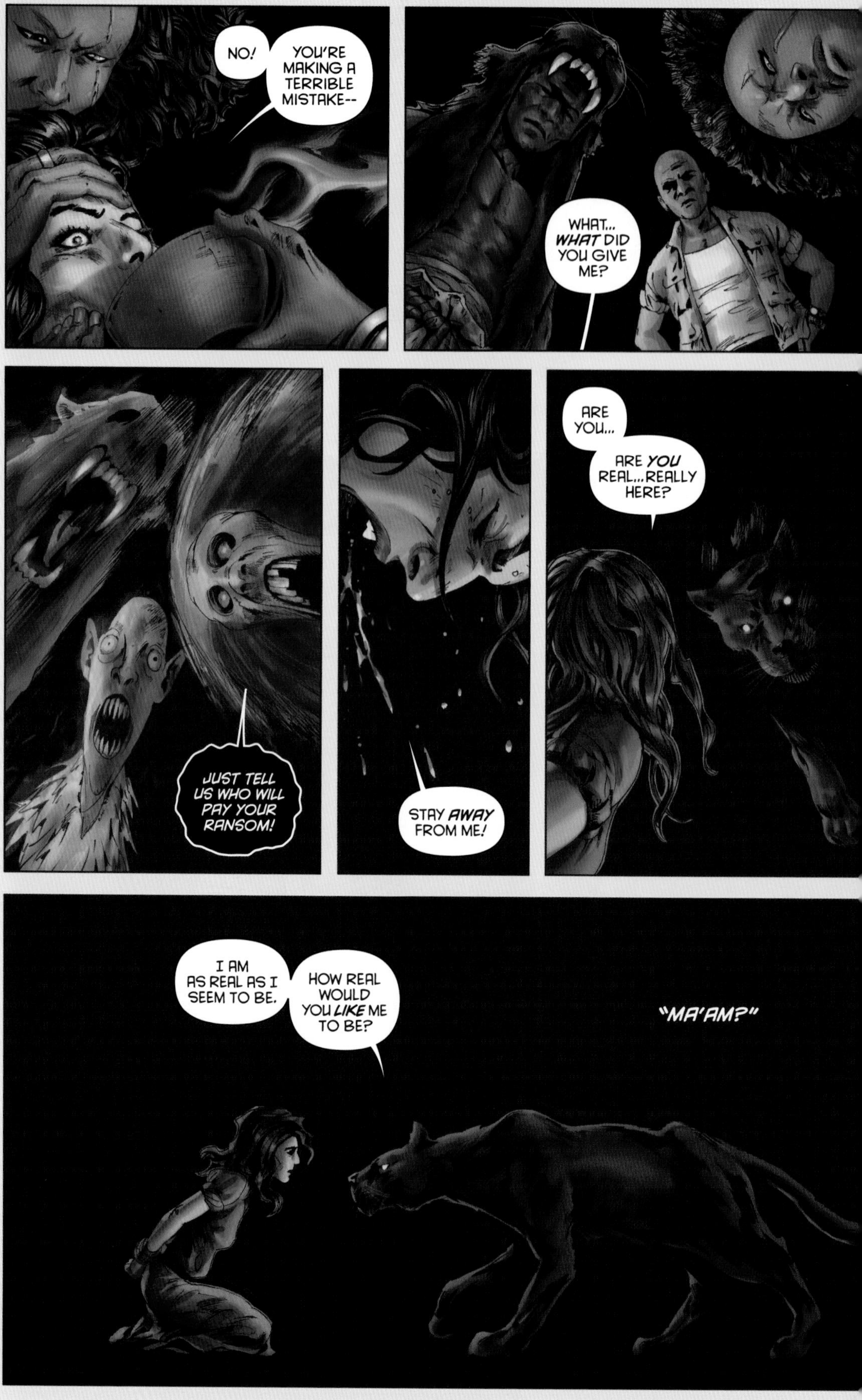
NO!
YOU'RE MAKING A TERRIBLE MISTAKE--
WHAT... *WHAT* DID YOU GIVE ME?
JUST TELL US WHO WILL PAY YOUR RANSOM!
STAY *AWAY* FROM ME!
ARE YOU...
ARE *YOU* REAL...REALLY HERE?
I AM AS REAL AS I SEEM TO BE.
HOW REAL WOULD YOU *LIKE* ME TO BE?
"MA'AM?"

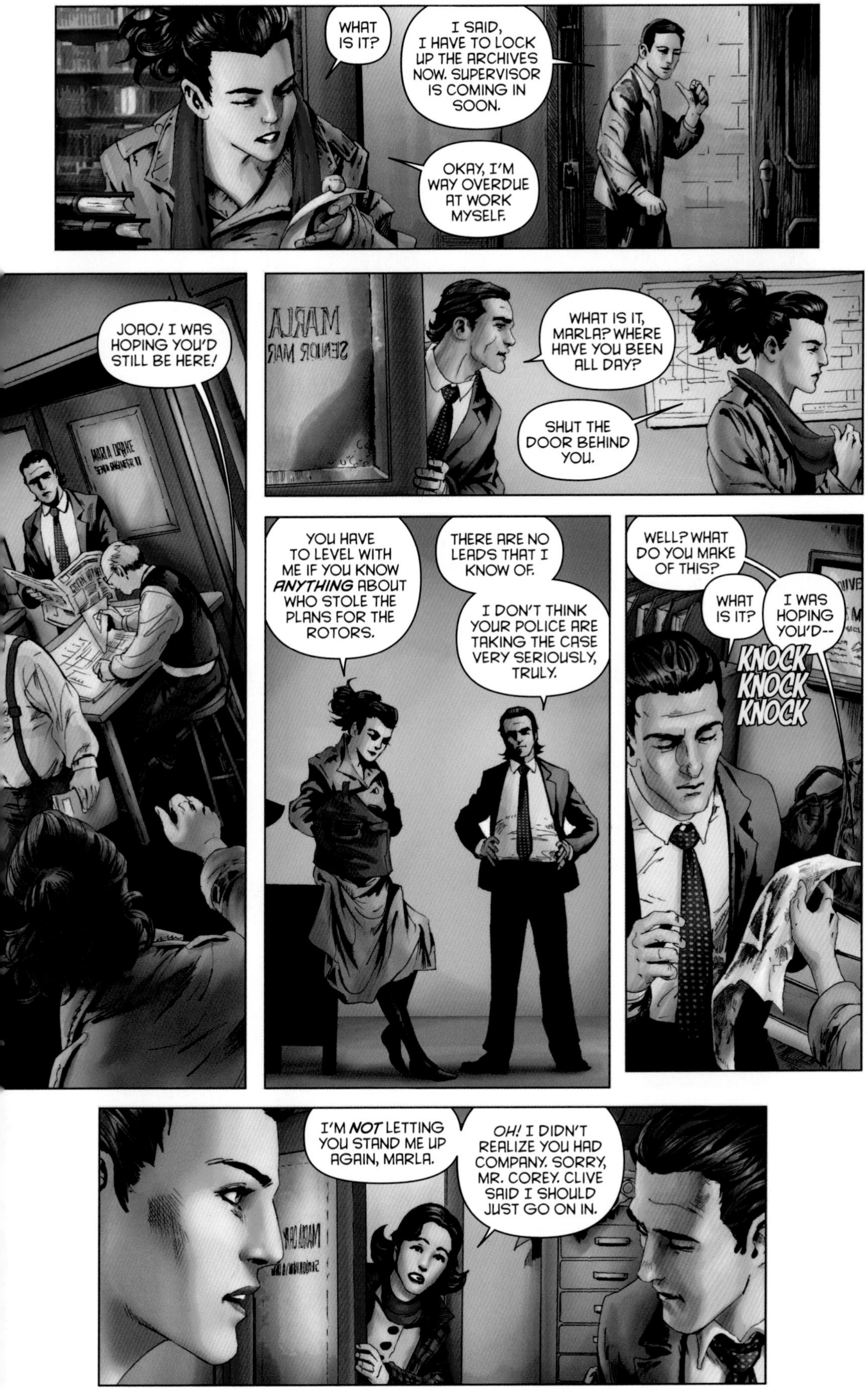
WHAT IS IT?
I SAID, I HAVE TO LOCK UP THE ARCHIVES NOW. SUPERVISOR IS COMING IN SOON.
OKAY, I'M WAY OVERDUE AT WORK MYSELF.
JOAO! I WAS HOPING YOU'D STILL BE HERE!
WHAT IS IT, MARLA? WHERE HAVE YOU BEEN ALL DAY?
SHUT THE DOOR BEHIND YOU.
YOU HAVE TO LEVEL WITH ME IF YOU KNOW ANYTHING ABOUT WHO STOLE THE PLANS FOR THE ROTORS.
THERE ARE NO LEADS THAT I KNOW OF.
I DON'T THINK YOUR POLICE ARE TAKING THE CASE VERY SERIOUSLY, TRULY.
WELL? WHAT DO YOU MAKE OF THIS?
WHAT IS IT?
I WAS HOPING YOU'D--
KNOCK KNOCK KNOCK
I'M NOT LETTING YOU STAND ME UP AGAIN, MARLA.
OH! I DIDN'T REALIZE YOU HAD COMPANY. SORRY, MR. COREY. CLIVE SAID I SHOULD JUST GO ON IN.

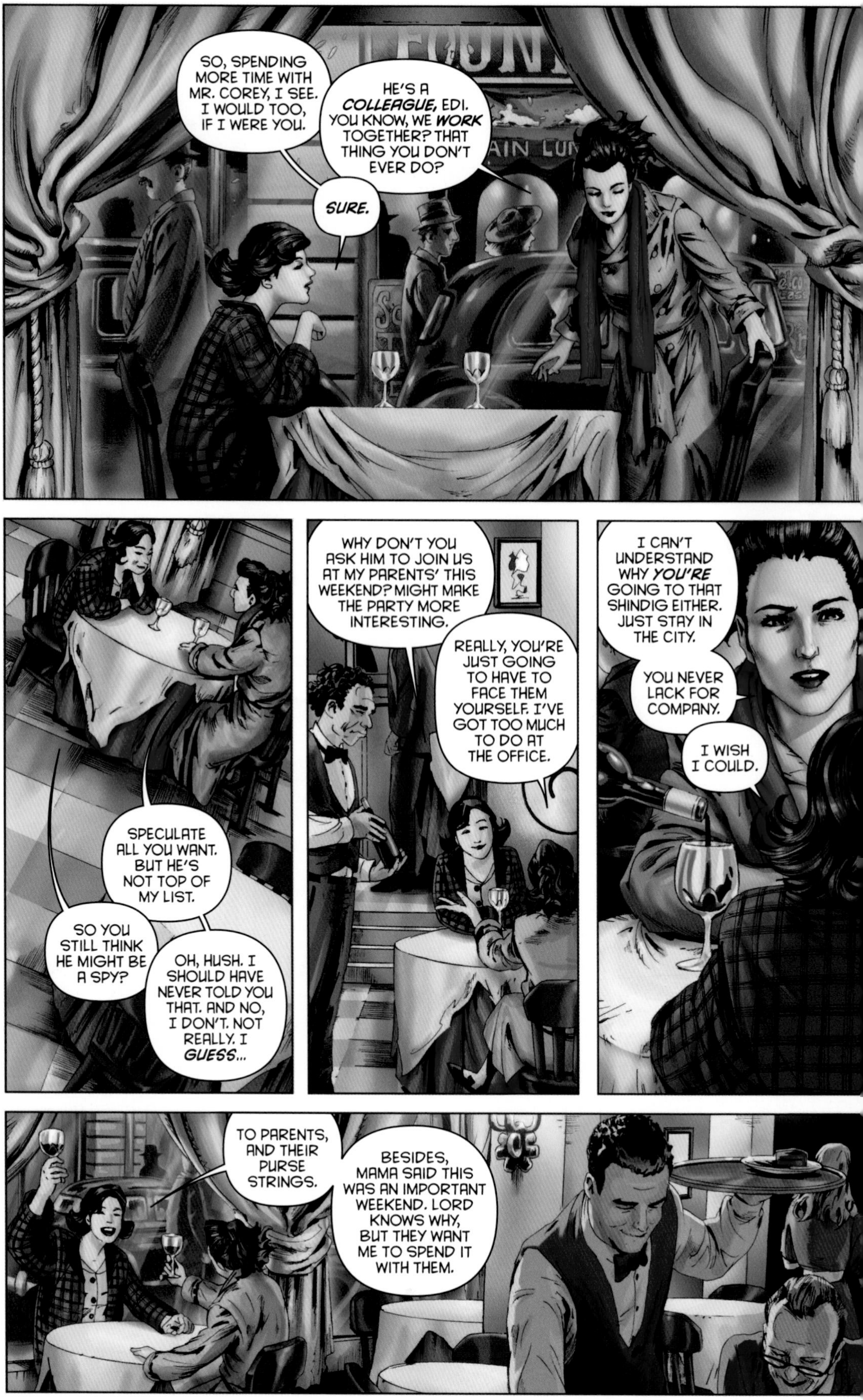
SO, SPENDING MORE TIME WITH MR. COREY, I SEE. I WOULD TOO, IF I WERE YOU.
HE'S A *COLLEAGUE,* EDI. YOU KNOW, WE *WORK* TOGETHER? THAT THING YOU DON'T EVER DO?
SURE.
SPECULATE ALL YOU WANT. BUT HE'S NOT TOP OF MY LIST.
SO YOU STILL THINK HE MIGHT BE A SPY?
OH, HUSH. I SHOULD HAVE NEVER TOLD YOU THAT. AND NO, I DON'T. NOT REALLY. I *GUESS...*
WHY DON'T YOU ASK HIM TO JOIN US AT MY PARENTS' THIS WEEKEND? MIGHT MAKE THE PARTY MORE INTERESTING.
REALLY, YOU'RE JUST GOING TO HAVE TO FACE THEM YOURSELF. I'VE GOT TOO MUCH TO DO AT THE OFFICE.
I CAN'T UNDERSTAND WHY *YOU'RE* GOING TO THAT SHINDIG EITHER. JUST STAY IN THE CITY.
YOU NEVER LACK FOR COMPANY.
I WISH I COULD.
TO PARENTS, AND THEIR PURSE STRINGS.
BESIDES, MAMA SAID THIS WAS AN IMPORTANT WEEKEND. LORD KNOWS WHY, BUT THEY WANT ME TO SPEND IT WITH THEM.

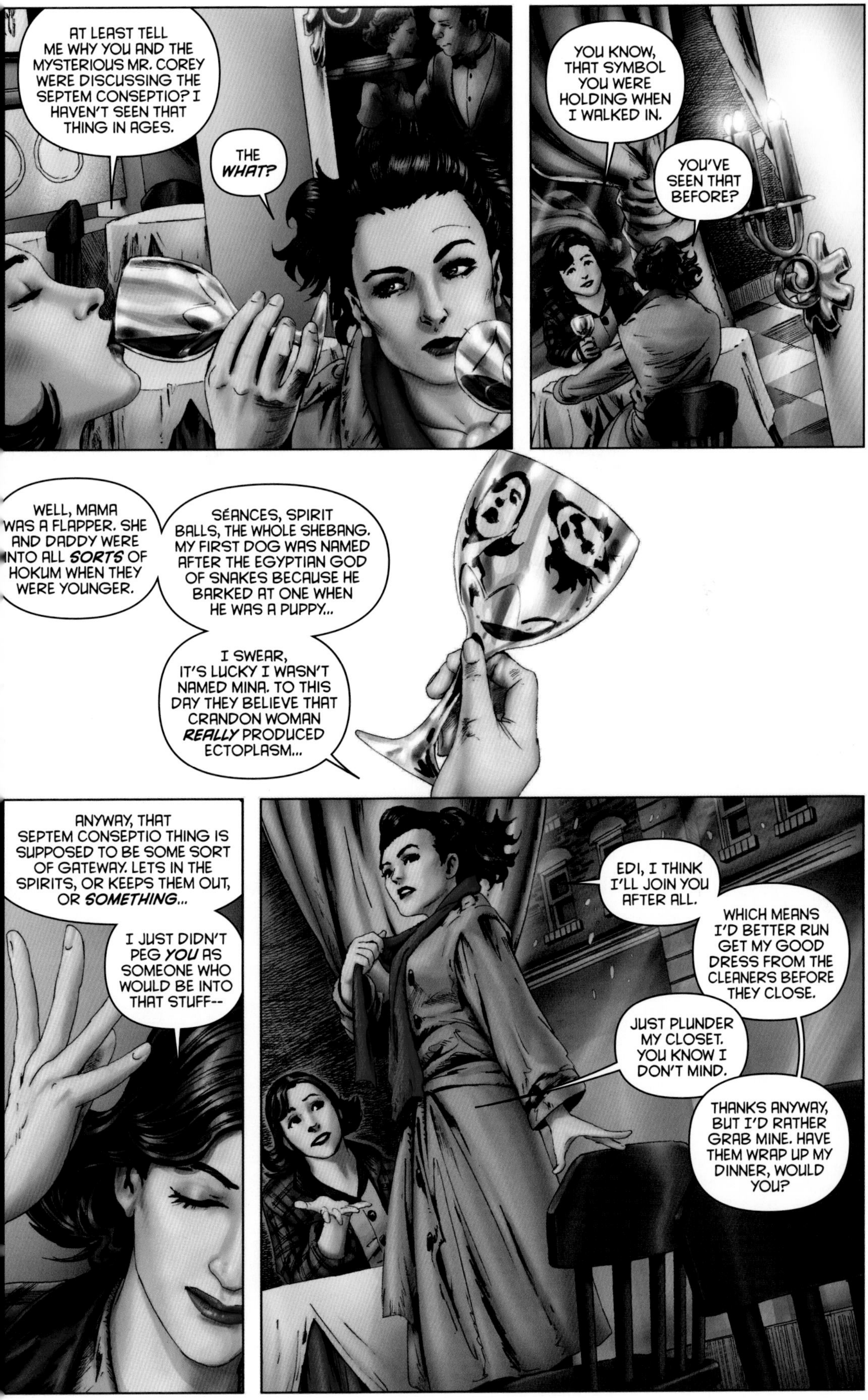
AT LEAST TELL ME WHY YOU AND THE MYSTERIOUS MR. COREY WERE DISCUSSING THE SEPTEM CONSEPTIO? I HAVEN'T SEEN THAT THING IN AGES.
THE *WHAT?*
YOU KNOW, THAT SYMBOL YOU WERE HOLDING WHEN I WALKED IN.
YOU'VE SEEN THAT BEFORE?
WELL, MAMA WAS A FLAPPER. SHE AND DADDY WERE INTO ALL *SORTS* OF HOKUM WHEN THEY WERE YOUNGER.
SÉANCES, SPIRIT BALLS, THE WHOLE SHEBANG. MY FIRST DOG WAS NAMED AFTER THE EGYPTIAN GOD OF SNAKES BECAUSE HE BARKED AT ONE WHEN HE WAS A PUPPY...
I SWEAR, IT'S LUCKY I WASN'T NAMED MINA. TO THIS DAY THEY BELIEVE THAT CRANDON WOMAN *REALLY* PRODUCED ECTOPLASM...
ANYWAY, THAT SEPTEM CONSEPTIO THING IS SUPPOSED TO BE SOME SORT OF GATEWAY. LETS IN THE SPIRITS, OR KEEPS THEM OUT, OR *SOMETHING*...
I JUST DIDN'T PEG *YOU* AS SOMEONE WHO WOULD BE INTO THAT STUFF--
EDI, I THINK I'LL JOIN YOU AFTER ALL.
WHICH MEANS I'D BETTER RUN GET MY GOOD DRESS FROM THE CLEANERS BEFORE THEY CLOSE.
JUST PLUNDER MY CLOSET. YOU KNOW I DON'T MIND.
THANKS ANYWAY, BUT I'D RATHER GRAB MINE. HAVE THEM WRAP UP MY DINNER, WOULD YOU?

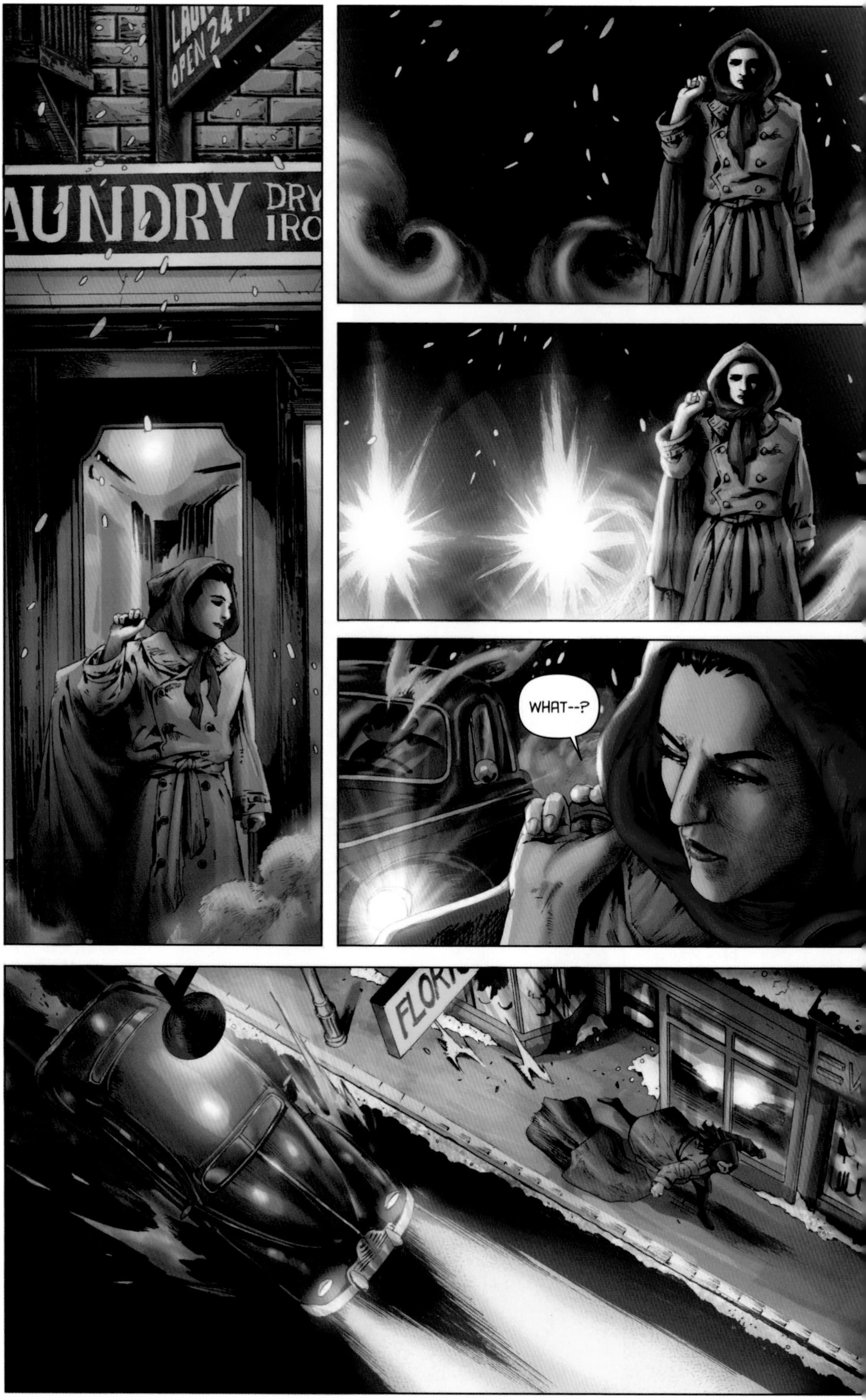
OPEN 24
AUNDRY
DRY
IRO
WHAT--?
FLOR

SKREEEE

SKREEET

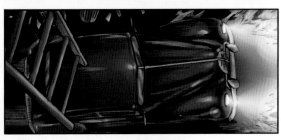

SHE'S GOTTA BE UP THERE!

C'MON DOWN, HON. IT'S GETTING AWFULLY COLD OUT AND WE GOT YOU TREED. ISN'T IT TIME TO BE REASONABLE?

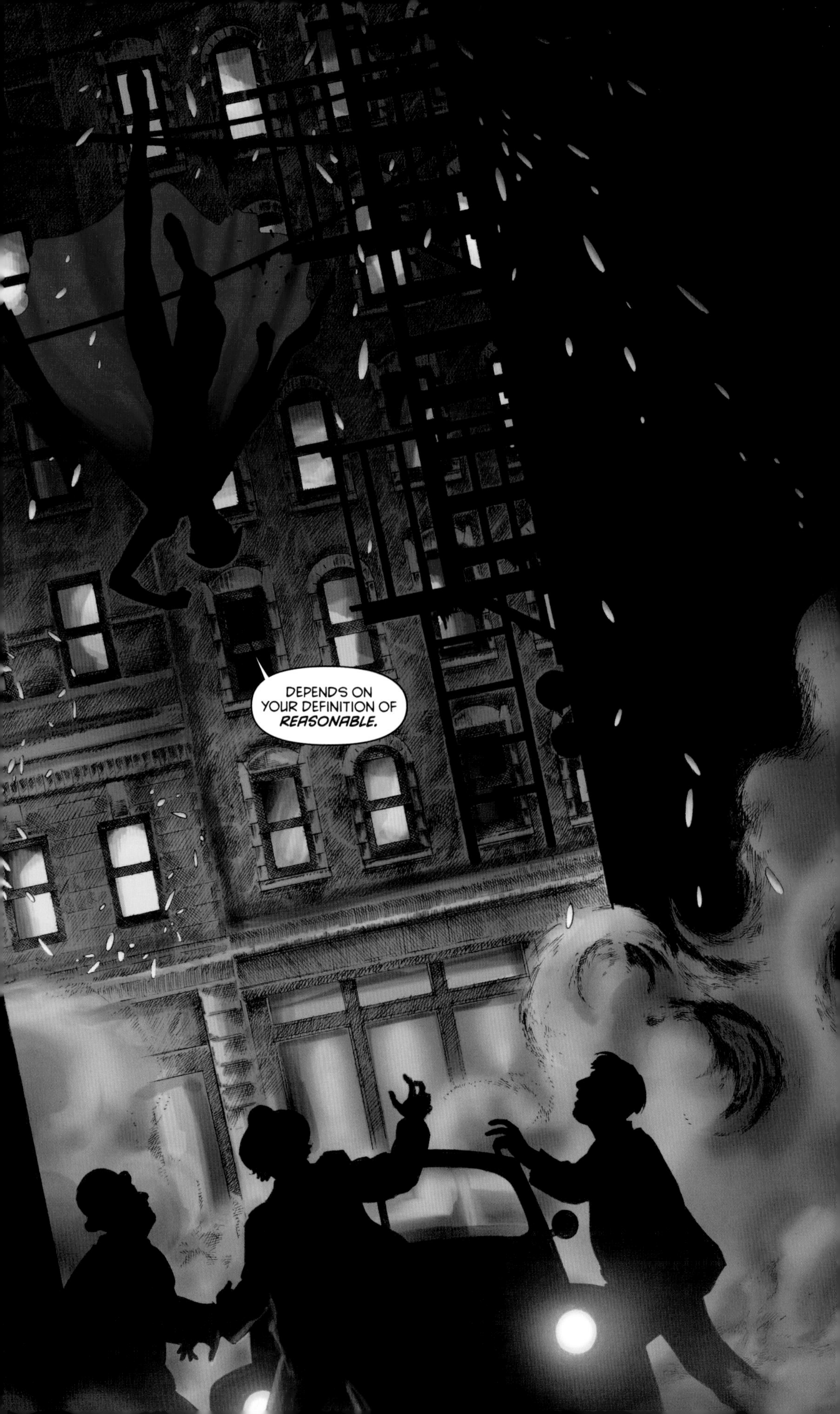
DEPENDS ON YOUR DEFINITION OF *REASONABLE.*

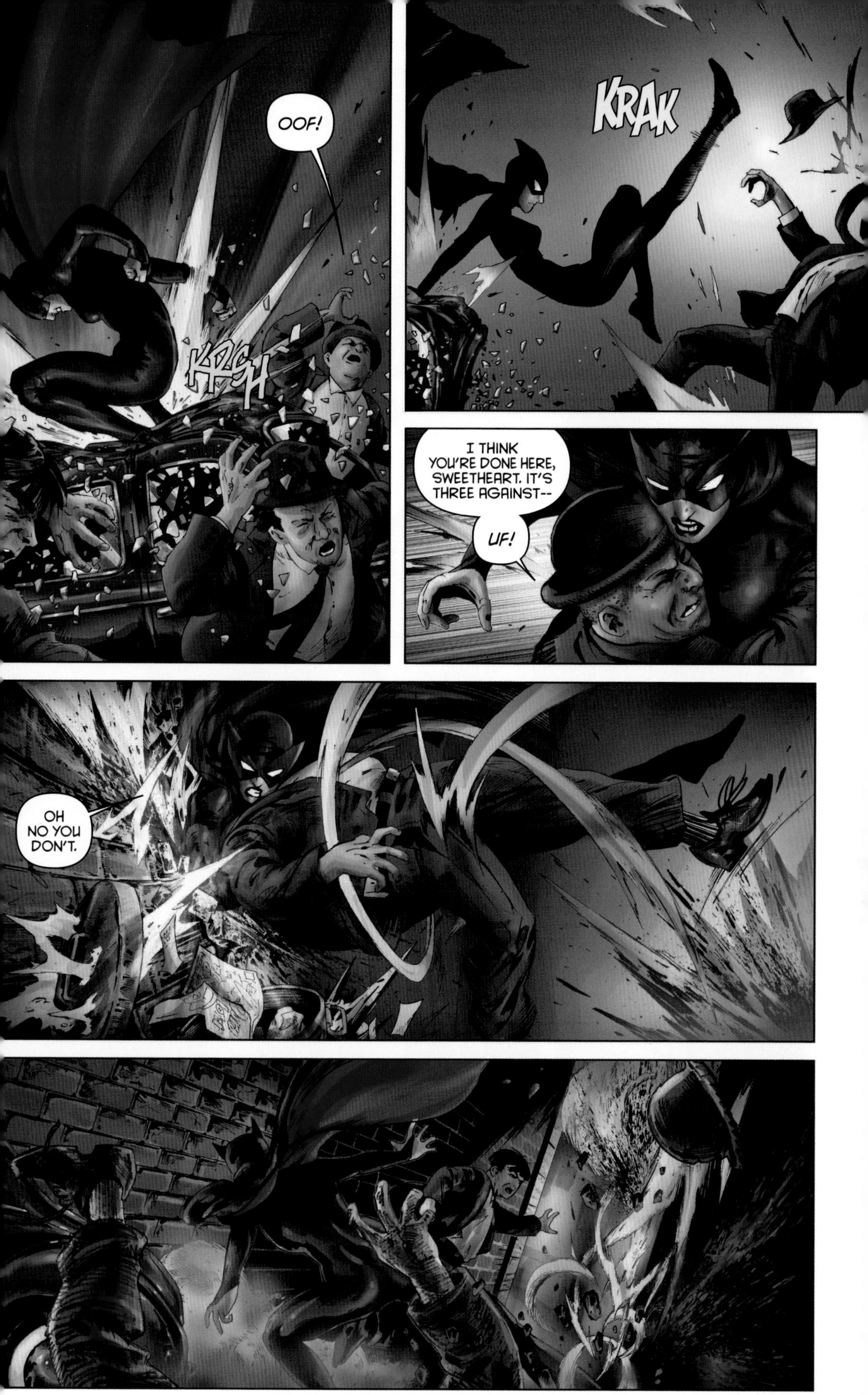
OOF!
KRASH
KRAK
I THINK YOU'RE DONE HERE, SWEETHEART. IT'S THREE AGAINST--
UF!
OH NO YOU DON'T.

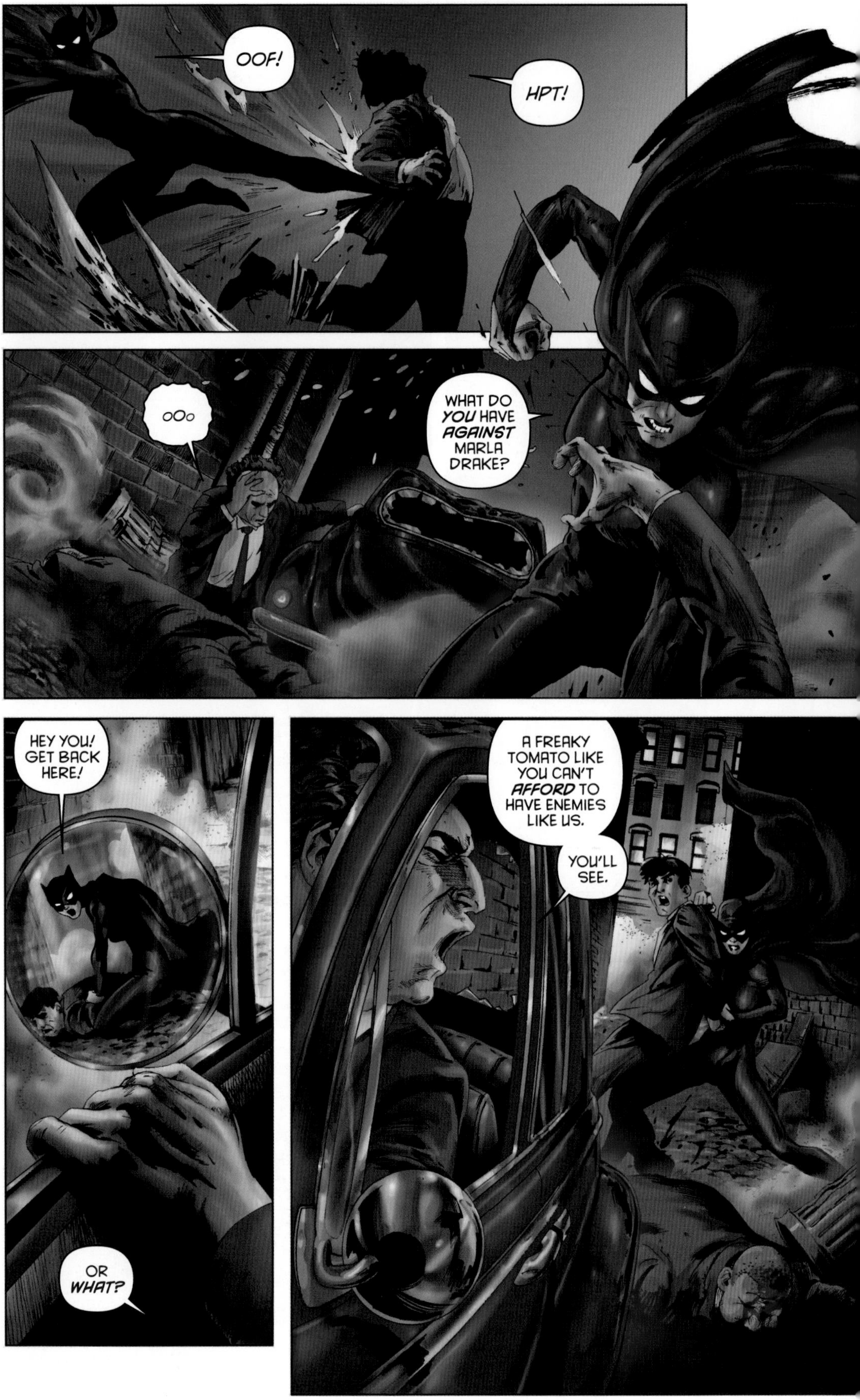
OOF!
HPT!
oOo
WHAT DO YOU HAVE AGAINST MARLA DRAKE?
HEY YOU! GET BACK HERE!
OR WHAT?
A FREAKY TOMATO LIKE YOU CAN'T AFFORD TO HAVE ENEMIES LIKE US.
YOU'LL SEE.

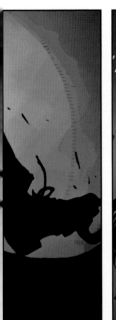

HEY! JOHN! WHAT ABOUT *ME?* YOU *CAN'T* LEAVE ME HERE!

NO! YOU'LL--

-:HRR-CHK:-

WHUMP

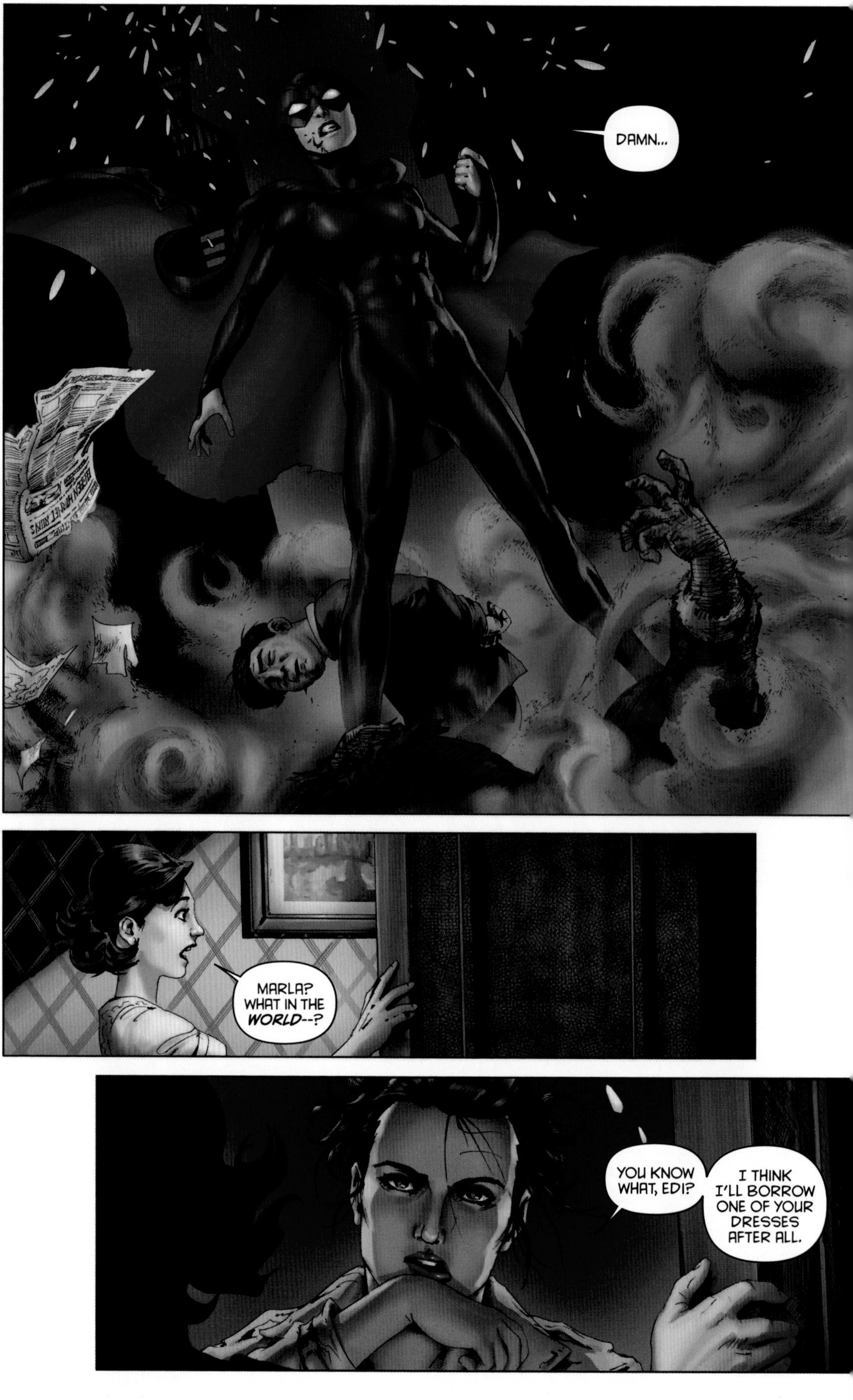
DAMN...
MARLA? WHAT IN THE *WORLD*--?
YOU KNOW WHAT, EDI?
I THINK I'LL BORROW ONE OF YOUR DRESSES AFTER ALL.

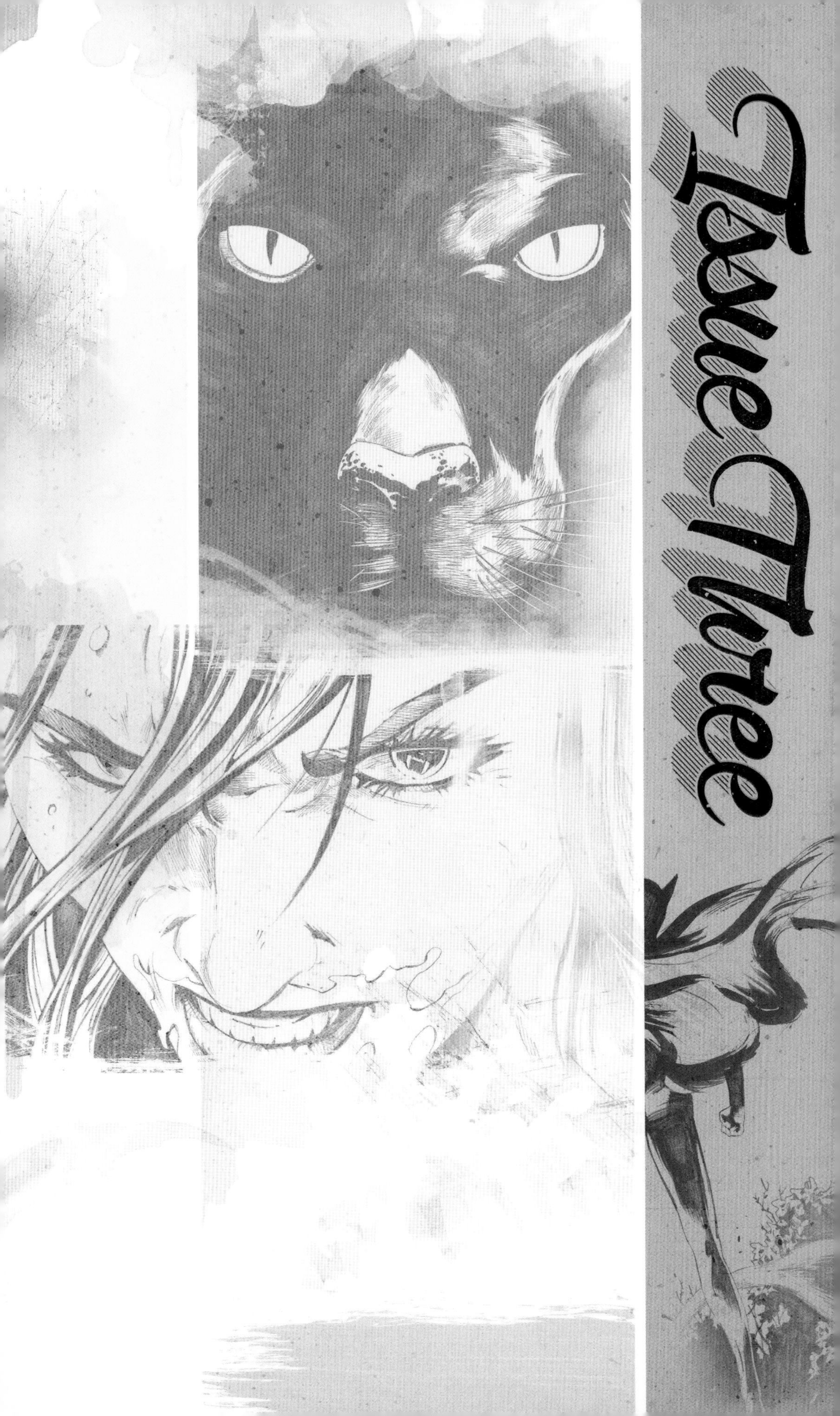
Issue Three

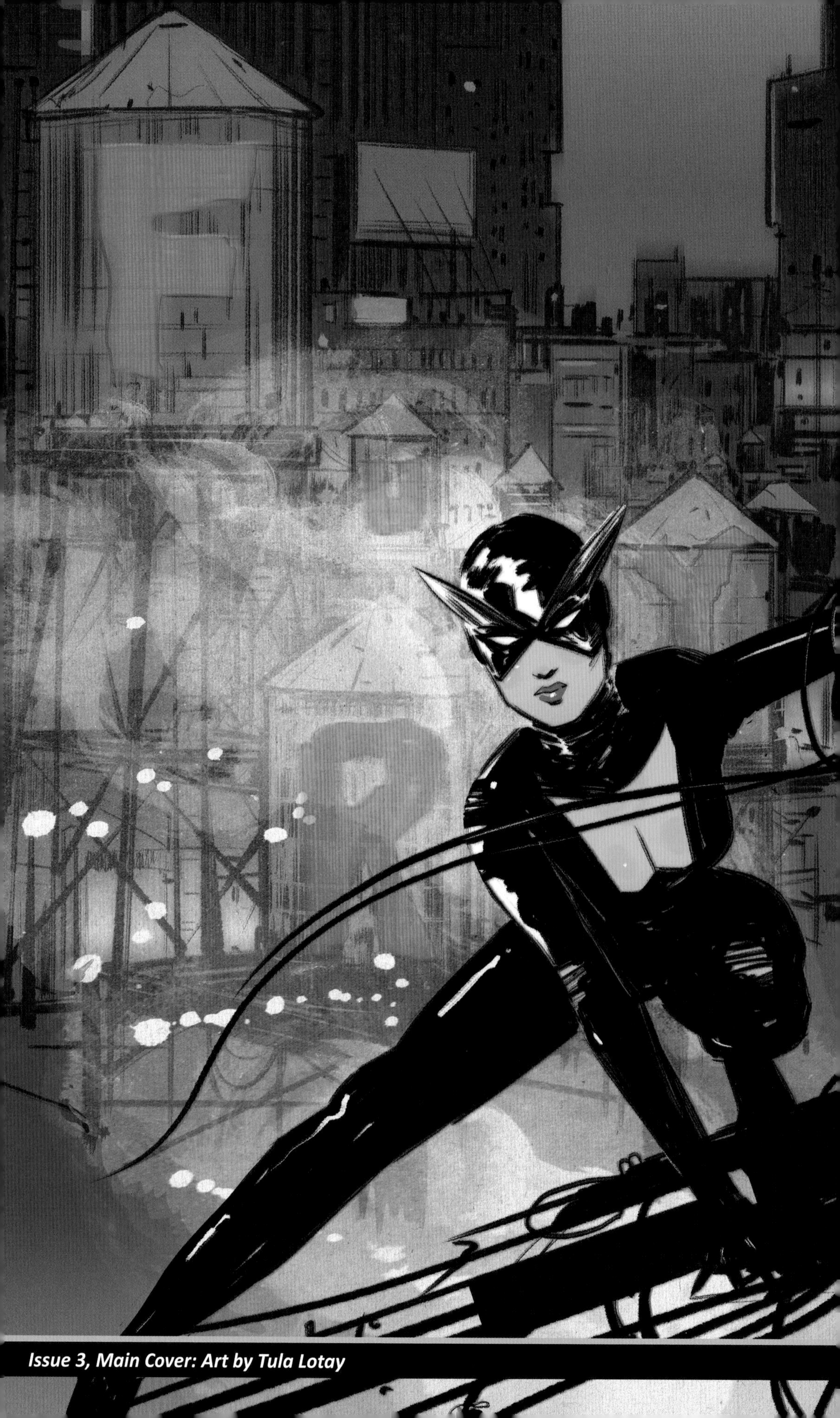

Issue 3, Main Cover: Art by Tula Lotay

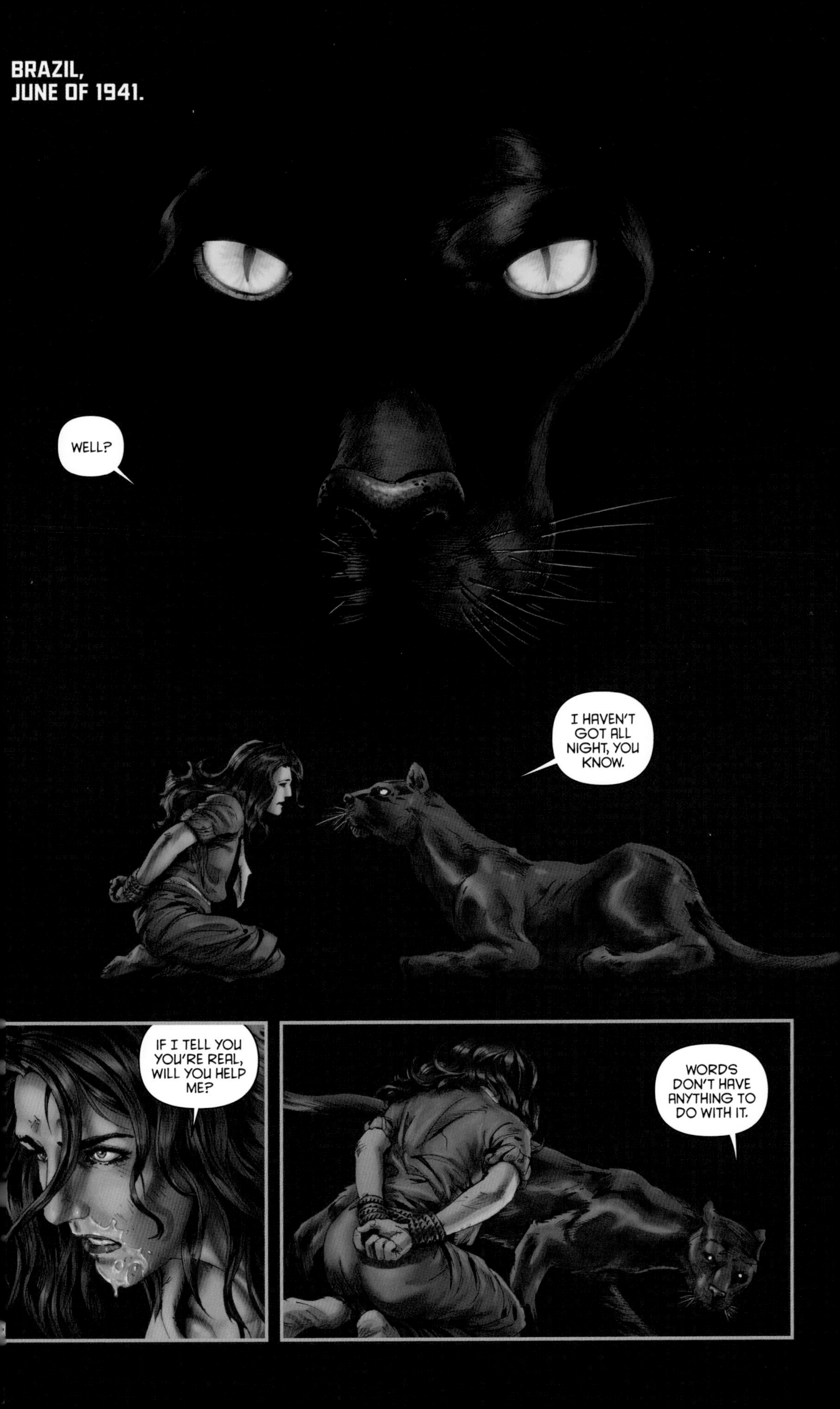
BRAZIL,
JUNE OF 1941.
WELL?
I HAVEN'T GOT ALL NIGHT, YOU KNOW.
IF I TELL YOU YOU'RE REAL, WILL YOU HELP ME?
WORDS DON'T HAVE ANYTHING TO DO WITH IT.

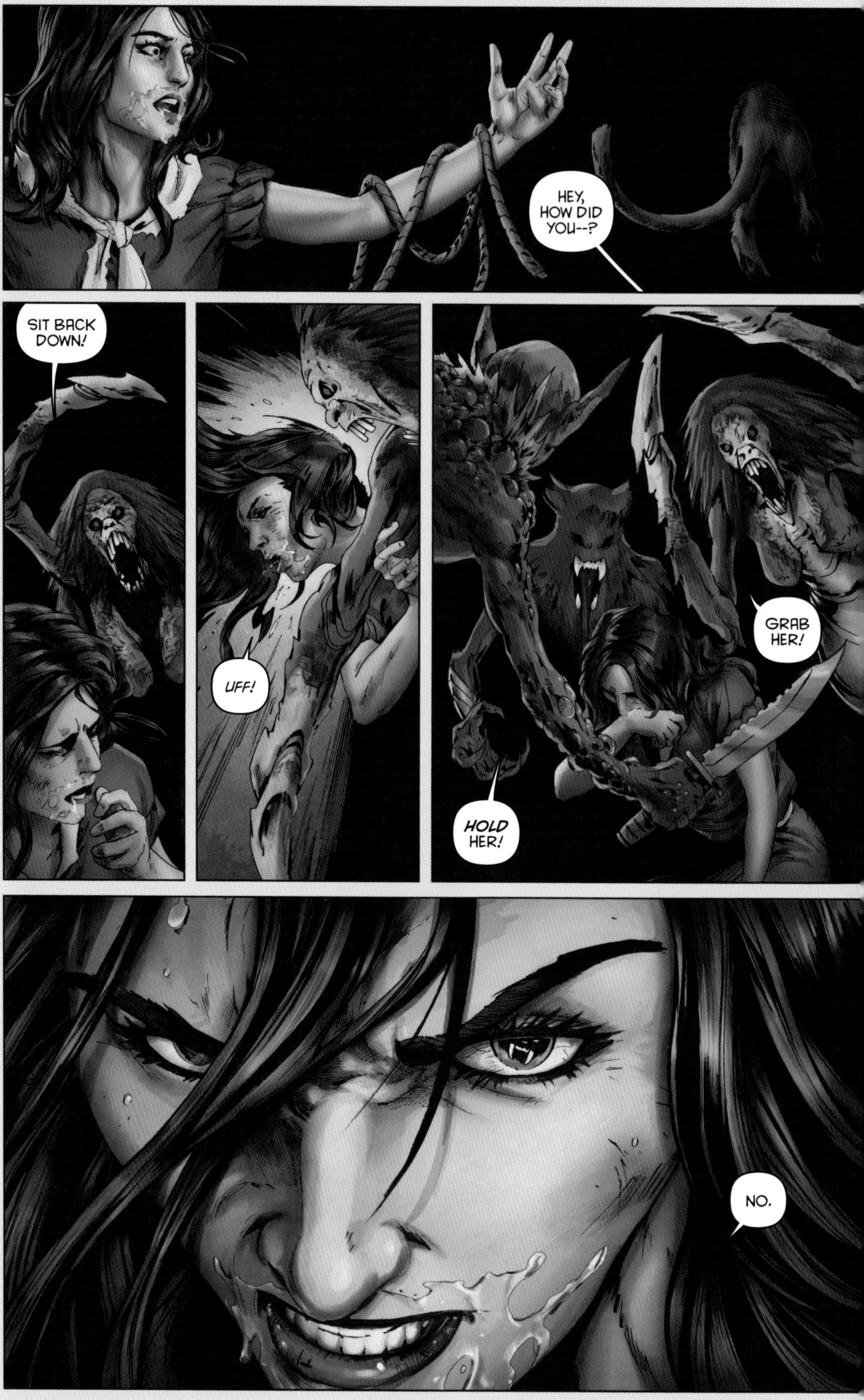
HEY, HOW DID YOU--?
SIT BACK DOWN!
UFF!
GRAB HER!
HOLD HER!
NO.

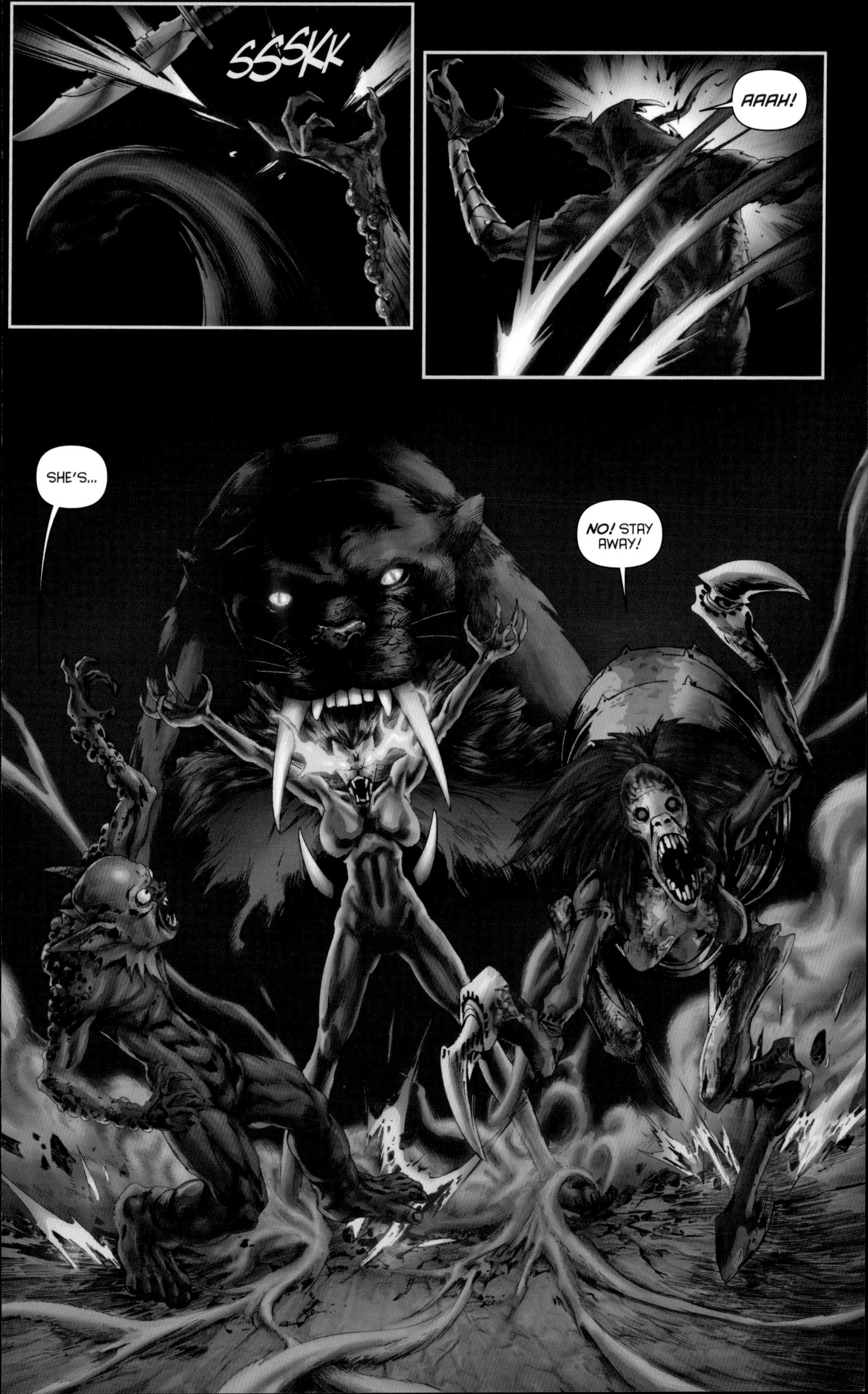
SSSKK
AAAH!
SHE'S...
NO! STAY AWAY!

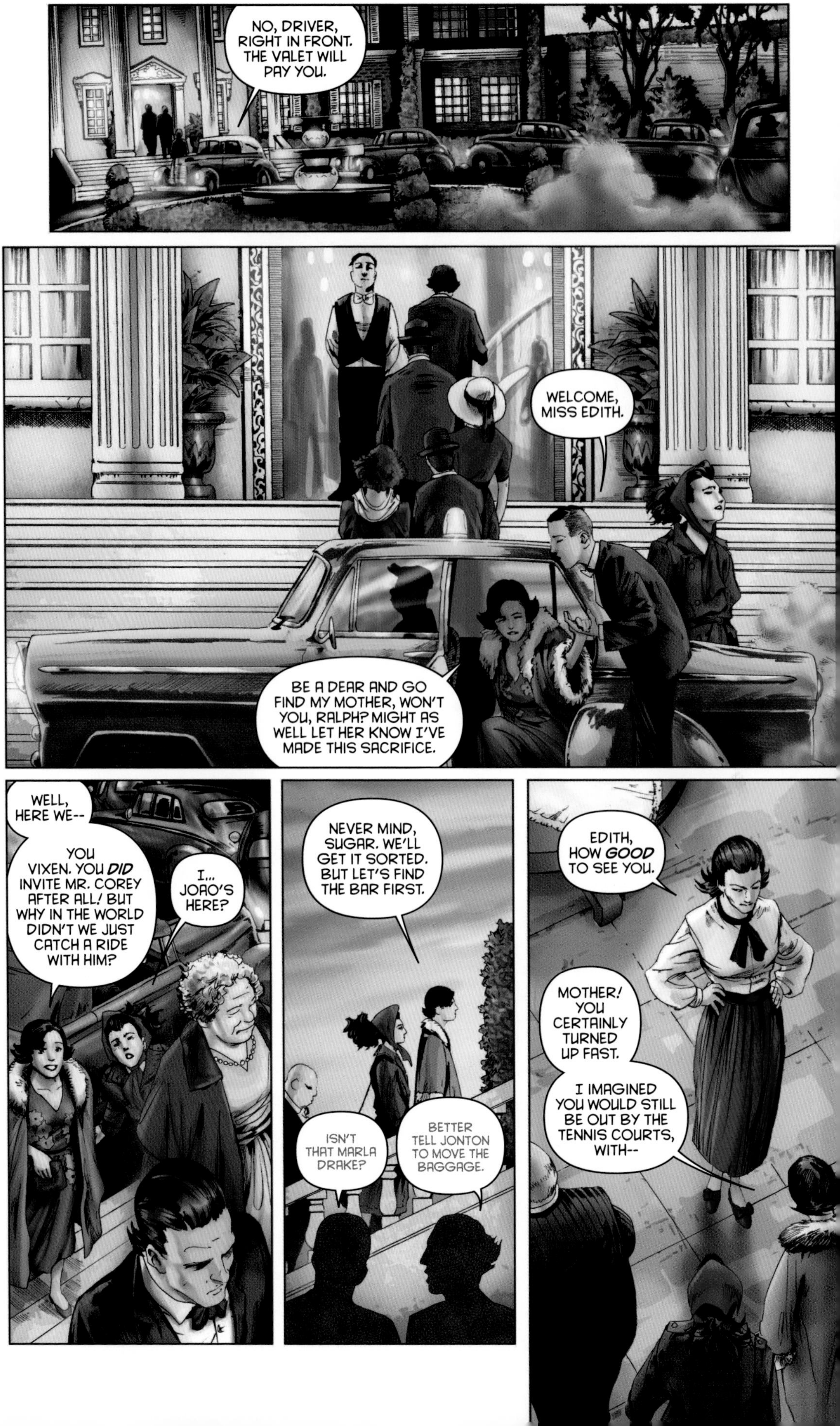
NO, DRIVER, RIGHT IN FRONT. THE VALET WILL PAY YOU.
WELCOME, MISS EDITH.
BE A DEAR AND GO FIND MY MOTHER, WON'T YOU, RALPH? MIGHT AS WELL LET HER KNOW I'VE MADE THIS SACRIFICE.
WELL, HERE WE--
YOU VIXEN. YOU *DID* INVITE MR. COREY AFTER ALL! BUT WHY IN THE WORLD DIDN'T WE JUST CATCH A RIDE WITH HIM?
I... JOAO'S HERE?
NEVER MIND, SUGAR. WE'LL GET IT SORTED. BUT LET'S FIND THE BAR FIRST.
ISN'T THAT MARLA DRAKE?
BETTER TELL JONTON TO MOVE THE BAGGAGE.
EDITH, HOW *GOOD* TO SEE YOU.
MOTHER! YOU CERTAINLY TURNED UP FAST.
I IMAGINED YOU WOULD STILL BE OUT BY THE TENNIS COURTS, WITH--

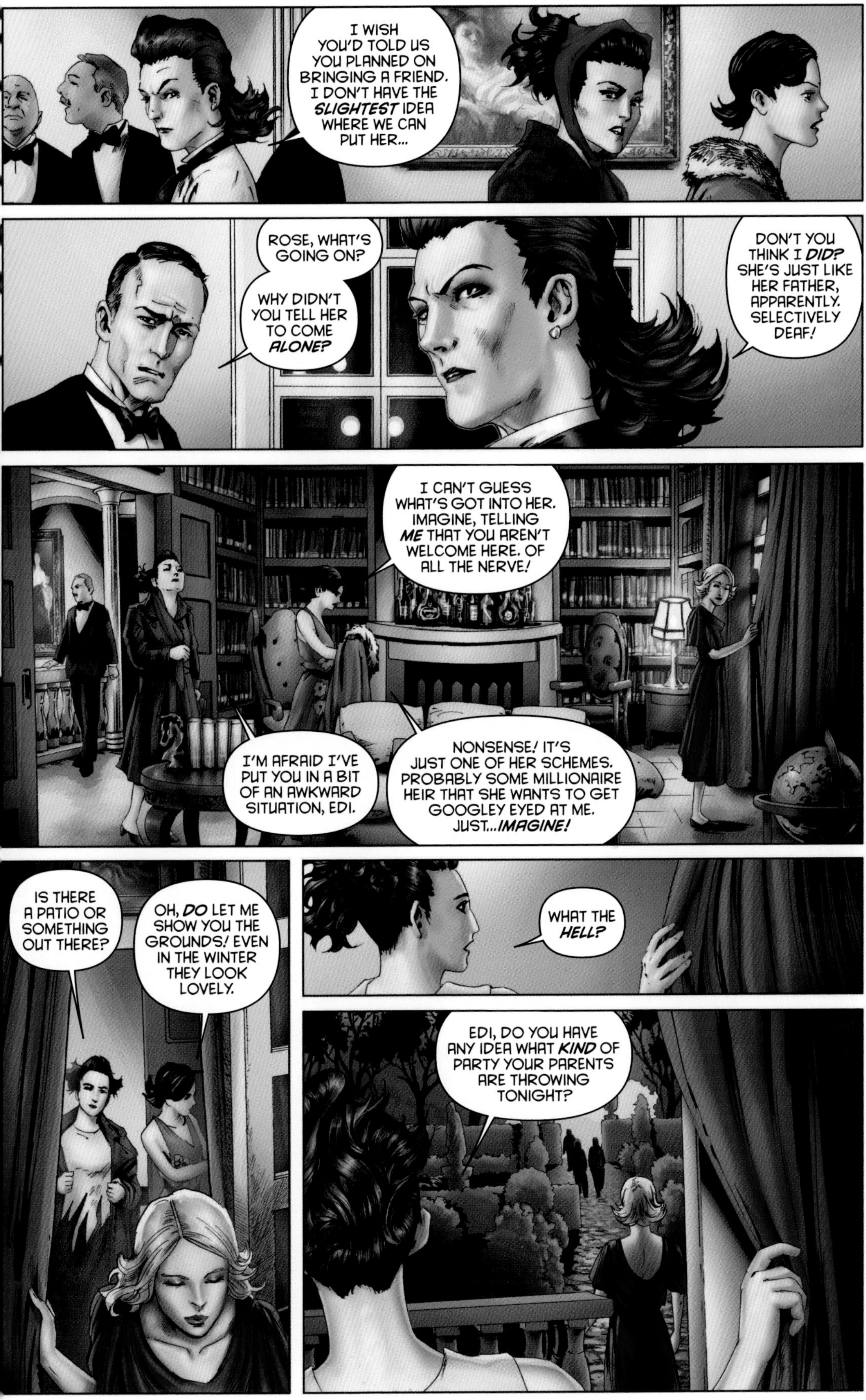

I WISH YOU'D TOLD US YOU PLANNED ON BRINGING A FRIEND. I DON'T HAVE THE SLIGHTEST IDEA WHERE WE CAN PUT HER...
ROSE, WHAT'S GOING ON?
WHY DIDN'T YOU TELL HER TO COME ALONE?
DON'T YOU THINK I DID? SHE'S JUST LIKE HER FATHER, APPARENTLY. SELECTIVELY DEAF!
I CAN'T GUESS WHAT'S GOT INTO HER. IMAGINE, TELLING ME THAT YOU AREN'T WELCOME HERE. OF ALL THE NERVE!
I'M AFRAID I'VE PUT YOU IN A BIT OF AN AWKWARD SITUATION, EDI.
NONSENSE! IT'S JUST ONE OF HER SCHEMES. PROBABLY SOME MILLIONAIRE HEIR THAT SHE WANTS TO GET GOOGLEY EYED AT ME. JUST...IMAGINE!
IS THERE A PATIO OR SOMETHING OUT THERE?
OH, DO LET ME SHOW YOU THE GROUNDS! EVEN IN THE WINTER THEY LOOK LOVELY.
WHAT THE HELL?
EDI, DO YOU HAVE ANY IDEA WHAT KIND OF PARTY YOUR PARENTS ARE THROWING TONIGHT?

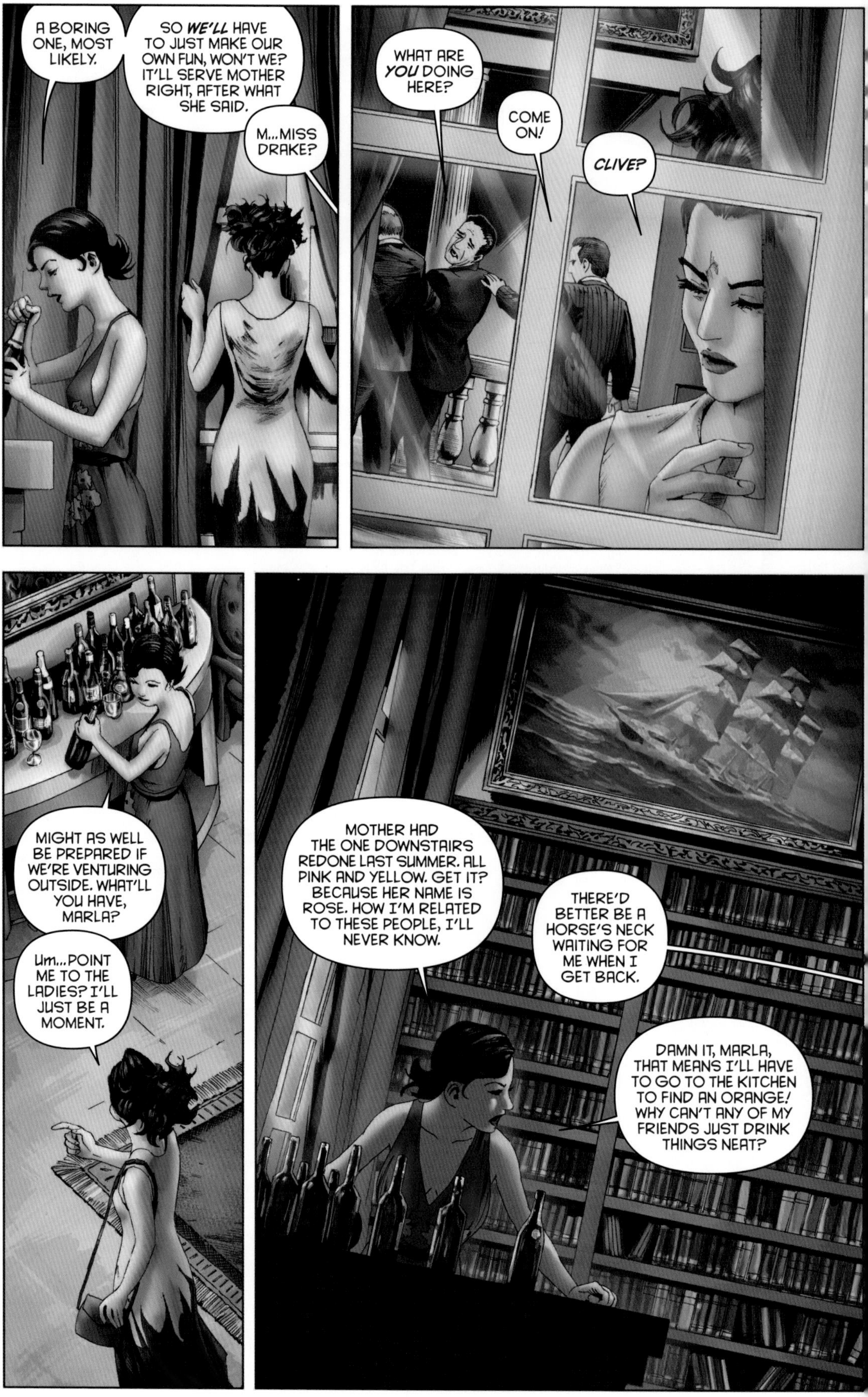
A BORING ONE, MOST LIKELY.
SO WE'LL HAVE TO JUST MAKE OUR OWN FUN, WON'T WE? IT'LL SERVE MOTHER RIGHT, AFTER WHAT SHE SAID.
M...MISS DRAKE?
WHAT ARE YOU DOING HERE?
COME ON!
CLIVE?
MIGHT AS WELL BE PREPARED IF WE'RE VENTURING OUTSIDE. WHAT'LL YOU HAVE, MARLA?
Um...POINT ME TO THE LADIES? I'LL JUST BE A MOMENT.
MOTHER HAD THE ONE DOWNSTAIRS REDONE LAST SUMMER. ALL PINK AND YELLOW. GET IT? BECAUSE HER NAME IS ROSE. HOW I'M RELATED TO THESE PEOPLE, I'LL NEVER KNOW.
THERE'D BETTER BE A HORSE'S NECK WAITING FOR ME WHEN I GET BACK.
DAMN IT, MARLA, THAT MEANS I'LL HAVE TO GO TO THE KITCHEN TO FIND AN ORANGE! WHY CAN'T ANY OF MY FRIENDS JUST DRINK THINGS NEAT?

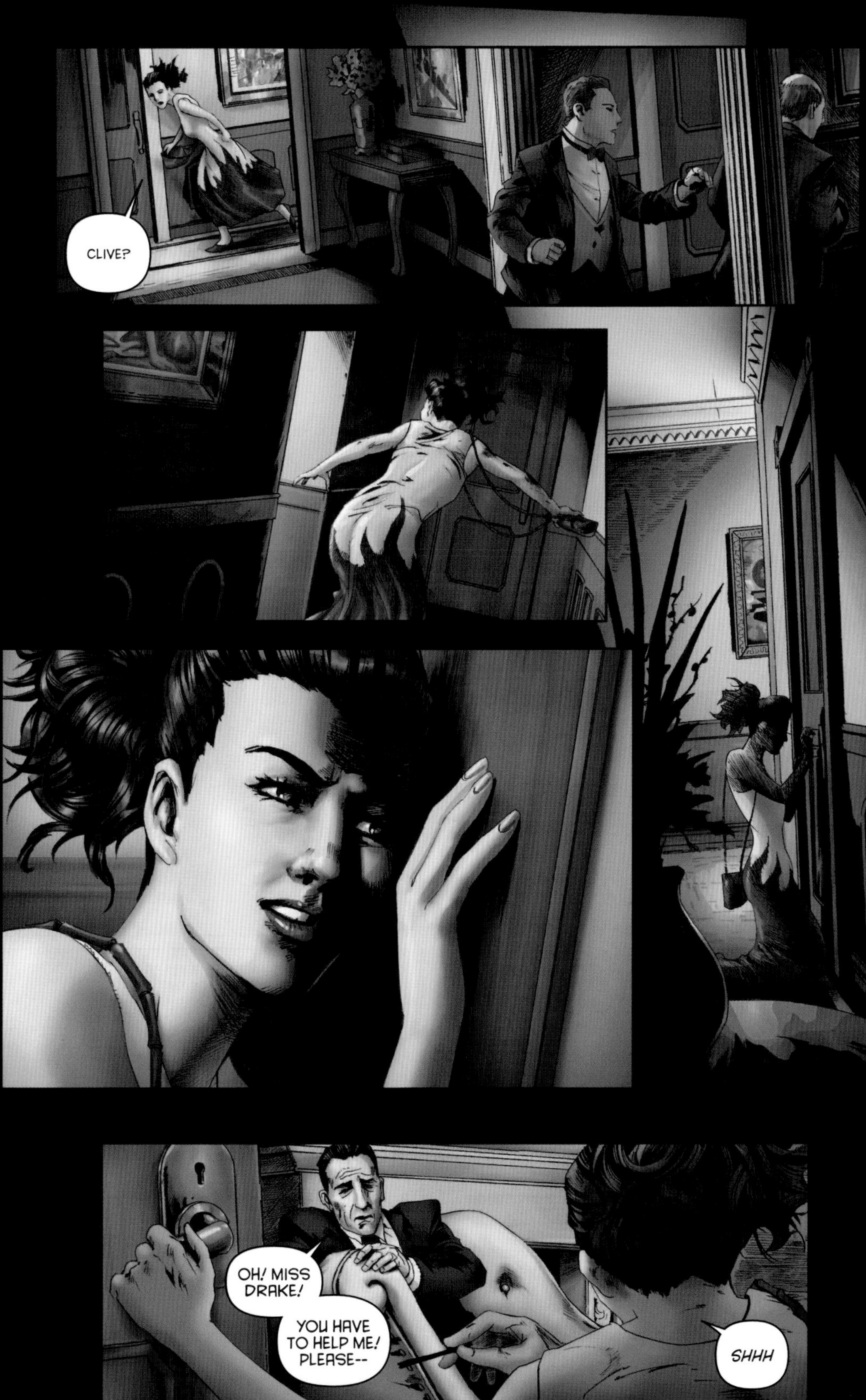
CLIVE?
OH! MISS DRAKE!
YOU HAVE TO HELP ME! PLEASE--
SHHH

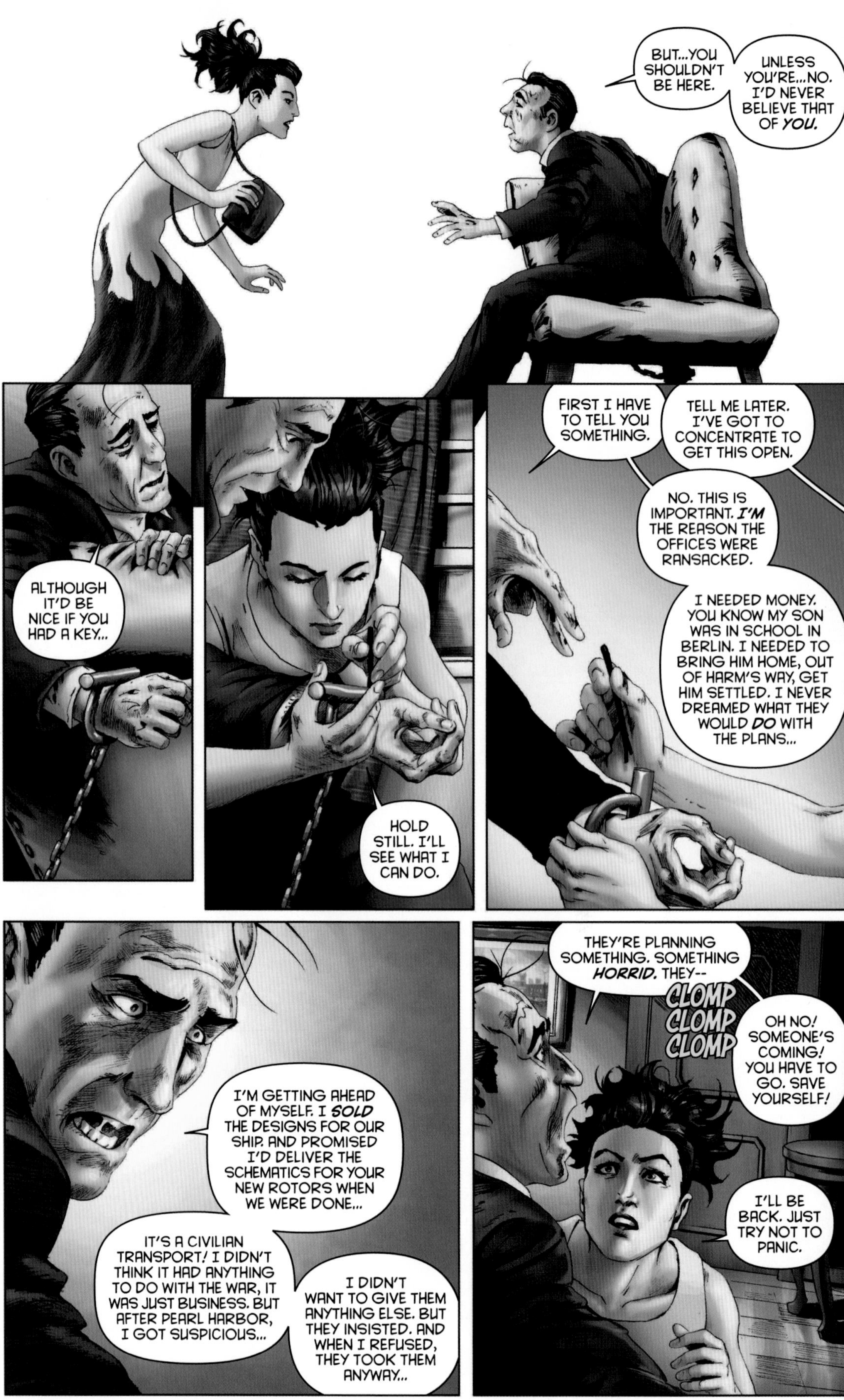
BUT...YOU SHOULDN'T BE HERE.
UNLESS YOU'RE...NO. I'D NEVER BELIEVE THAT OF *YOU.*
ALTHOUGH IT'D BE NICE IF YOU HAD A KEY...
HOLD STILL. I'LL SEE WHAT I CAN DO.
FIRST I HAVE TO TELL YOU SOMETHING.
TELL ME LATER. I'VE GOT TO CONCENTRATE TO GET THIS OPEN.
NO. THIS IS IMPORTANT. *I'M* THE REASON THE OFFICES WERE RANSACKED.
I NEEDED MONEY. YOU KNOW MY SON WAS IN SCHOOL IN BERLIN. I NEEDED TO BRING HIM HOME, OUT OF HARM'S WAY, GET HIM SETTLED. I NEVER DREAMED WHAT THEY WOULD *DO* WITH THE PLANS...
I'M GETTING AHEAD OF MYSELF. I *SOLD* THE DESIGNS FOR OUR SHIP. AND PROMISED I'D DELIVER THE SCHEMATICS FOR YOUR NEW ROTORS WHEN WE WERE DONE...
IT'S A CIVILIAN TRANSPORT! I DIDN'T THINK IT HAD ANYTHING TO DO WITH THE WAR, IT WAS JUST BUSINESS. BUT AFTER PEARL HARBOR, I GOT SUSPICIOUS...
I DIDN'T WANT TO GIVE THEM ANYTHING ELSE. BUT THEY INSISTED. AND WHEN I REFUSED, THEY TOOK THEM ANYWAY...
THEY'RE PLANNING SOMETHING. SOMETHING *HORRID.* THEY--
CLOMP CLOMP CLOMP
OH NO! SOMEONE'S COMING! YOU HAVE TO GO. SAVE YOURSELF!
I'LL BE BACK. JUST TRY NOT TO PANIC.

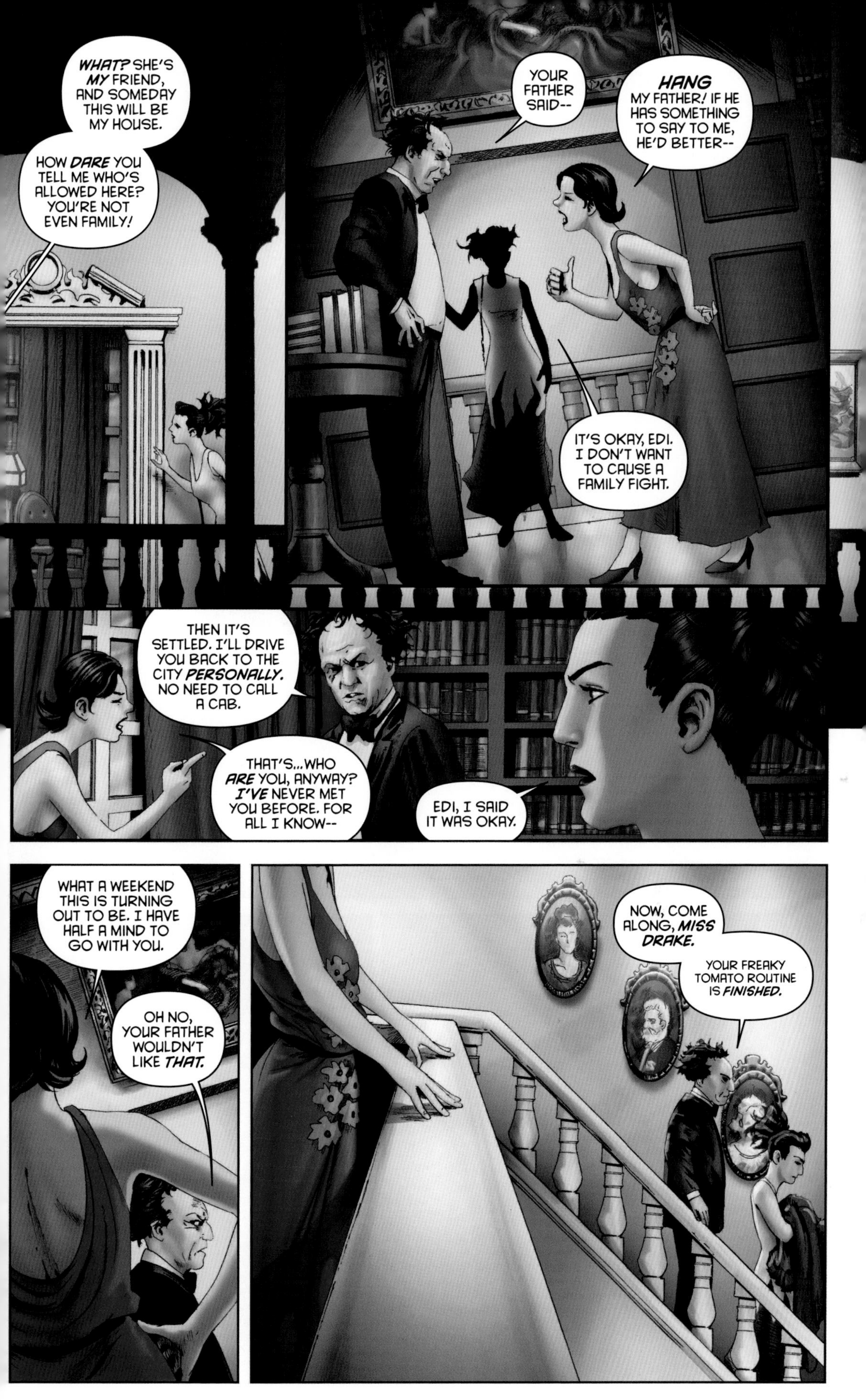
WHAT? SHE'S MY FRIEND, AND SOMEDAY THIS WILL BE MY HOUSE.
HOW DARE YOU TELL ME WHO'S ALLOWED HERE? YOU'RE NOT EVEN FAMILY!
YOUR FATHER SAID--
HANG MY FATHER! IF HE HAS SOMETHING TO SAY TO ME, HE'D BETTER--
IT'S OKAY, EDI. I DON'T WANT TO CAUSE A FAMILY FIGHT.
THEN IT'S SETTLED. I'LL DRIVE YOU BACK TO THE CITY PERSONALLY. NO NEED TO CALL A CAB.
THAT'S...WHO ARE YOU, ANYWAY? I'VE NEVER MET YOU BEFORE. FOR ALL I KNOW--
EDI, I SAID IT WAS OKAY.
WHAT A WEEKEND THIS IS TURNING OUT TO BE. I HAVE HALF A MIND TO GO WITH YOU.
OH NO, YOUR FATHER WOULDN'T LIKE THAT.
NOW, COME ALONG, MISS DRAKE.
YOUR FREAKY TOMATO ROUTINE IS FINISHED.

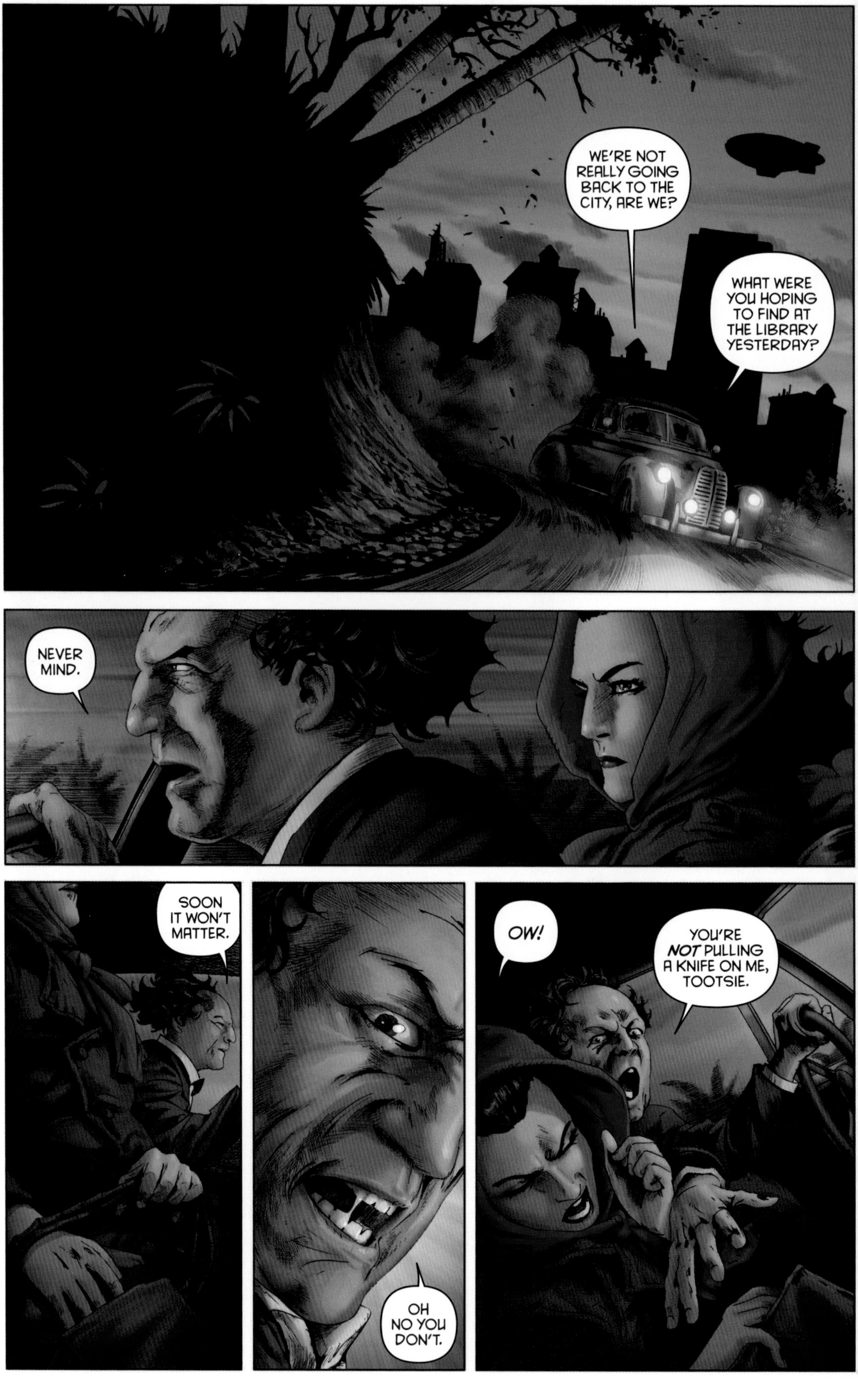

WE'RE NOT REALLY GOING BACK TO THE CITY, ARE WE?
WHAT WERE YOU HOPING TO FIND AT THE LIBRARY YESTERDAY?
NEVER MIND.
SOON IT WON'T MATTER.
OH NO YOU DON'T.
OW!
YOU'RE *NOT* PULLING A KNIFE ON ME, TOOTSIE.

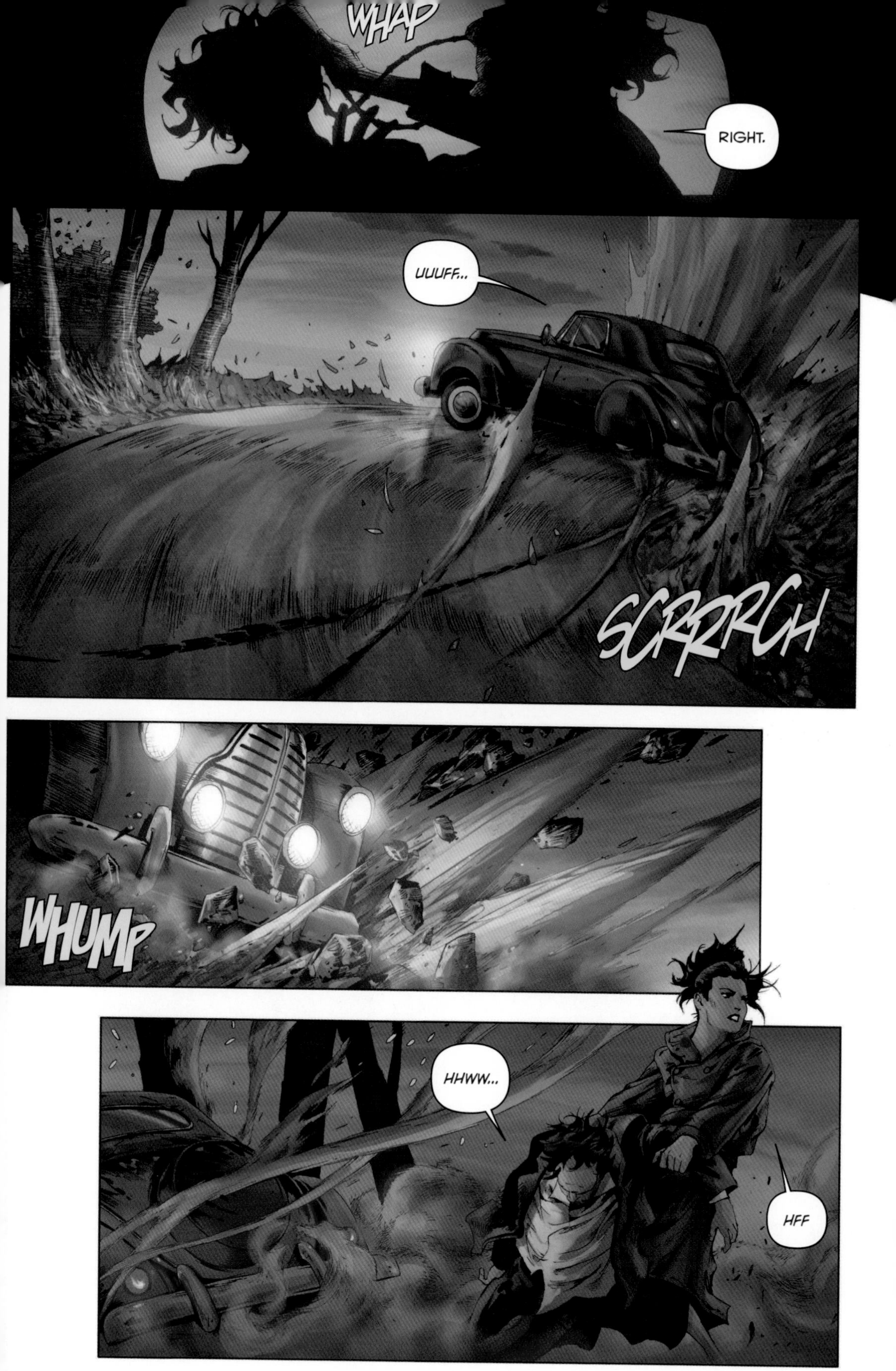
WHAP
RIGHT.
UUUFF...
SCRRRCH
WHUMP
HHWW...
HFF

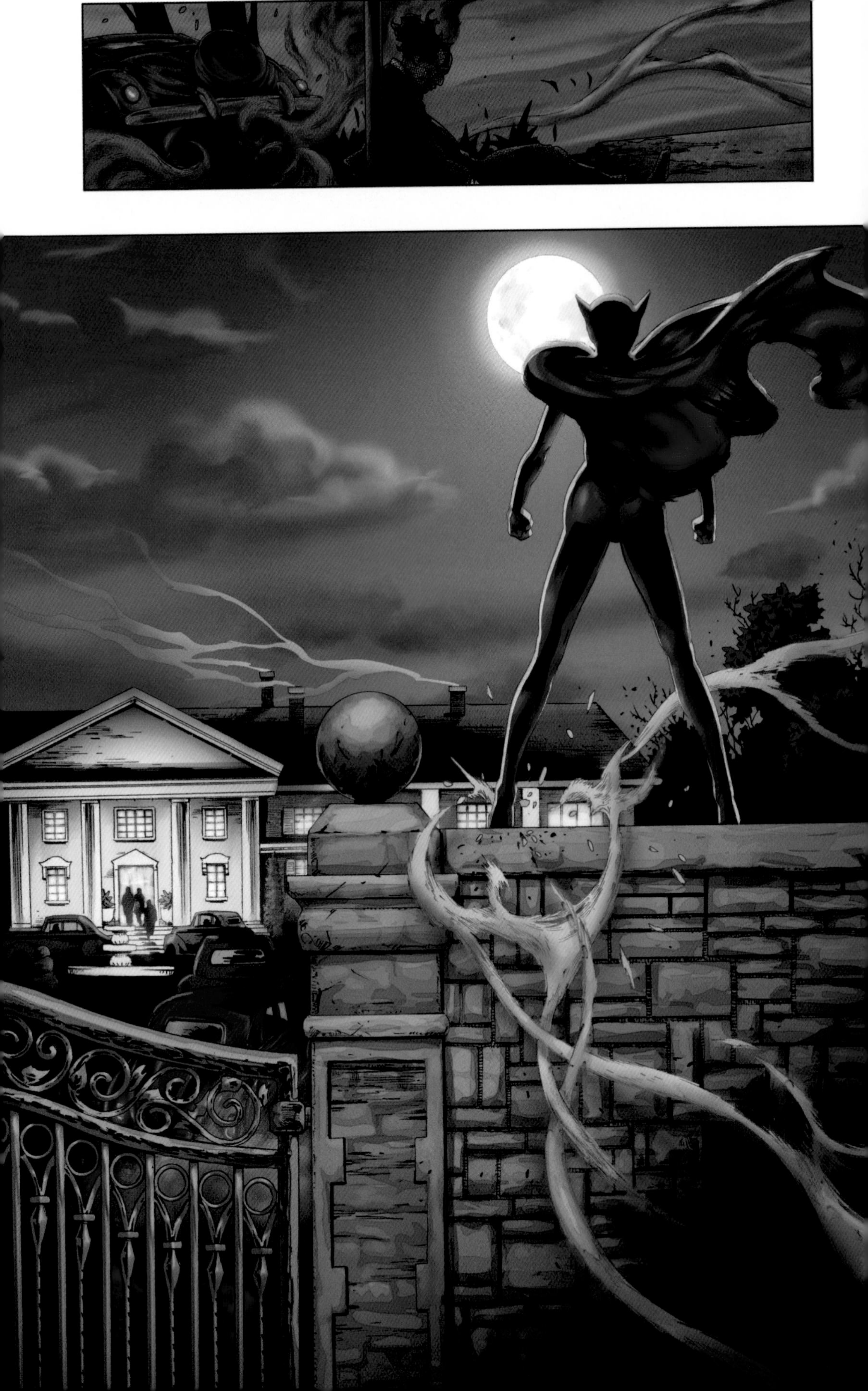

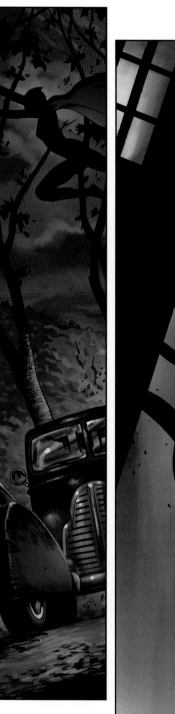

TP TP TP

HEY!

YOU'LL NEED TO SHIELD YOUR EYES, OKAY?

KSSHH

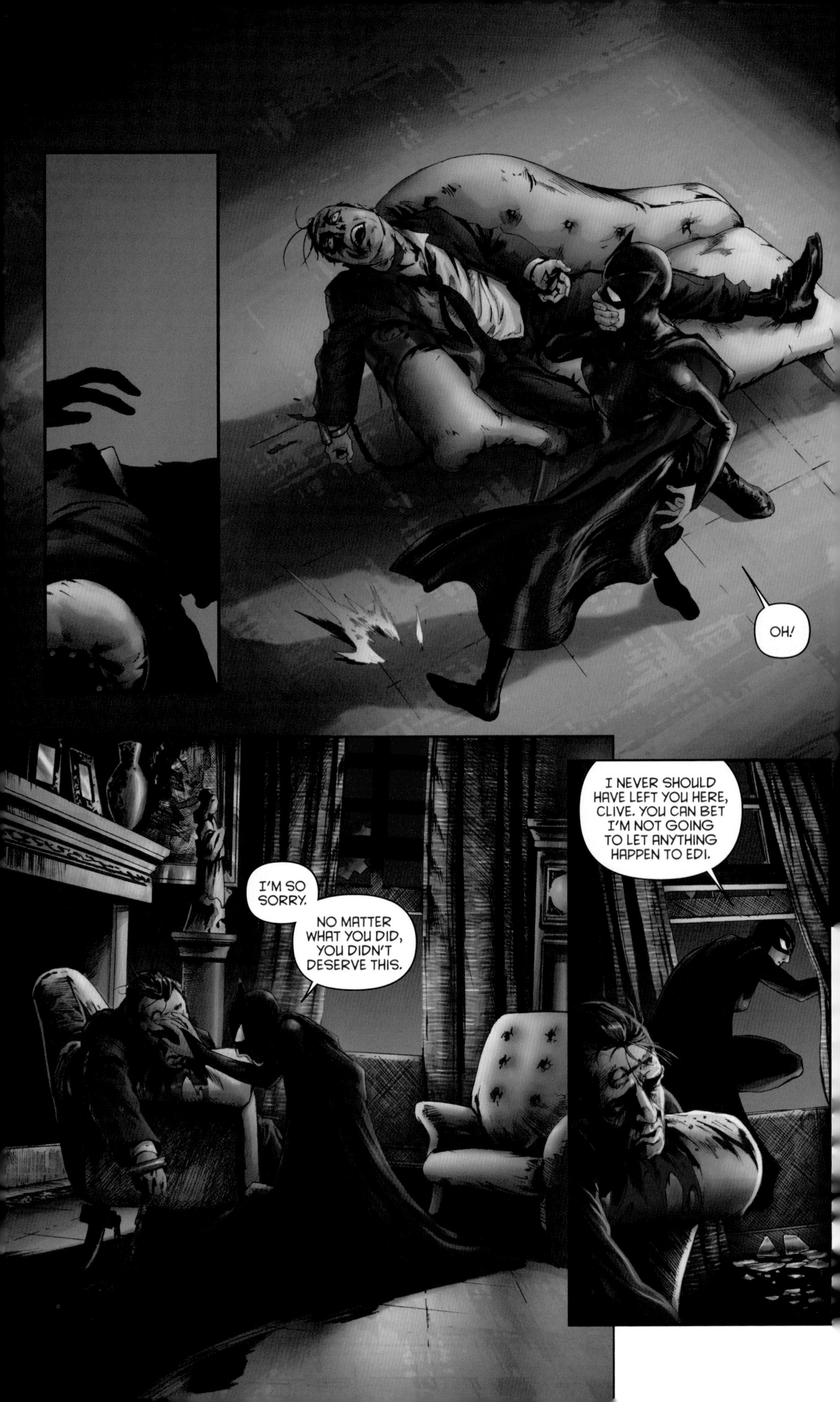
OH!
I'M SO SORRY.
NO MATTER WHAT YOU DID, YOU DIDN'T DESERVE THIS.
I NEVER SHOULD HAVE LEFT YOU HERE, CLIVE. YOU CAN BET I'M NOT GOING TO LET ANYTHING HAPPEN TO EDI.

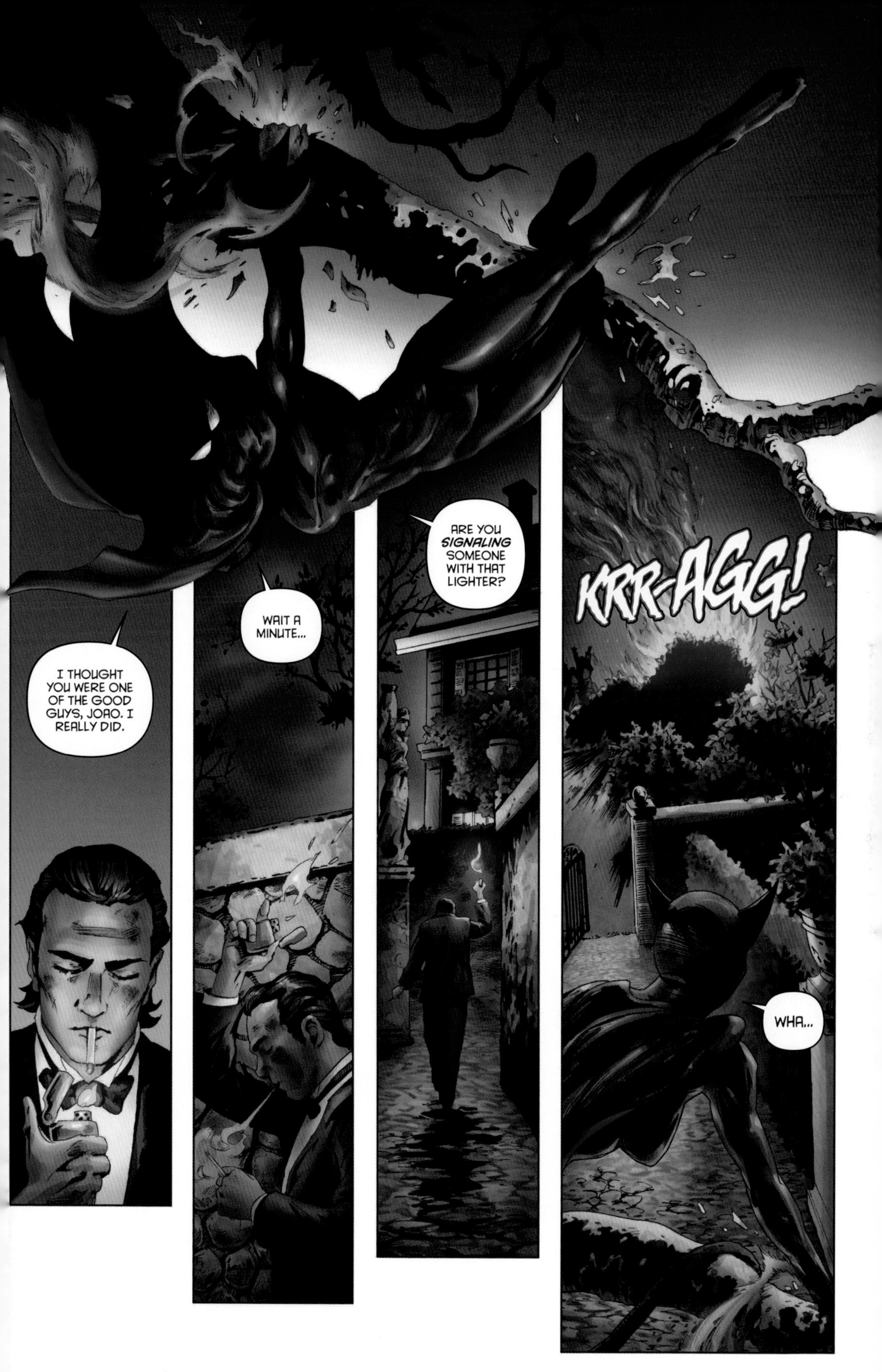
I THOUGHT YOU WERE ONE OF THE GOOD GUYS, JOAO. I REALLY DID.
WAIT A MINUTE...
ARE YOU SIGNALING SOMEONE WITH THAT LIGHTER?
KRR-AGG!
WHA...

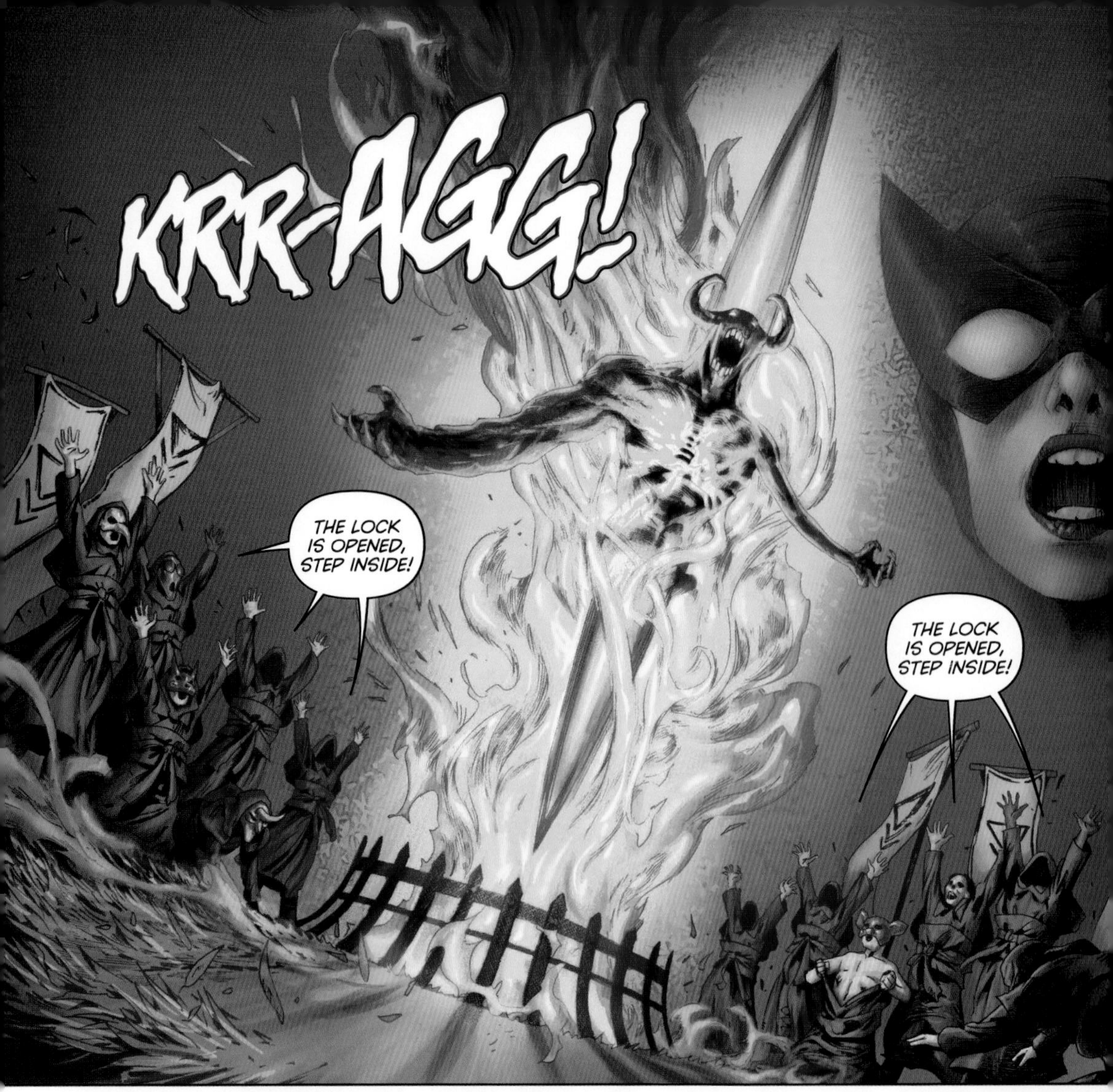
KRR-AGG!
THE LOCK IS OPENED, STEP INSIDE!
THE LOCK IS OPENED, STEP INSIDE!

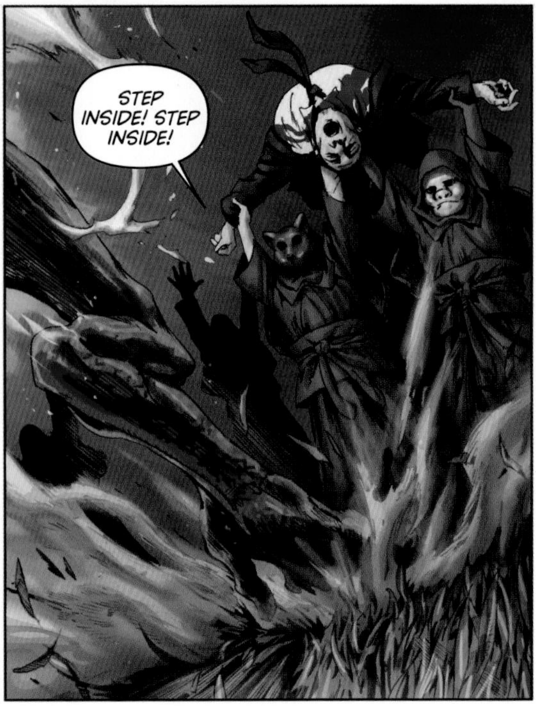
STEP INSIDE! STEP INSIDE!

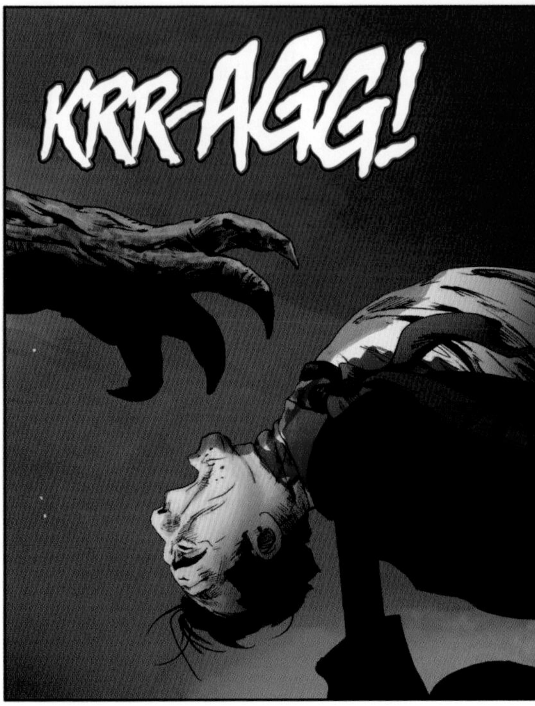
KRR-AGG!

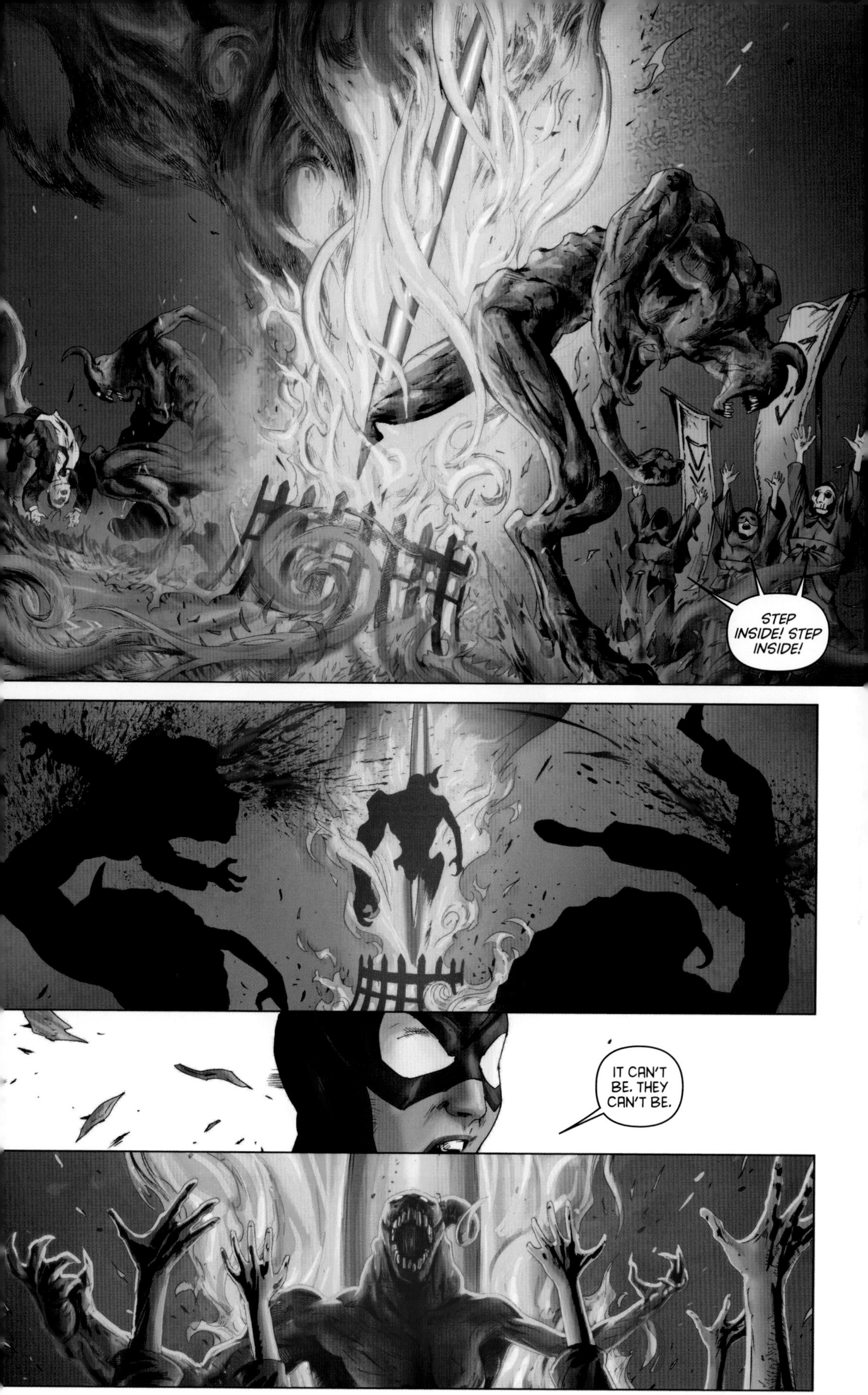
STEP INSIDE! STEP INSIDE!
IT CAN'T BE. THEY CAN'T BE.

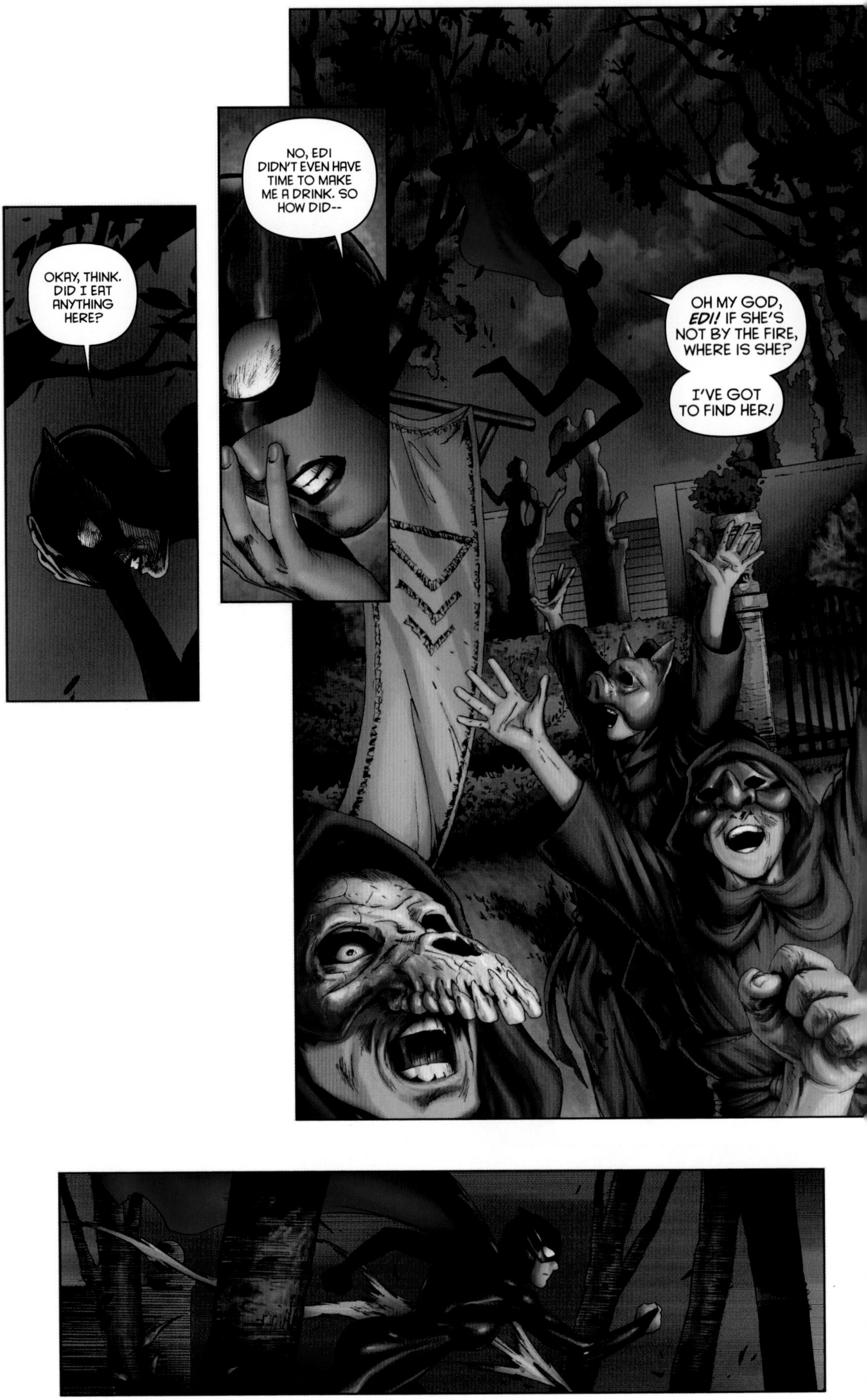
OKAY, THINK. DID I EAT ANYTHING HERE?
NO, EDI DIDN'T EVEN HAVE TIME TO MAKE ME A DRINK. SO HOW DID--
OH MY GOD, EDI! IF SHE'S NOT BY THE FIRE, WHERE IS SHE?
I'VE GOT TO FIND HER!

SNAP

JOAO?

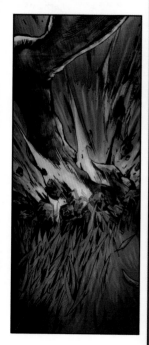

YOU AREN'T REAL.

YOU CAN'T BE REAL.

YOU'RE JUST A HALLUCINATION, LIKE--

KRR-AGG!

SSSKK

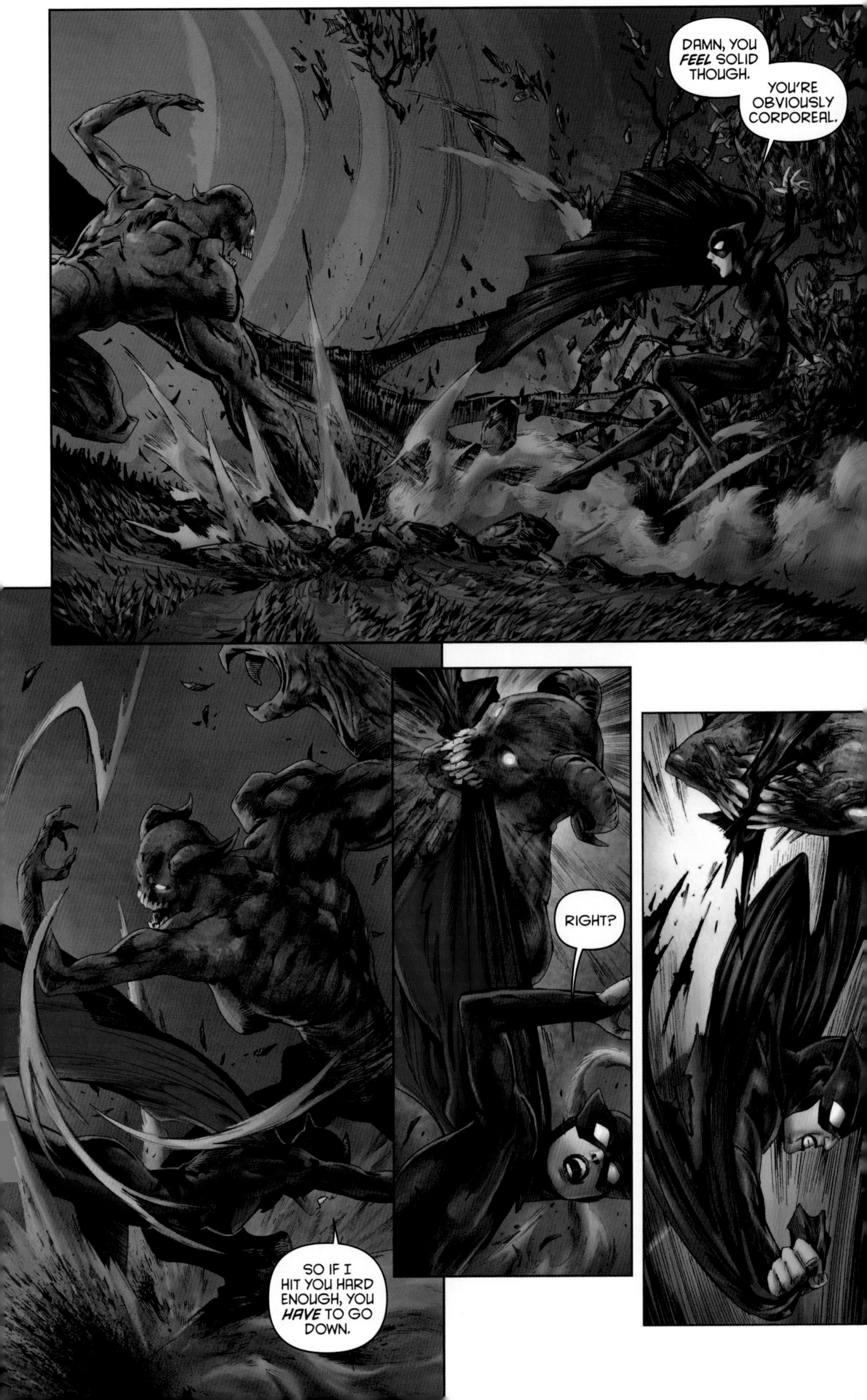
DAMN, YOU *FEEL* SOLID THOUGH.
YOU'RE OBVIOUSLY CORPOREAL.
SO IF I HIT YOU HARD ENOUGH, YOU *HAVE* TO GO DOWN.
RIGHT?

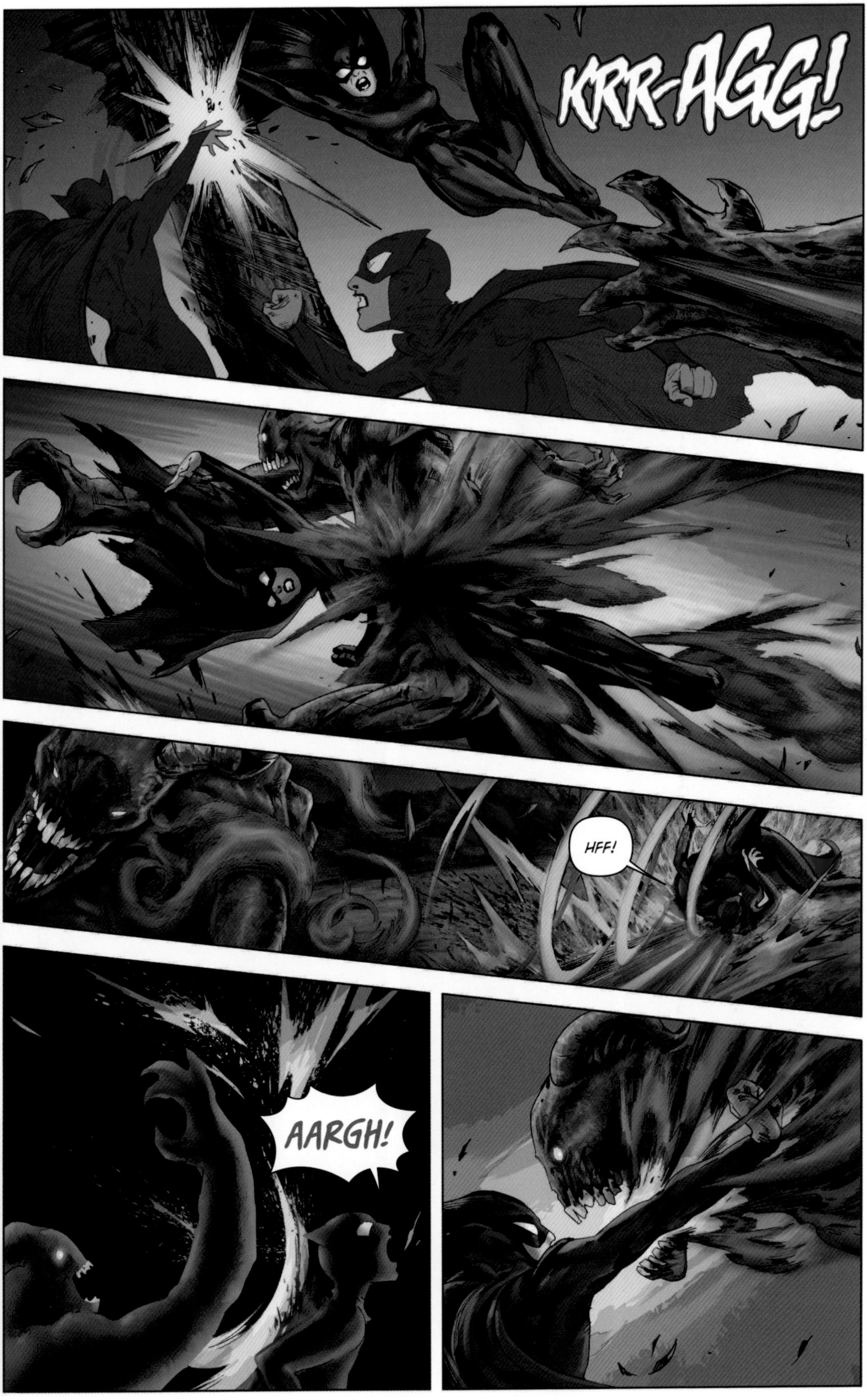
KRR-AGG!
HFF!
AARGH!

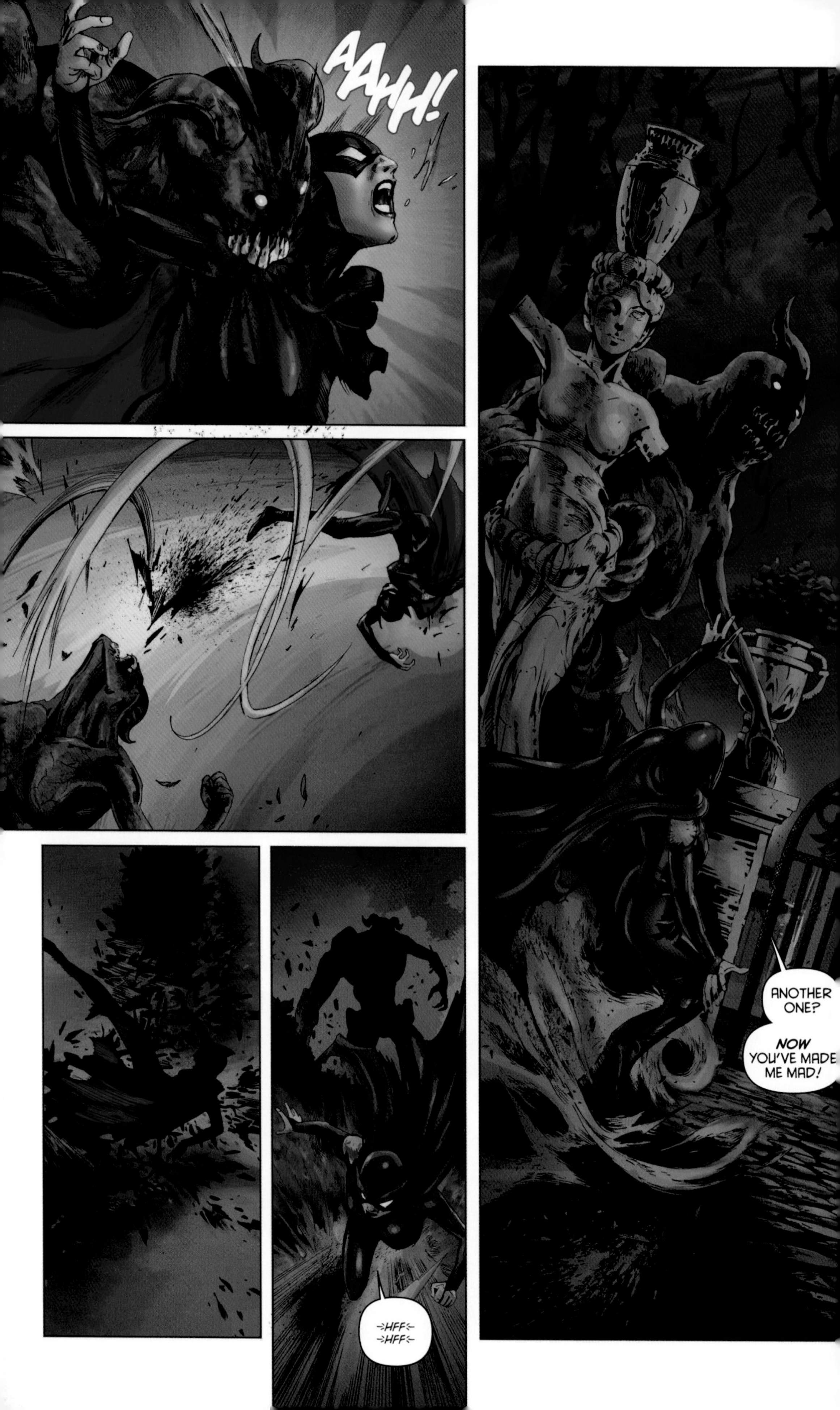
AAHH!
-HFF-
-HFF-
ANOTHER ONE?
NOW YOU'VE MADE ME MAD!

Issue Four

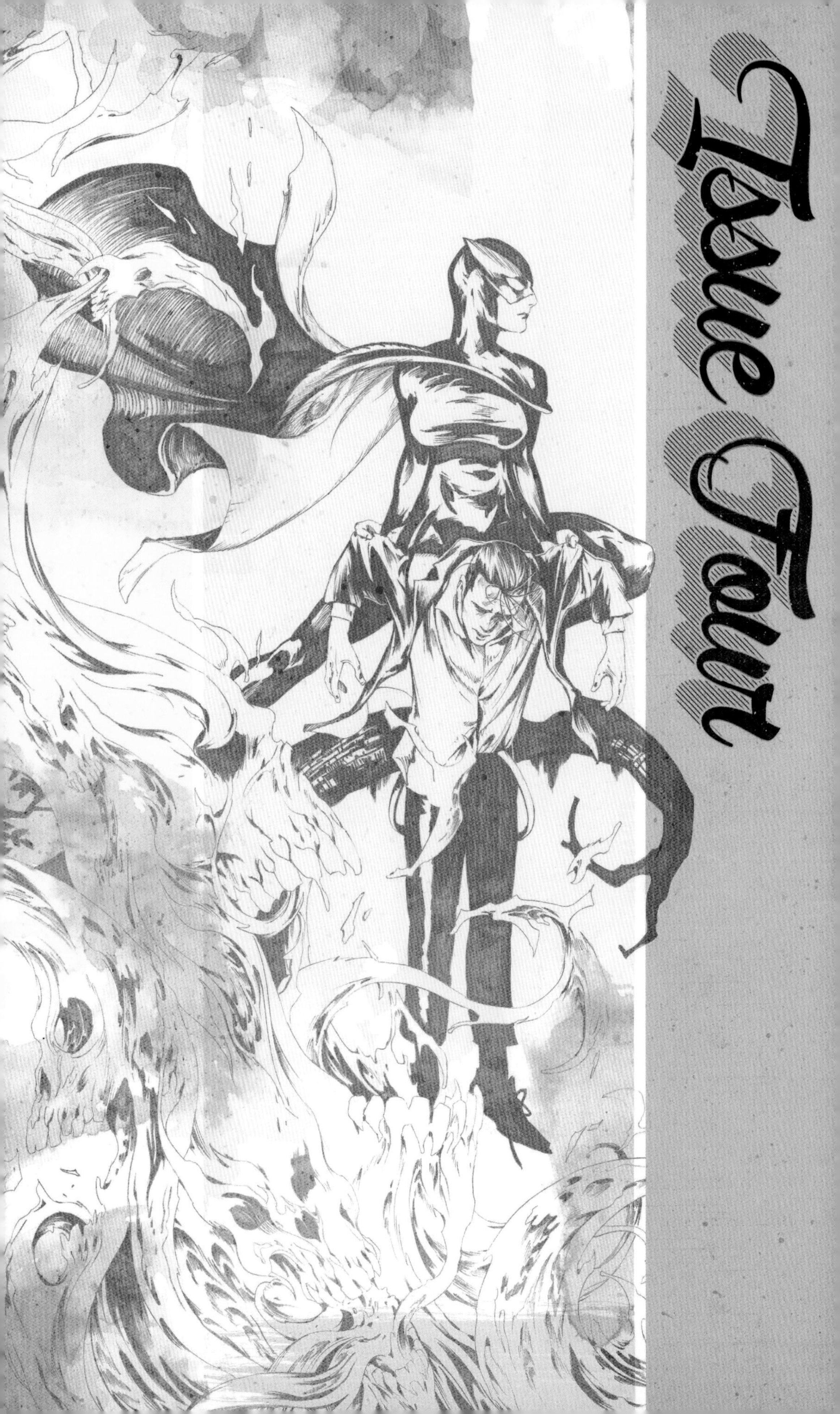

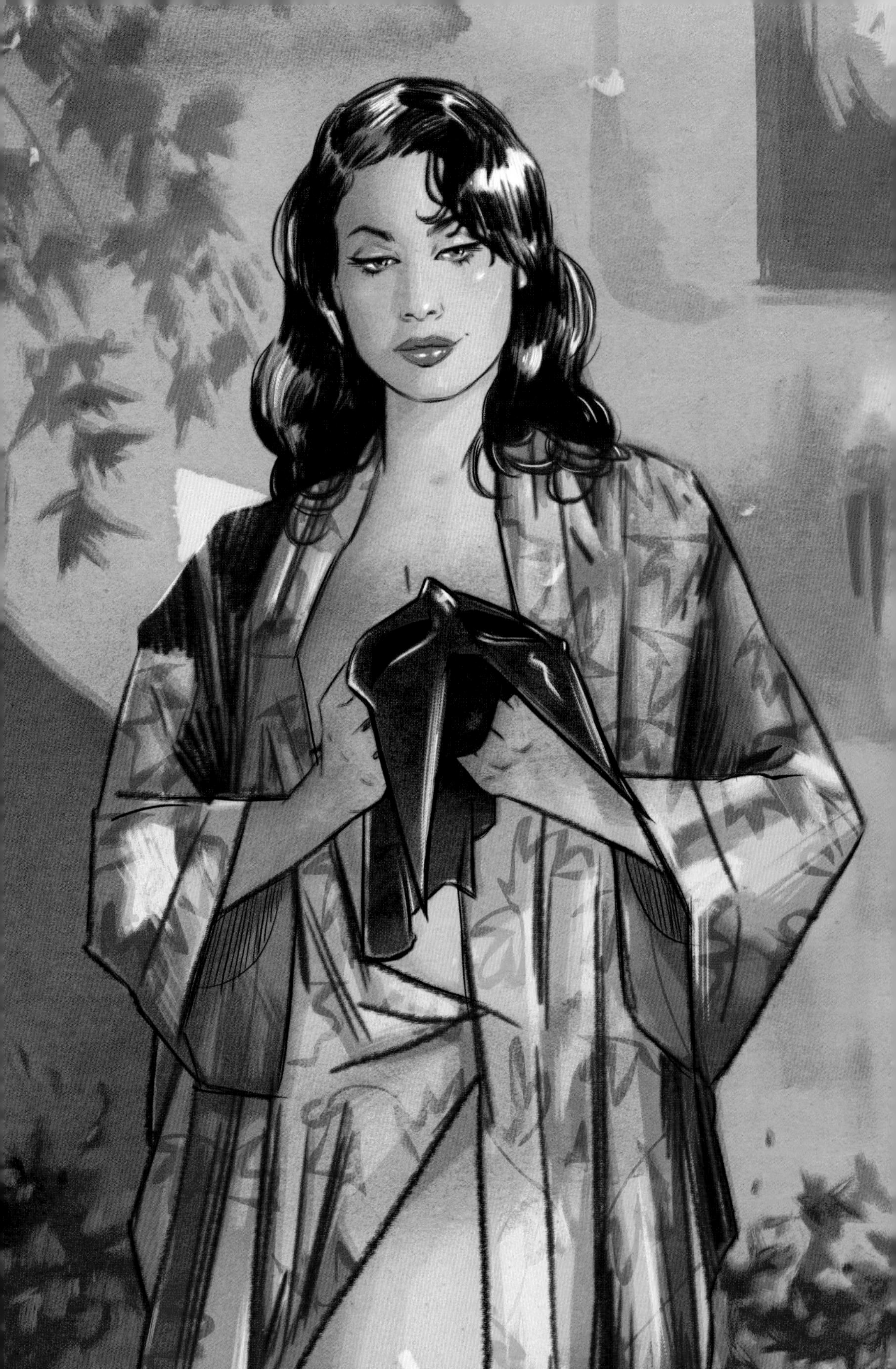

Issue 4, Main Cover: Art by Tula Lotay

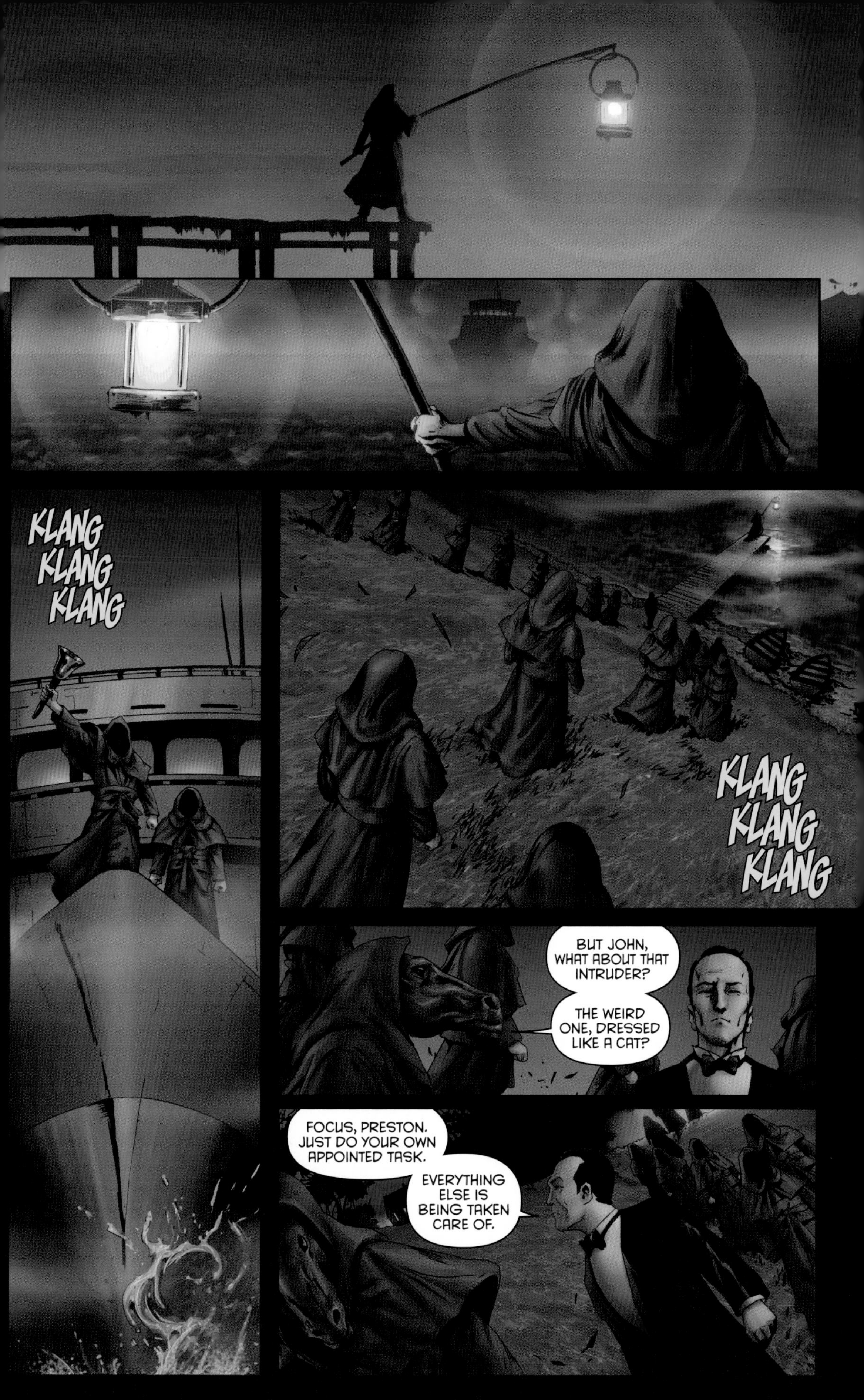

KLANG KLANG KLANG
KLANG KLANG KLANG
BUT JOHN, WHAT ABOUT THAT INTRUDER?
THE WEIRD ONE, DRESSED LIKE A CAT?
FOCUS, PRESTON. JUST DO YOUR OWN APPOINTED TASK.
EVERYTHING ELSE IS BEING TAKEN CARE OF.

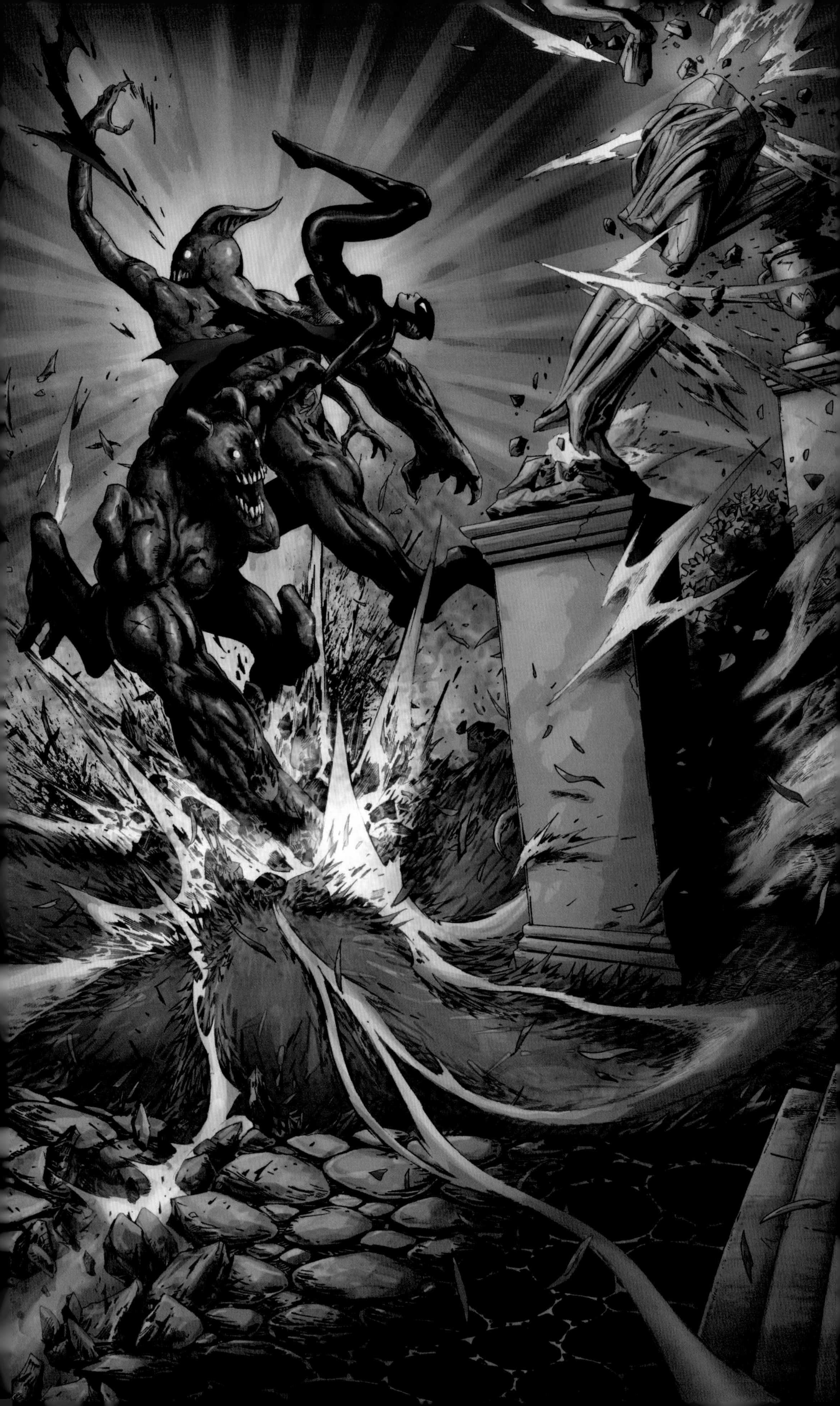

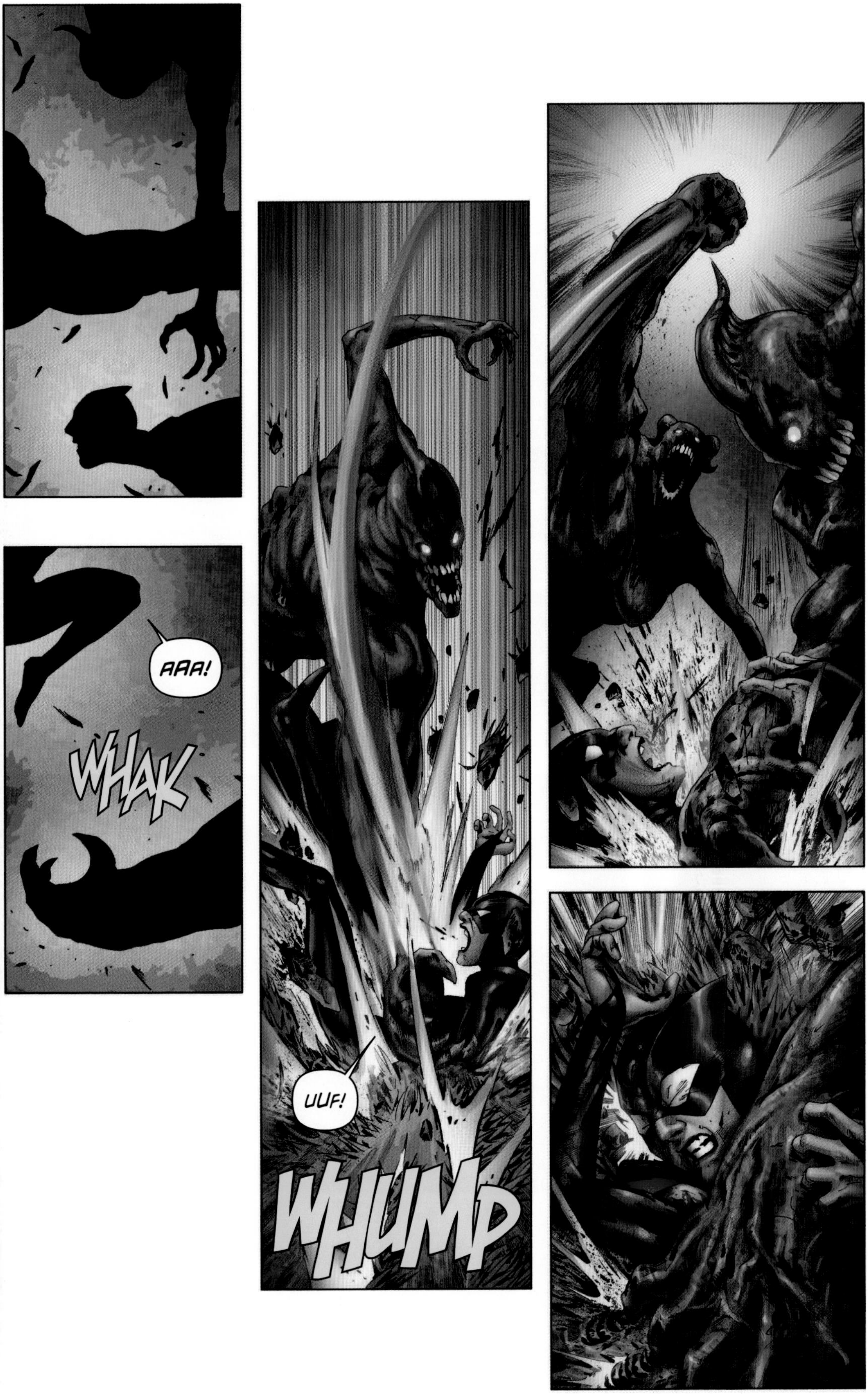
AAA!
WHAK
UUF!
WHUMP

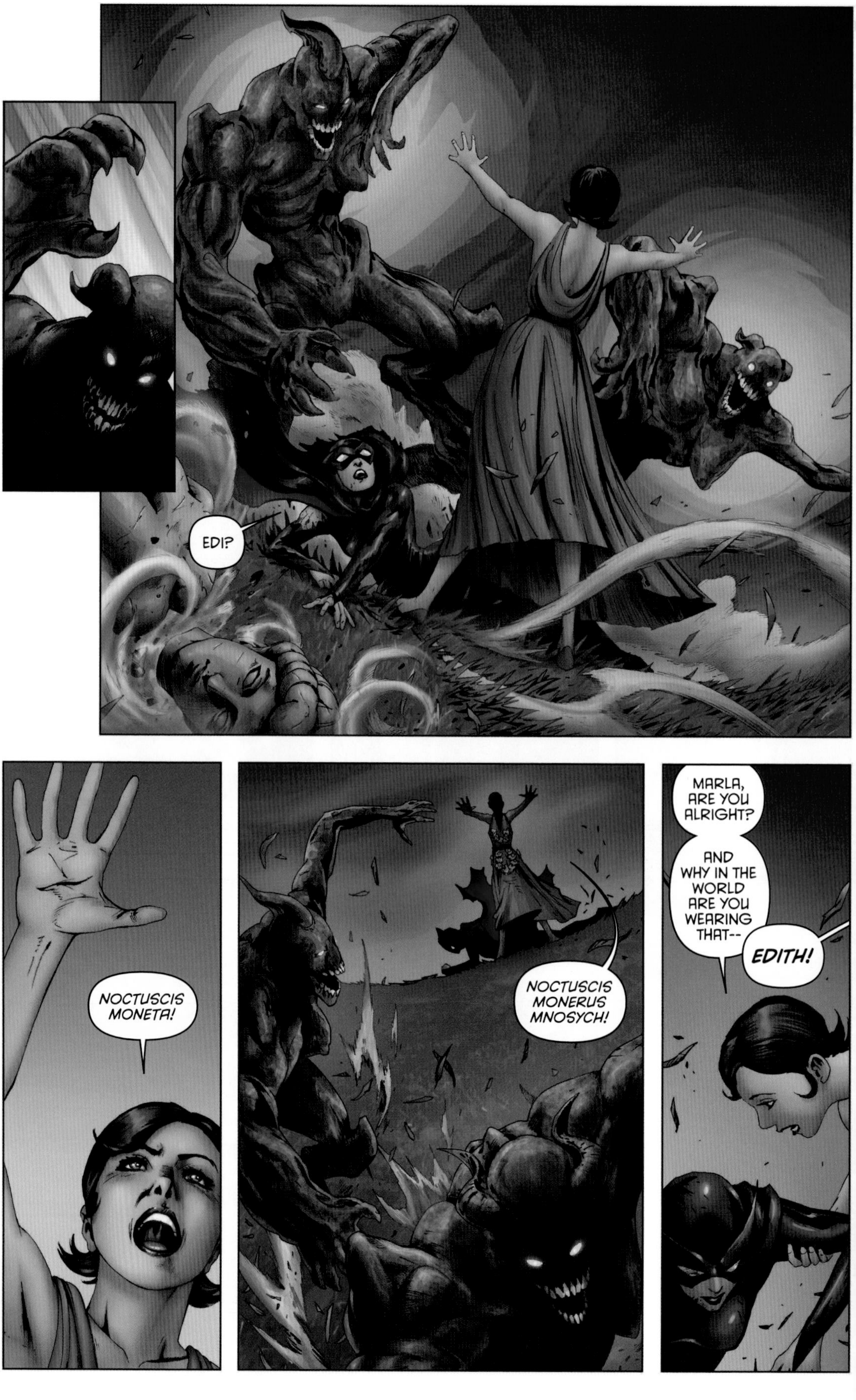

EDI?
NOCTUSCIS MONETA!
NOCTUSCIS MONERUS MNOSYCH!
MARLA, ARE YOU ALRIGHT?
AND WHY IN THE WORLD ARE YOU WEARING THAT--
EDITH!

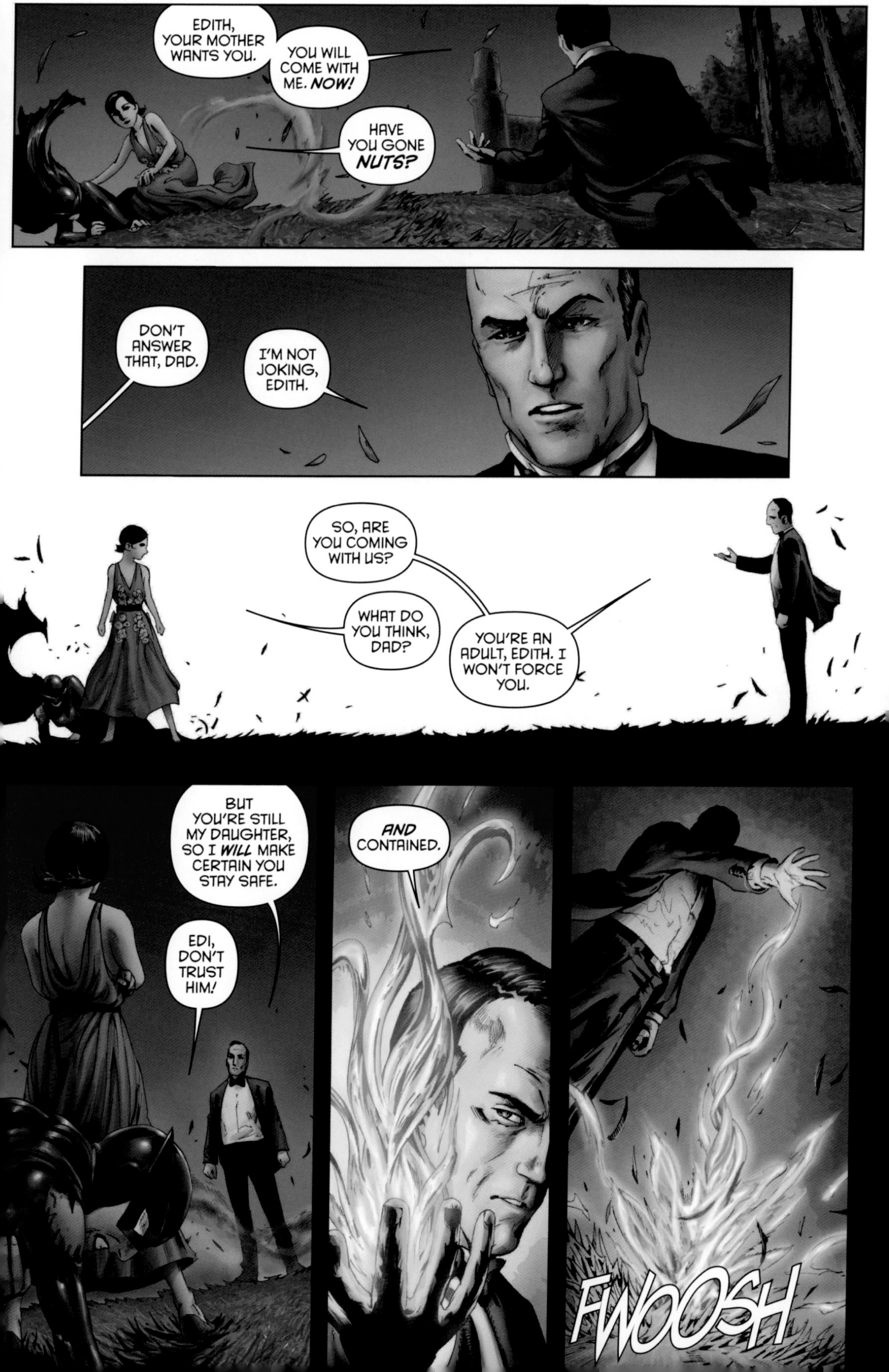
EDITH, YOUR MOTHER WANTS YOU.
YOU WILL COME WITH ME. NOW!
HAVE YOU GONE NUTS?
DON'T ANSWER THAT, DAD.
I'M NOT JOKING, EDITH.
SO, ARE YOU COMING WITH US?
WHAT DO YOU THINK, DAD?
YOU'RE AN ADULT, EDITH. I WON'T FORCE YOU.
BUT YOU'RE STILL MY DAUGHTER, SO I WILL MAKE CERTAIN YOU STAY SAFE.
EDI, DON'T TRUST HIM!
AND CONTAINED.
FWOOSH

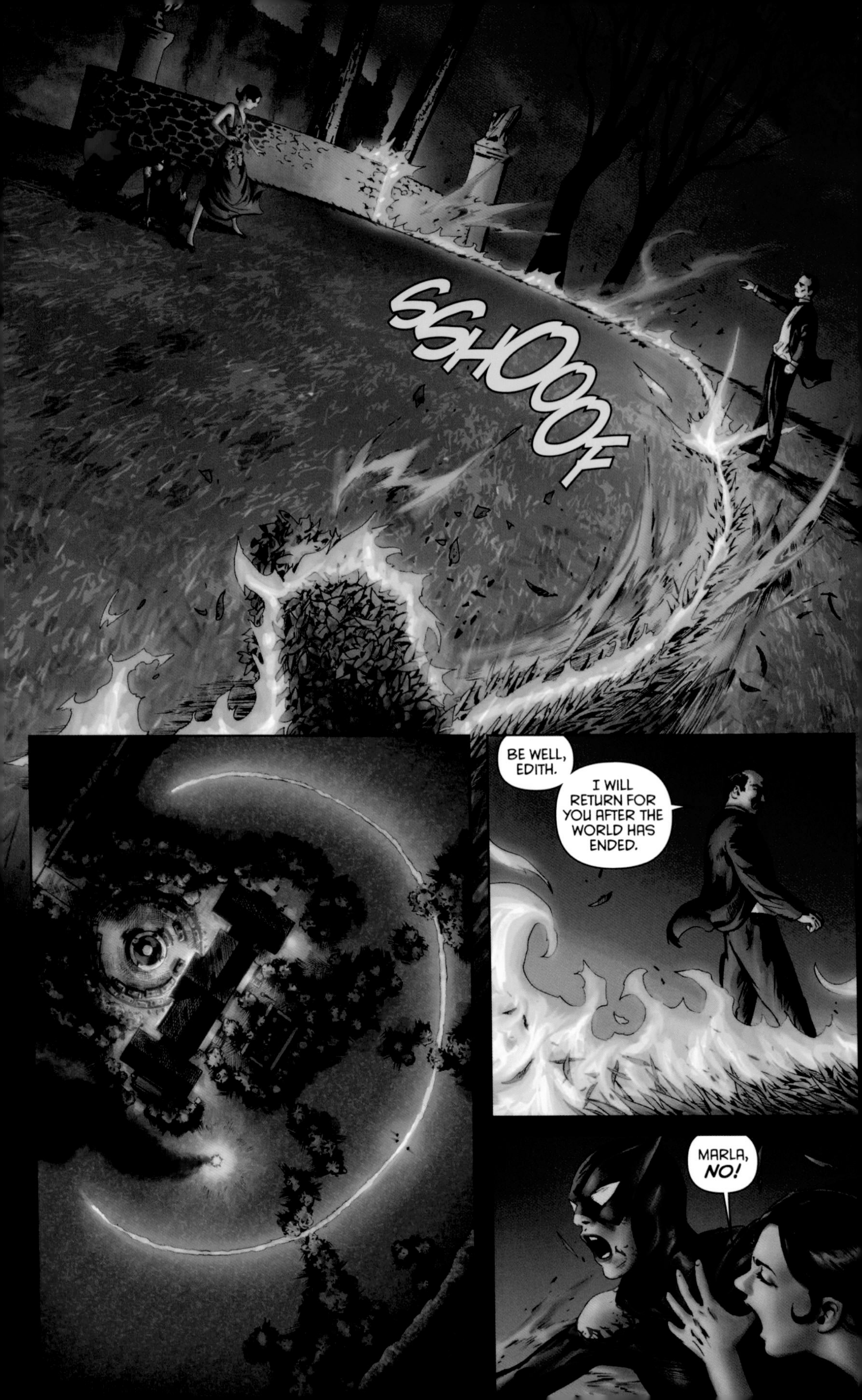
SSHOOOOF
BE WELL, EDITH.
I WILL RETURN FOR YOU AFTER THE WORLD HAS ENDED.
MARLA, NO!

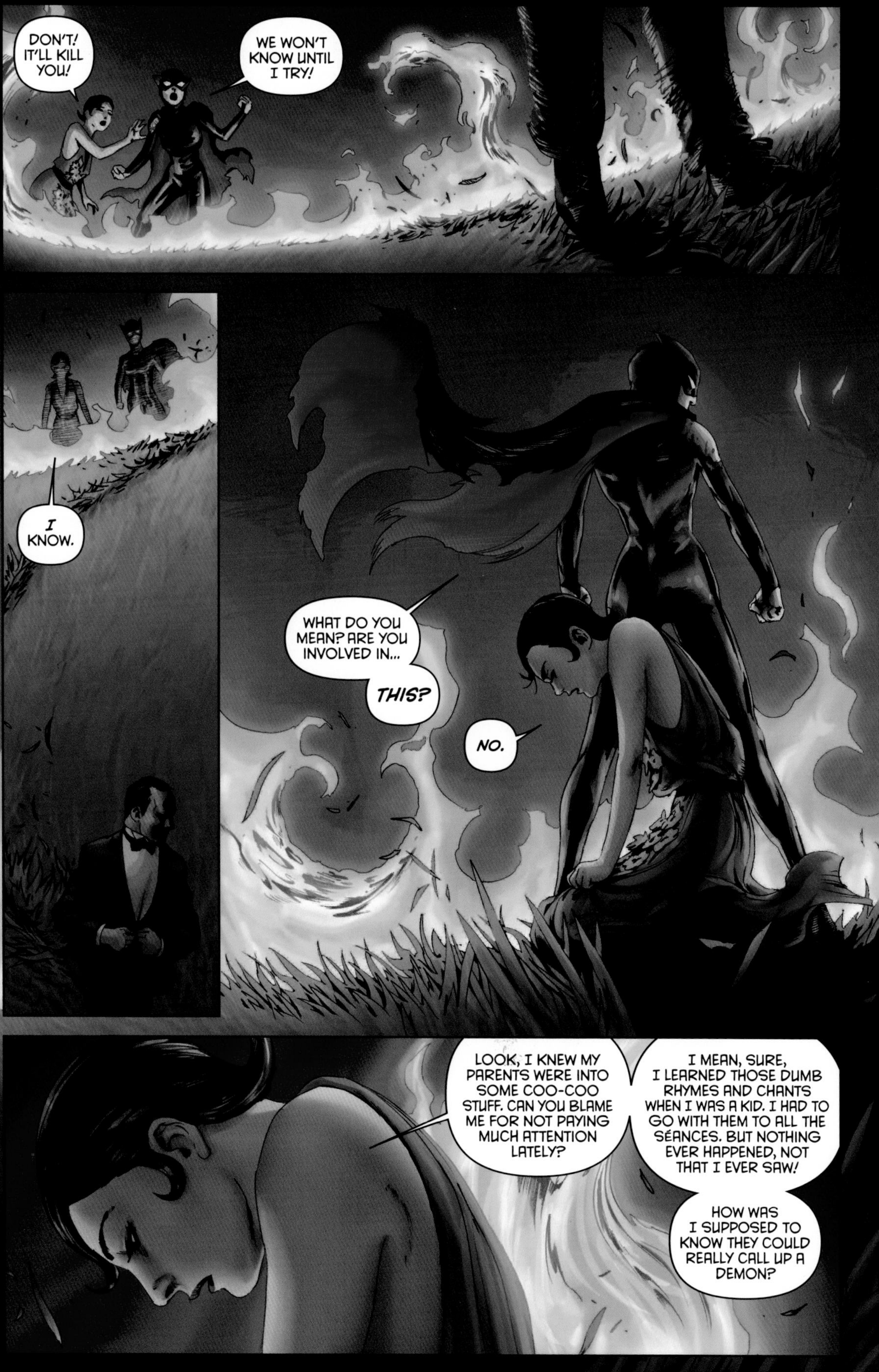
DON'T! IT'LL KILL YOU!
WE WON'T KNOW UNTIL I TRY!
I KNOW.
WHAT DO YOU MEAN? ARE YOU INVOLVED IN...
THIS?
NO.
LOOK, I KNEW MY PARENTS WERE INTO SOME COO-COO STUFF. CAN YOU BLAME ME FOR NOT PAYING MUCH ATTENTION LATELY?
I MEAN, SURE, I LEARNED THOSE DUMB RHYMES AND CHANTS WHEN I WAS A KID. I HAD TO GO WITH THEM TO ALL THE SÉANCES. BUT NOTHING EVER HAPPENED, NOT THAT I EVER SAW!
HOW WAS I SUPPOSED TO KNOW THEY COULD REALLY CALL UP A DEMON?

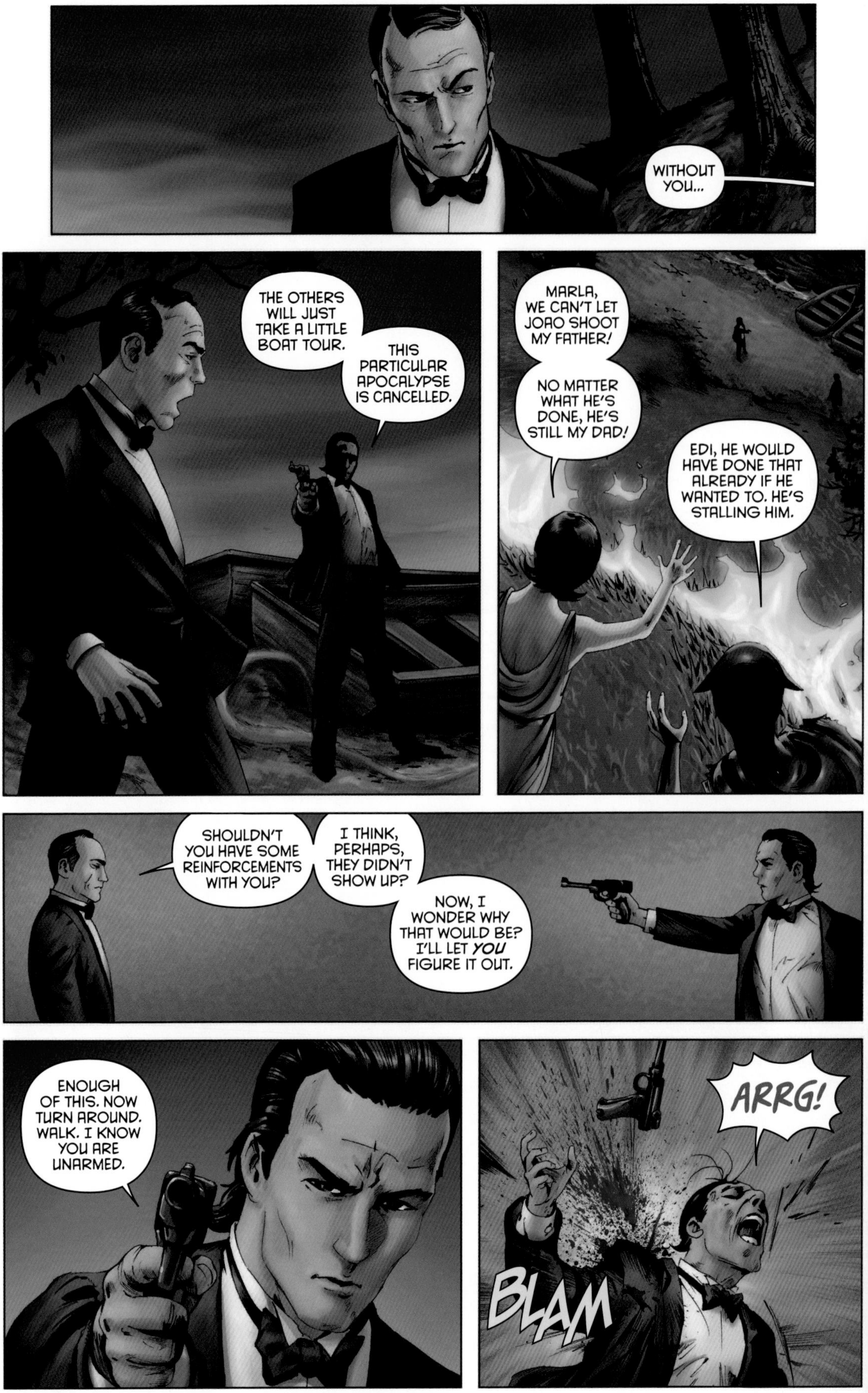

WITHOUT YOU...
THE OTHERS WILL JUST TAKE A LITTLE BOAT TOUR.
THIS PARTICULAR APOCALYPSE IS CANCELLED.
MARLA, WE CAN'T LET JOAO SHOOT MY FATHER!
NO MATTER WHAT HE'S DONE, HE'S STILL MY DAD!
EDI, HE WOULD HAVE DONE THAT ALREADY IF HE WANTED TO. HE'S STALLING HIM.
SHOULDN'T YOU HAVE SOME REINFORCEMENTS WITH YOU?
I THINK, PERHAPS, THEY DIDN'T SHOW UP?
NOW, I WONDER WHY THAT WOULD BE? I'LL LET YOU FIGURE IT OUT.
ENOUGH OF THIS. NOW TURN AROUND. WALK. I KNOW YOU ARE UNARMED.
ARRG!
BLAM

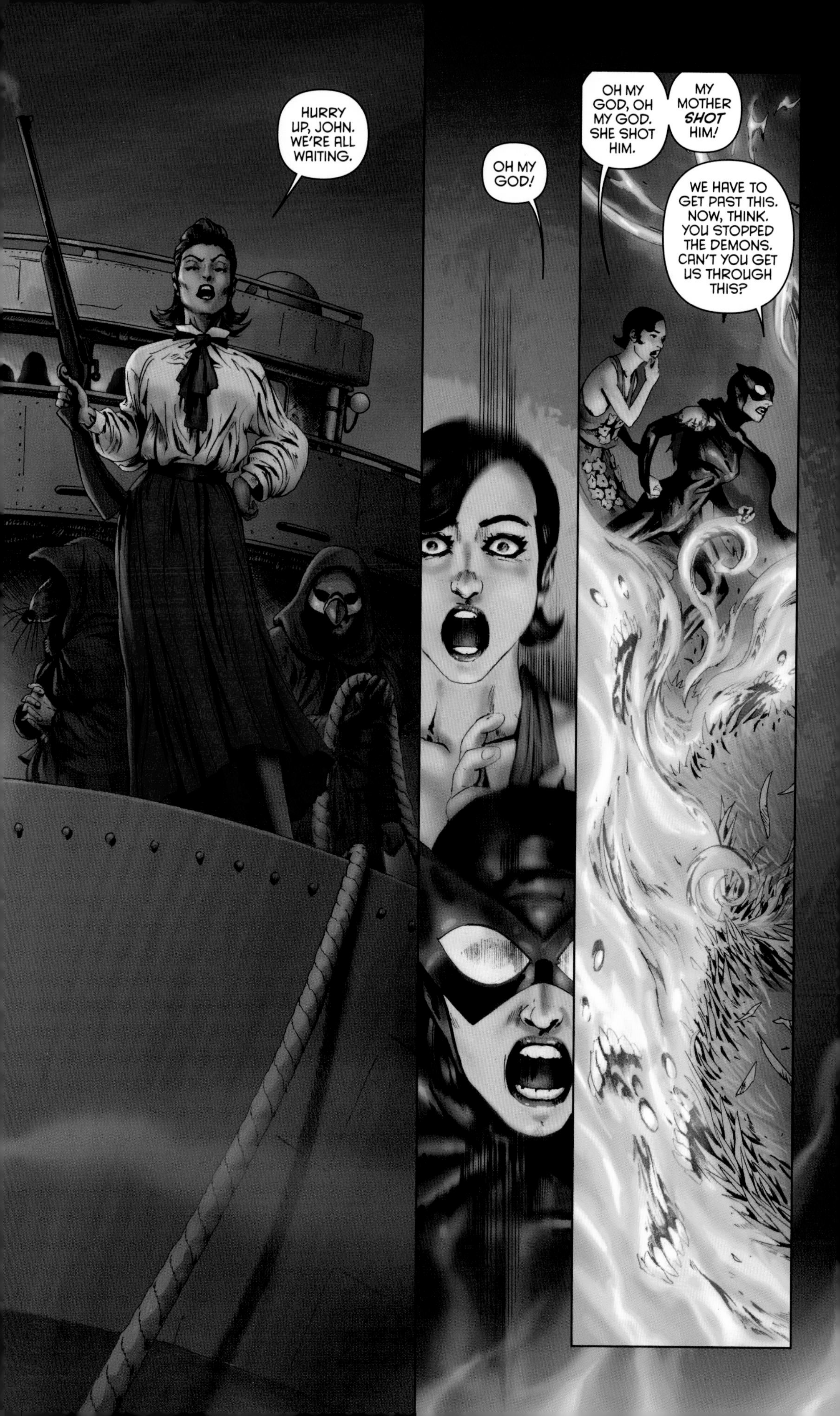
HURRY UP, JOHN. WE'RE ALL WAITING.
OH MY GOD!
OH MY GOD, OH MY GOD. SHE SHOT HIM.
MY MOTHER *SHOT* HIM!
WE HAVE TO GET PAST THIS. NOW, THINK. YOU STOPPED THE DEMONS. CAN'T YOU GET US THROUGH THIS?

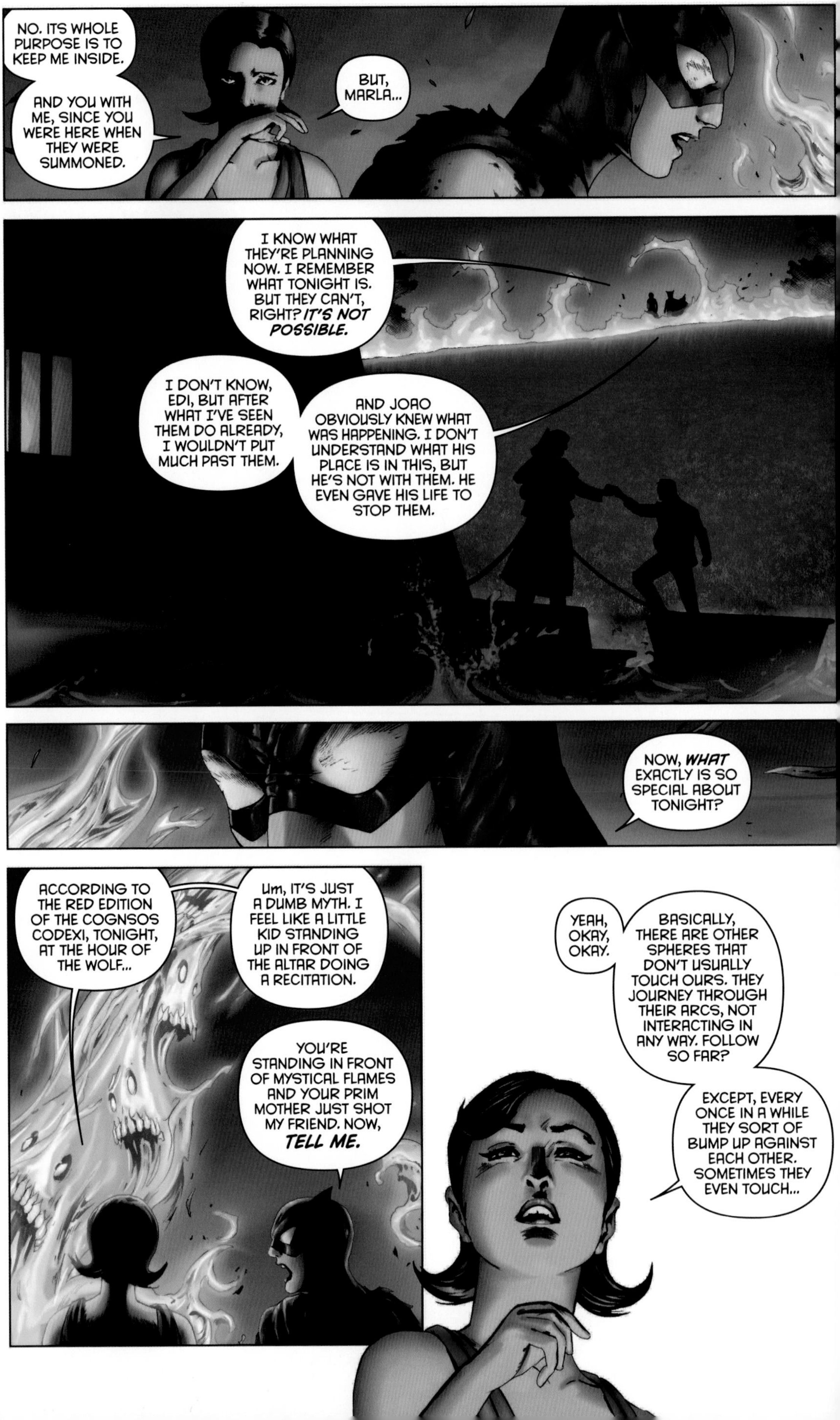
NO. ITS WHOLE PURPOSE IS TO KEEP ME INSIDE.
AND YOU WITH ME, SINCE YOU WERE HERE WHEN THEY WERE SUMMONED.
BUT, MARLA...
I KNOW WHAT THEY'RE PLANNING NOW. I REMEMBER WHAT TONIGHT IS. BUT THEY CAN'T, RIGHT? *IT'S NOT POSSIBLE.*
I DON'T KNOW, EDI, BUT AFTER WHAT I'VE SEEN THEM DO ALREADY, I WOULDN'T PUT MUCH PAST THEM.
AND JOAO OBVIOUSLY KNEW WHAT WAS HAPPENING. I DON'T UNDERSTAND WHAT HIS PLACE IS IN THIS, BUT HE'S NOT WITH THEM. HE EVEN GAVE HIS LIFE TO STOP THEM.
NOW, *WHAT* EXACTLY IS SO SPECIAL ABOUT TONIGHT?
ACCORDING TO THE RED EDITION OF THE COGNSOS CODEXI, TONIGHT, AT THE HOUR OF THE WOLF...
UM, IT'S JUST A DUMB MYTH. I FEEL LIKE A LITTLE KID STANDING UP IN FRONT OF THE ALTAR DOING A RECITATION.
YOU'RE STANDING IN FRONT OF MYSTICAL FLAMES AND YOUR PRIM MOTHER JUST SHOT MY FRIEND. NOW, **TELL ME.**
YEAH, OKAY, OKAY.
BASICALLY, THERE ARE OTHER SPHERES THAT DON'T USUALLY TOUCH OURS. THEY JOURNEY THROUGH THEIR ARCS, NOT INTERACTING IN ANY WAY. FOLLOW SO FAR?
EXCEPT, EVERY ONCE IN A WHILE THEY SORT OF BUMP UP AGAINST EACH OTHER. SOMETIMES THEY EVEN TOUCH...

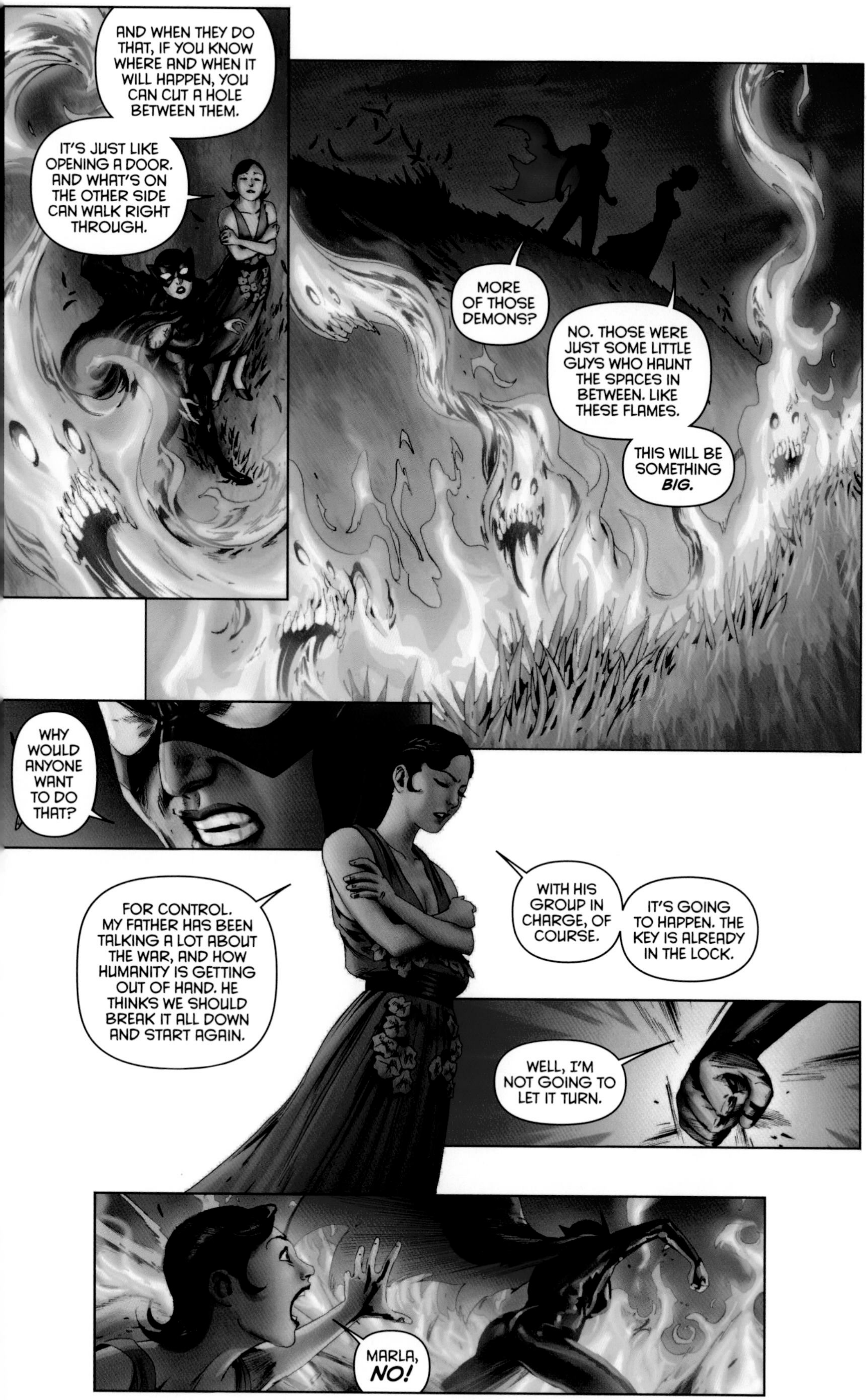
AND WHEN THEY DO THAT, IF YOU KNOW WHERE AND WHEN IT WILL HAPPEN, YOU CAN CUT A HOLE BETWEEN THEM.
IT'S JUST LIKE OPENING A DOOR. AND WHAT'S ON THE OTHER SIDE CAN WALK RIGHT THROUGH.
MORE OF THOSE DEMONS?
NO. THOSE WERE JUST SOME LITTLE GUYS WHO HAUNT THE SPACES IN BETWEEN. LIKE THESE FLAMES.
THIS WILL BE SOMETHING *BIG.*
WHY WOULD ANYONE WANT TO DO THAT?
FOR CONTROL. MY FATHER HAS BEEN TALKING A LOT ABOUT THE WAR, AND HOW HUMANITY IS GETTING OUT OF HAND. HE THINKS WE SHOULD BREAK IT ALL DOWN AND START AGAIN.
WITH HIS GROUP IN CHARGE, OF COURSE.
IT'S GOING TO HAPPEN. THE KEY IS ALREADY IN THE LOCK.
WELL, I'M NOT GOING TO LET IT TURN.
MARLA, *NO!*

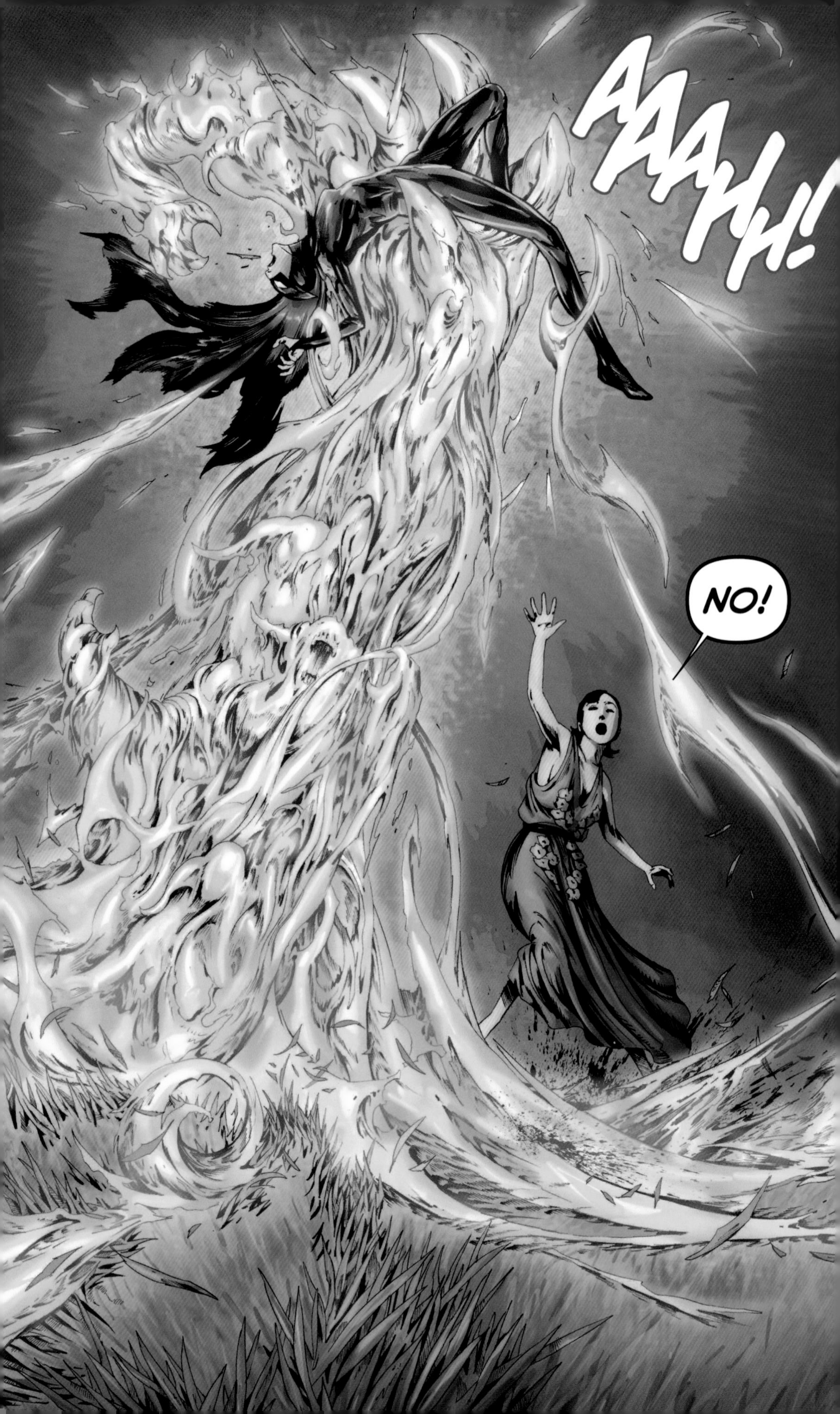
AAAAHH!
NO!

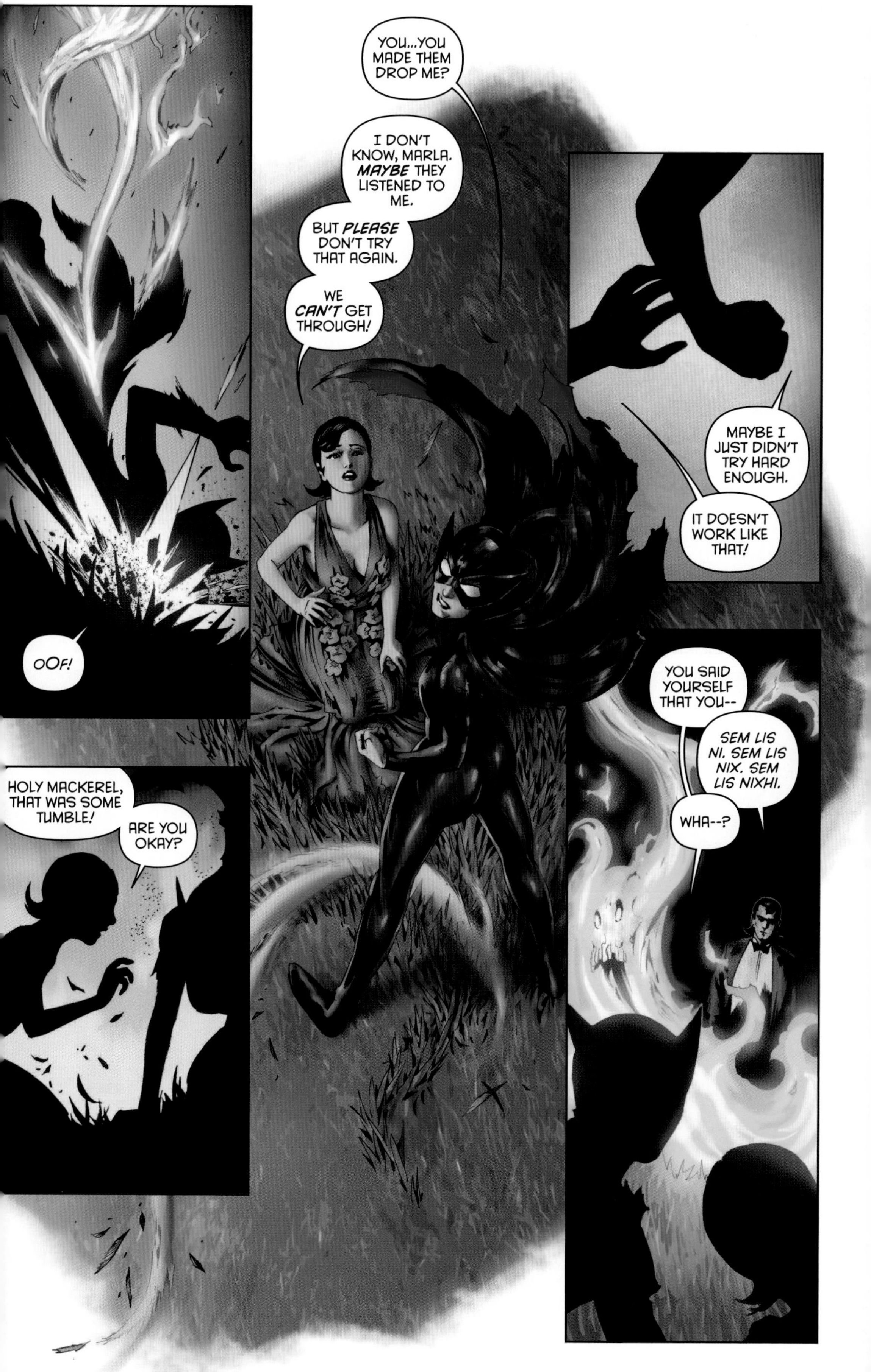
OOF!
HOLY MACKEREL, THAT WAS SOME TUMBLE!
ARE YOU OKAY?
YOU...YOU MADE THEM DROP ME?
I DON'T KNOW, MARLA. *MAYBE* THEY LISTENED TO ME.
BUT *PLEASE* DON'T TRY THAT AGAIN.
WE *CAN'T* GET THROUGH!
MAYBE I JUST DIDN'T TRY HARD ENOUGH.
IT DOESN'T WORK LIKE THAT!
YOU SAID YOURSELF THAT YOU--
SEM LIS NI. SEM LIS NIX. SEM LIS NIXHI.
WHA--?

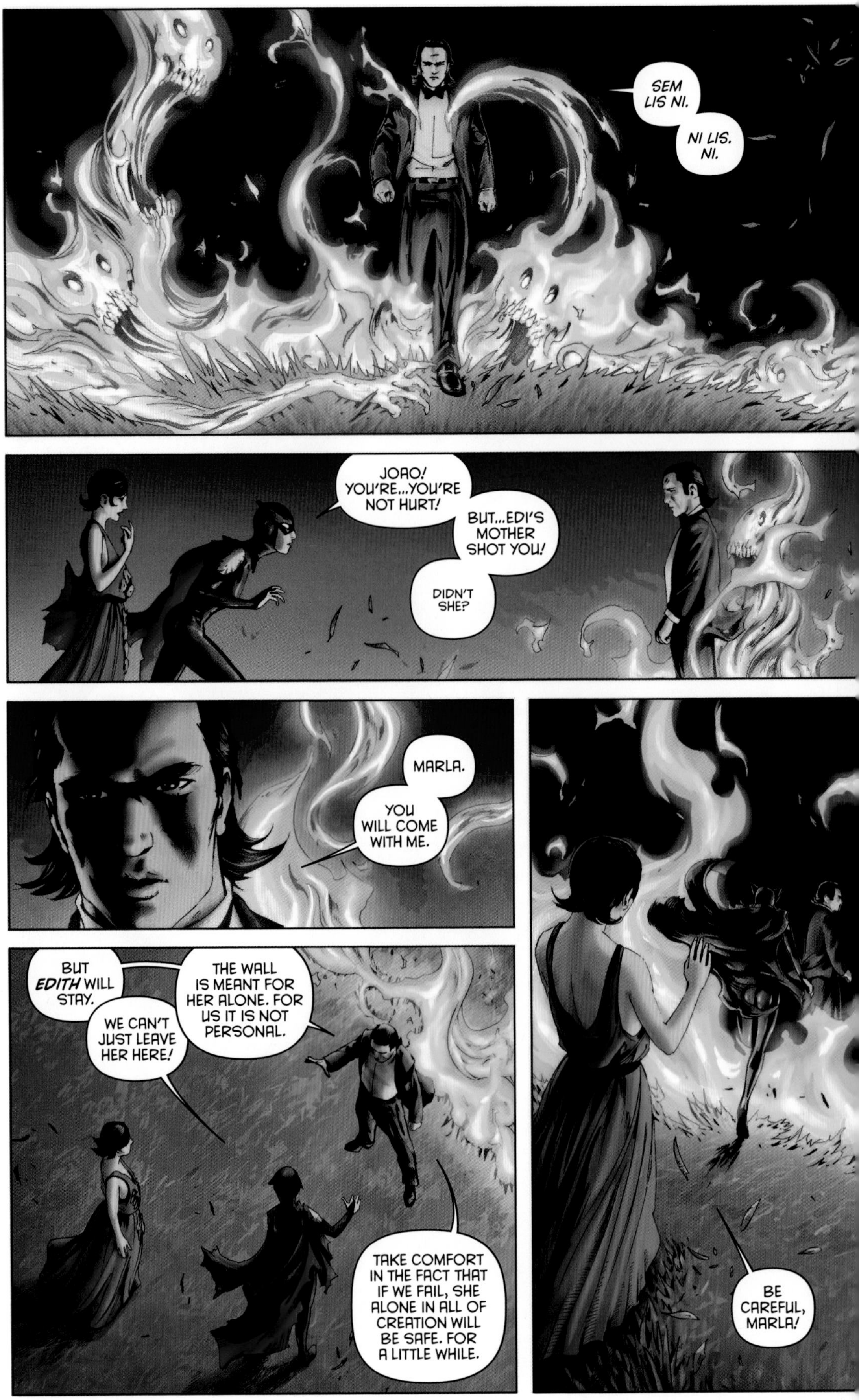
SEM LIS NI.
NI LIS. NI.
JOAO! YOU'RE...YOU'RE NOT HURT!
BUT...EDI'S MOTHER SHOT YOU!
DIDN'T SHE?
MARLA.
YOU WILL COME WITH ME.
BUT *EDITH* WILL STAY.
THE WALL IS MEANT FOR HER ALONE. FOR US IT IS NOT PERSONAL.
WE CAN'T JUST LEAVE HER HERE!
TAKE COMFORT IN THE FACT THAT IF WE FAIL, SHE ALONE IN ALL OF CREATION WILL BE SAFE. FOR A LITTLE WHILE.
BE CAREFUL, MARLA!

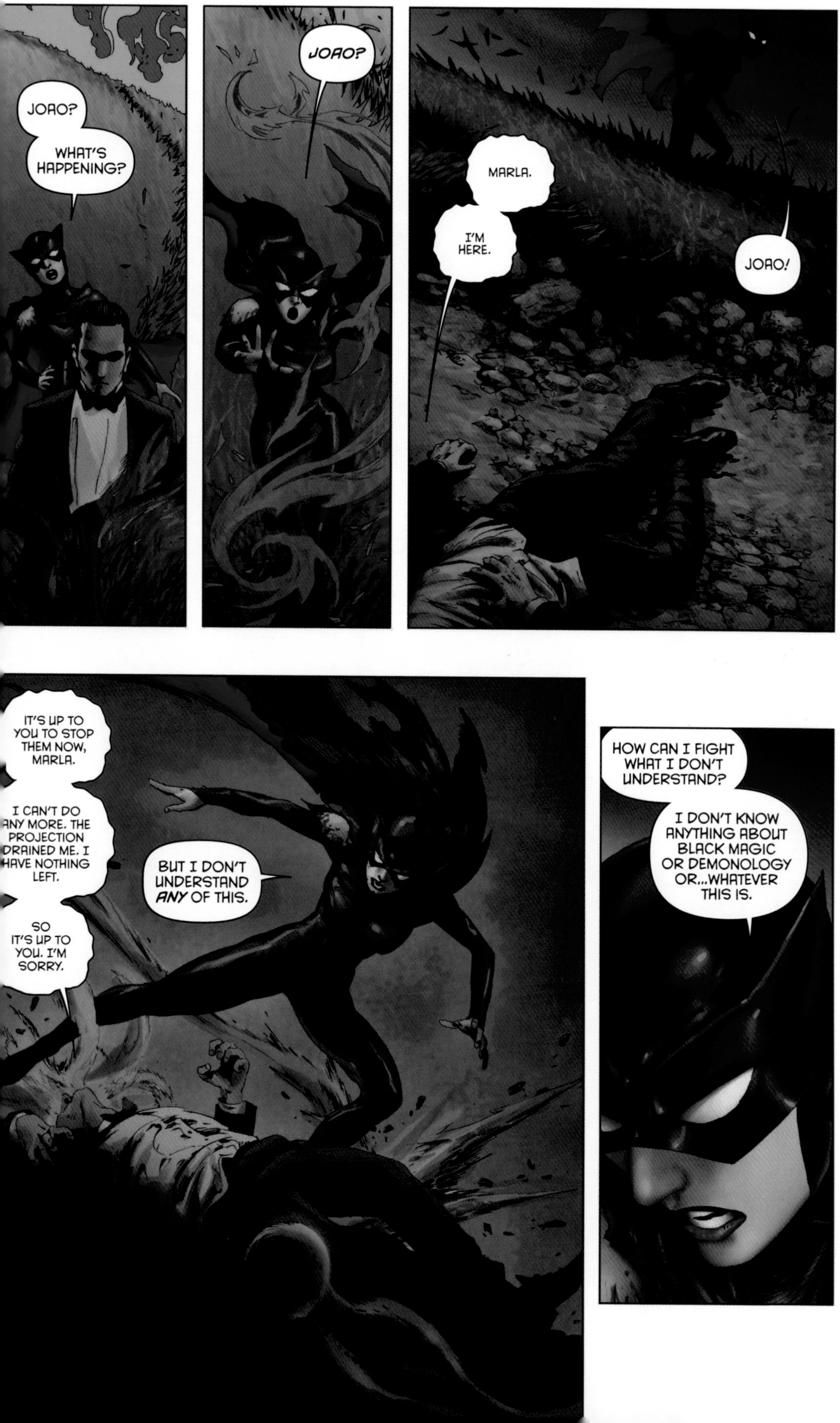
JOAO?
WHAT'S HAPPENING?
JOAO?
MARLA.
I'M HERE.
JOAO!
IT'S UP TO YOU TO STOP THEM NOW, MARLA.
I CAN'T DO ANY MORE. THE PROJECTION DRAINED ME. I HAVE NOTHING LEFT.
BUT I DON'T UNDERSTAND ANY OF THIS.
SO IT'S UP TO YOU. I'M SORRY.
HOW CAN I FIGHT WHAT I DON'T UNDERSTAND?
I DON'T KNOW ANYTHING ABOUT BLACK MAGIC OR DEMONOLOGY OR...WHATEVER THIS IS.

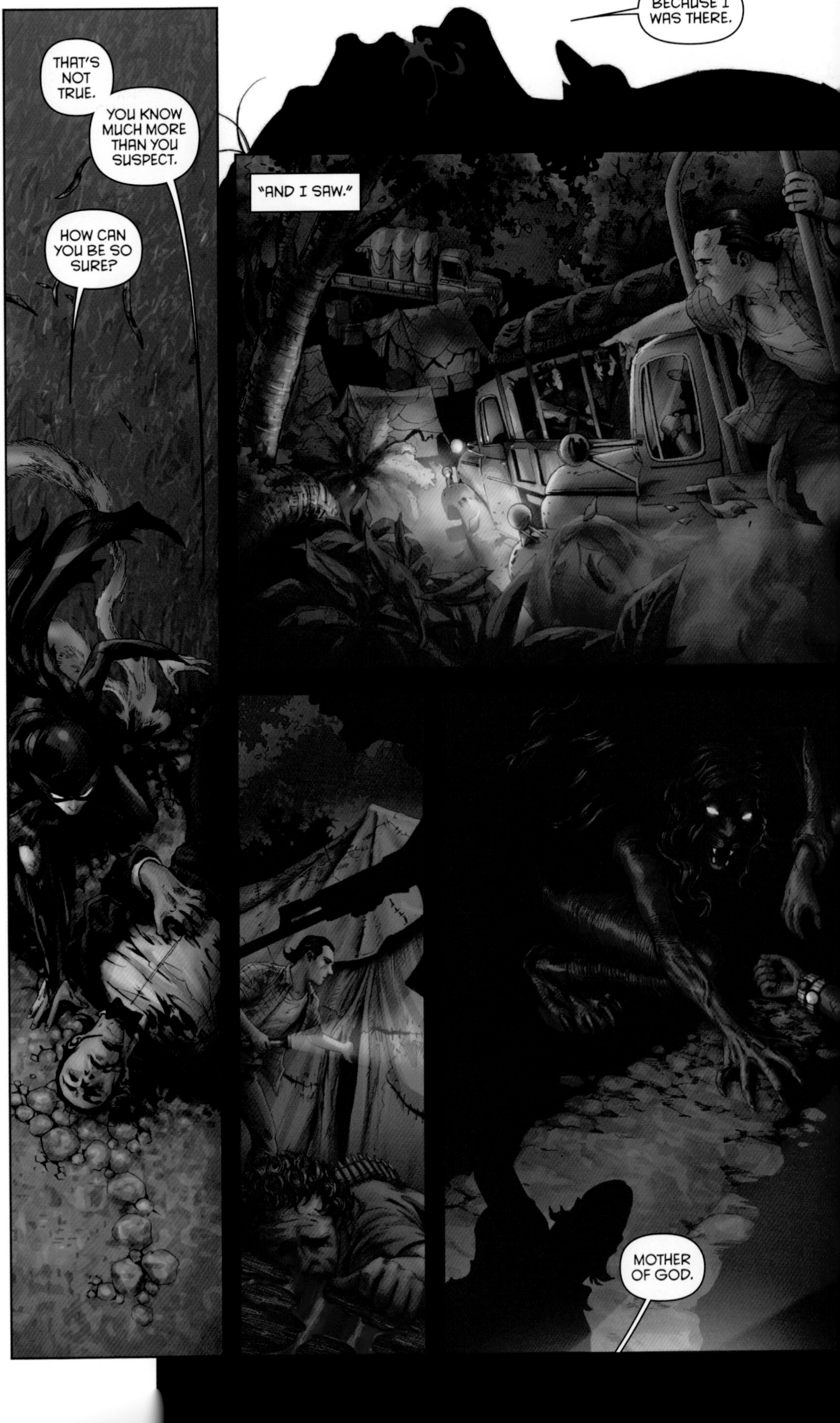
THAT'S NOT TRUE.
YOU KNOW MUCH MORE THAN YOU SUSPECT.
HOW CAN YOU BE SO SURE?
BECAUSE I WAS THERE.
"AND I SAW."
MOTHER OF GOD.

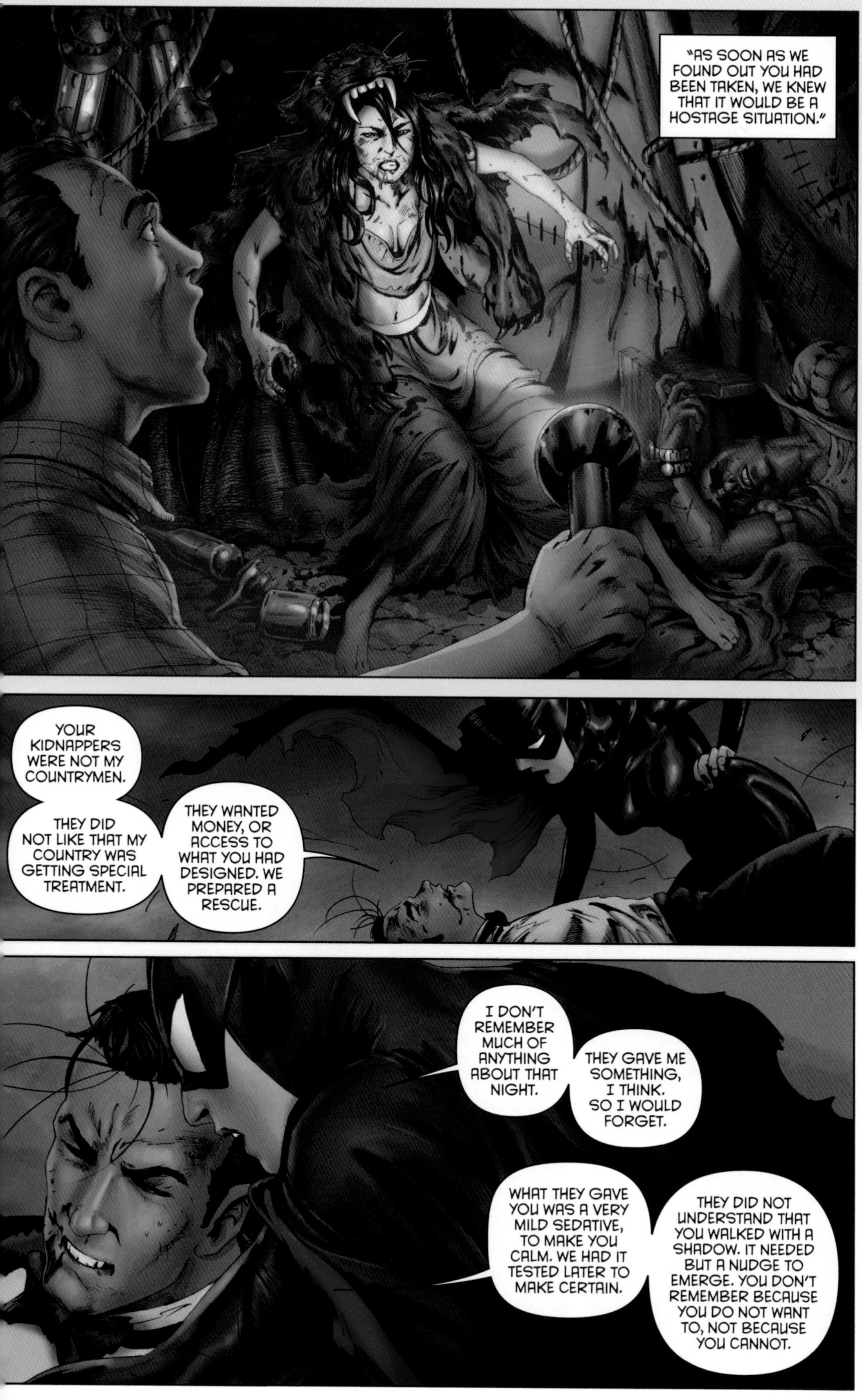

"AS SOON AS WE FOUND OUT YOU HAD BEEN TAKEN, WE KNEW THAT IT WOULD BE A HOSTAGE SITUATION."
YOUR KIDNAPPERS WERE NOT MY COUNTRYMEN.
THEY DID NOT LIKE THAT MY COUNTRY WAS GETTING SPECIAL TREATMENT.
THEY WANTED MONEY, OR ACCESS TO WHAT YOU HAD DESIGNED. WE PREPARED A RESCUE.
I DON'T REMEMBER MUCH OF ANYTHING ABOUT THAT NIGHT.
THEY GAVE ME SOMETHING, I THINK. SO I WOULD FORGET.
WHAT THEY GAVE YOU WAS A VERY MILD SEDATIVE, TO MAKE YOU CALM. WE HAD IT TESTED LATER TO MAKE CERTAIN.
THEY DID NOT UNDERSTAND THAT YOU WALKED WITH A SHADOW. IT NEEDED BUT A NUDGE TO EMERGE. YOU DON'T REMEMBER BECAUSE YOU DO NOT WANT TO, NOT BECAUSE YOU CANNOT.

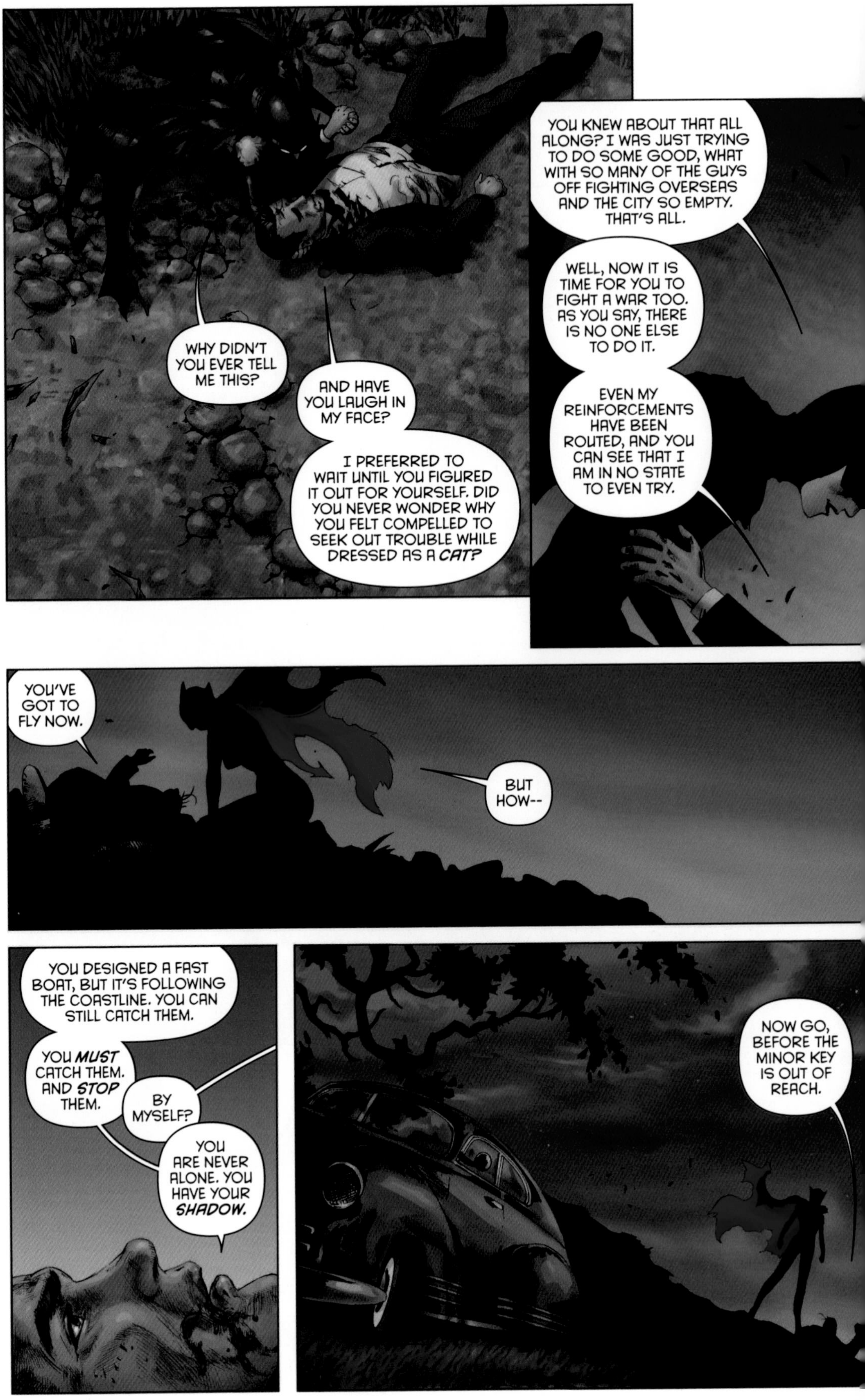
WHY DIDN'T YOU EVER TELL ME THIS?
AND HAVE YOU LAUGH IN MY FACE?
I PREFERRED TO WAIT UNTIL YOU FIGURED IT OUT FOR YOURSELF. DID YOU NEVER WONDER WHY YOU FELT COMPELLED TO SEEK OUT TROUBLE WHILE DRESSED AS A *CAT?*
YOU KNEW ABOUT THAT ALL ALONG? I WAS JUST TRYING TO DO SOME GOOD, WHAT WITH SO MANY OF THE GUYS OFF FIGHTING OVERSEAS AND THE CITY SO EMPTY. THAT'S ALL.
WELL, NOW IT IS TIME FOR YOU TO FIGHT A WAR TOO. AS YOU SAY, THERE IS NO ONE ELSE TO DO IT.
EVEN MY REINFORCEMENTS HAVE BEEN ROUTED, AND YOU CAN SEE THAT I AM IN NO STATE TO EVEN TRY.
YOU'VE GOT TO FLY NOW.
BUT HOW--
YOU DESIGNED A FAST BOAT, BUT IT'S FOLLOWING THE COASTLINE. YOU CAN STILL CATCH THEM.
YOU ***MUST*** CATCH THEM. AND ***STOP*** THEM.
BY MYSELF?
YOU ARE NEVER ALONE. YOU HAVE YOUR ***SHADOW.***
NOW GO, BEFORE THE MINOR KEY IS OUT OF REACH.

SEE THAT? THERE'S A CAR FOLLOWING US.

MAYBE IT'S A COINCIDENCE. THERE ARE A FEW HOUSES EVEN THIS FAR OUT.

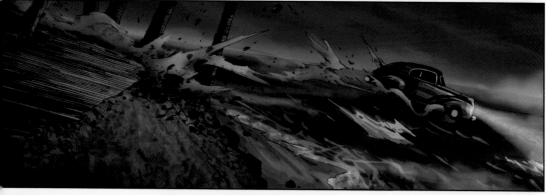

SEE? NOTHING TO DO WITH US AT ALL.

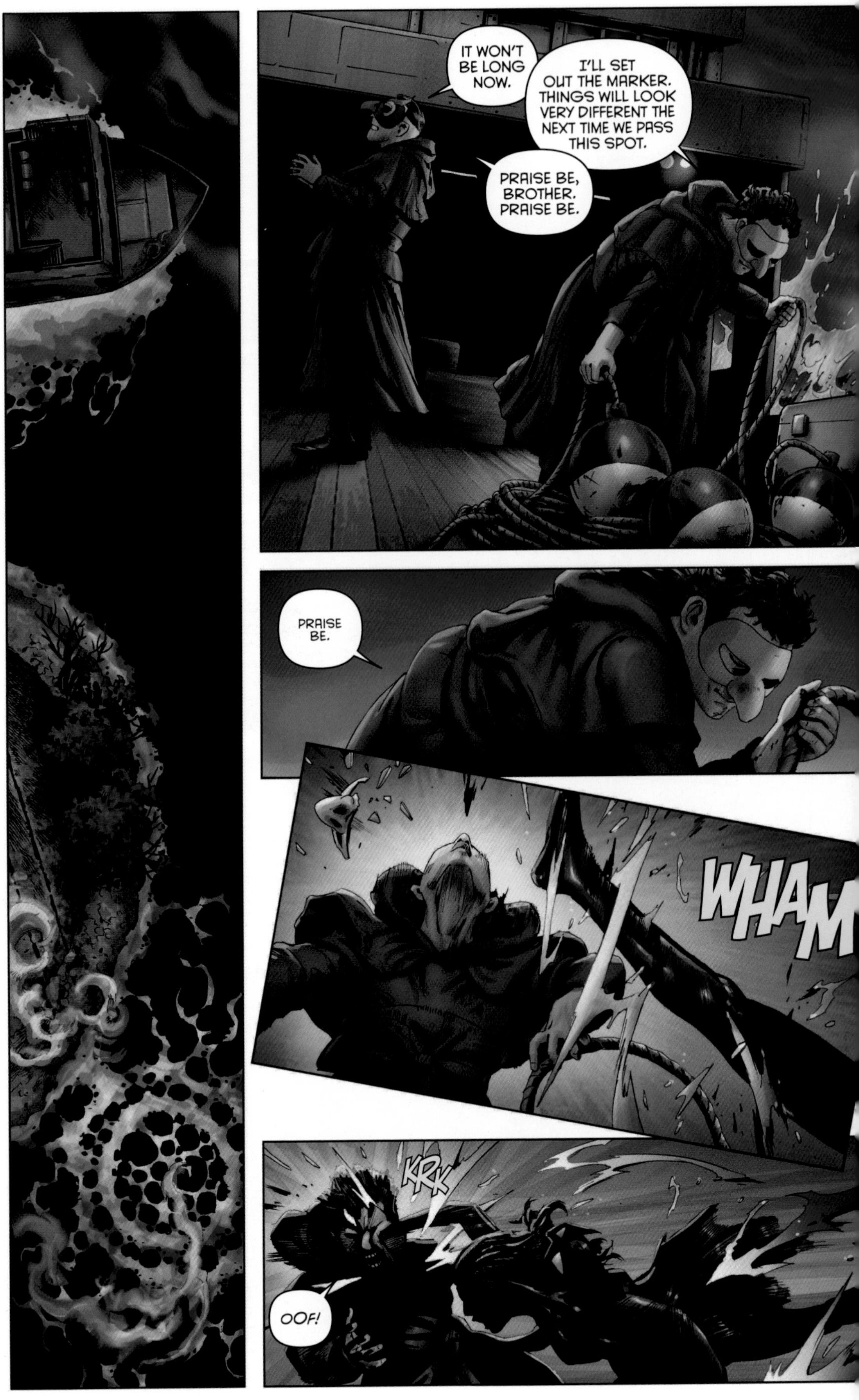
IT WON'T BE LONG NOW.
I'LL SET OUT THE MARKER. THINGS WILL LOOK VERY DIFFERENT THE NEXT TIME WE PASS THIS SPOT.
PRAISE BE, BROTHER. PRAISE BE.
PRAISE BE.
WHAM
KRK
OOF!

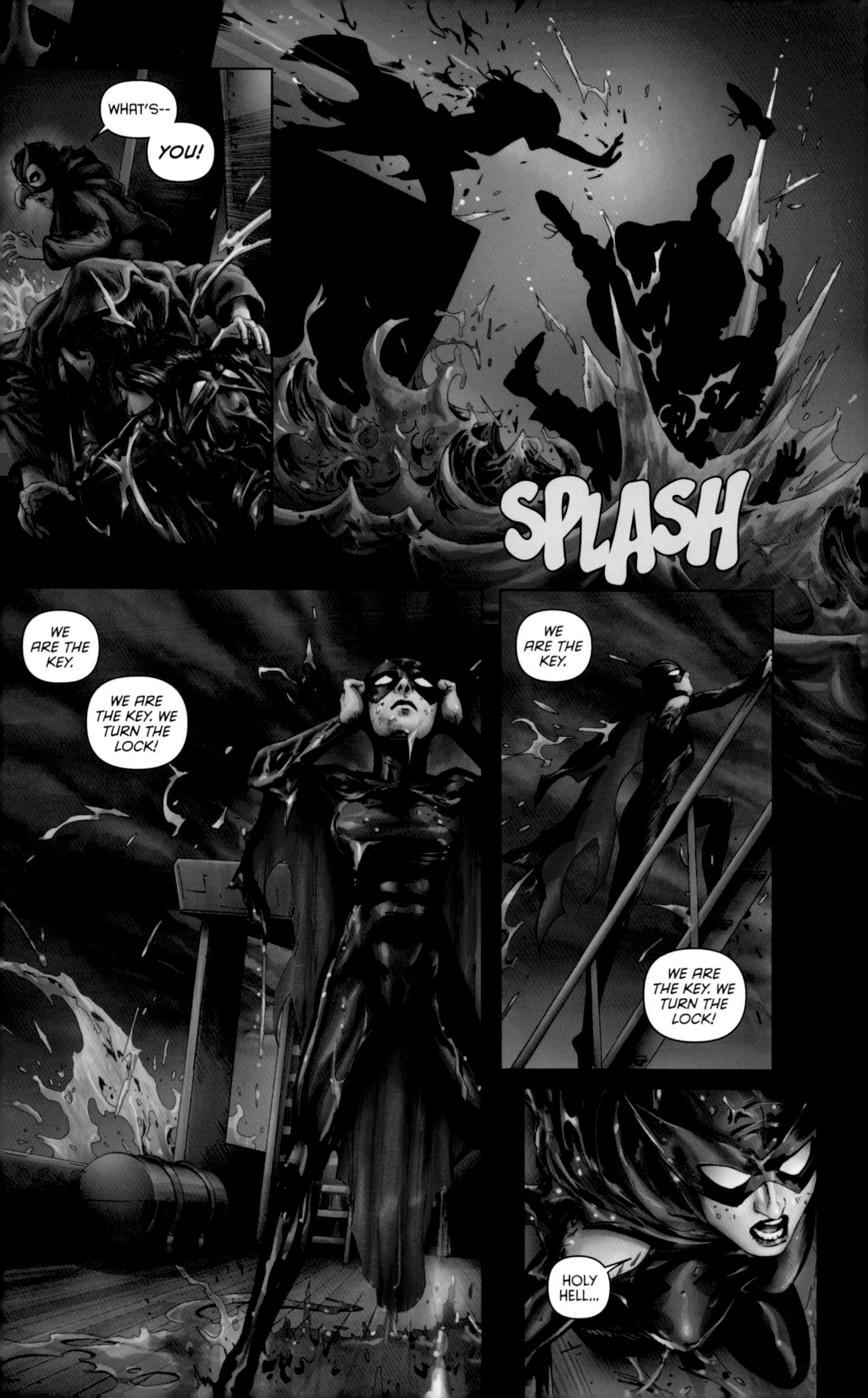
WHAT'S--
YOU!
SPLASH
WE ARE THE KEY.
WE ARE THE KEY. WE TURN THE LOCK!
WE ARE THE KEY.
WE ARE THE KEY. WE TURN THE LOCK!
HOLY HELL...

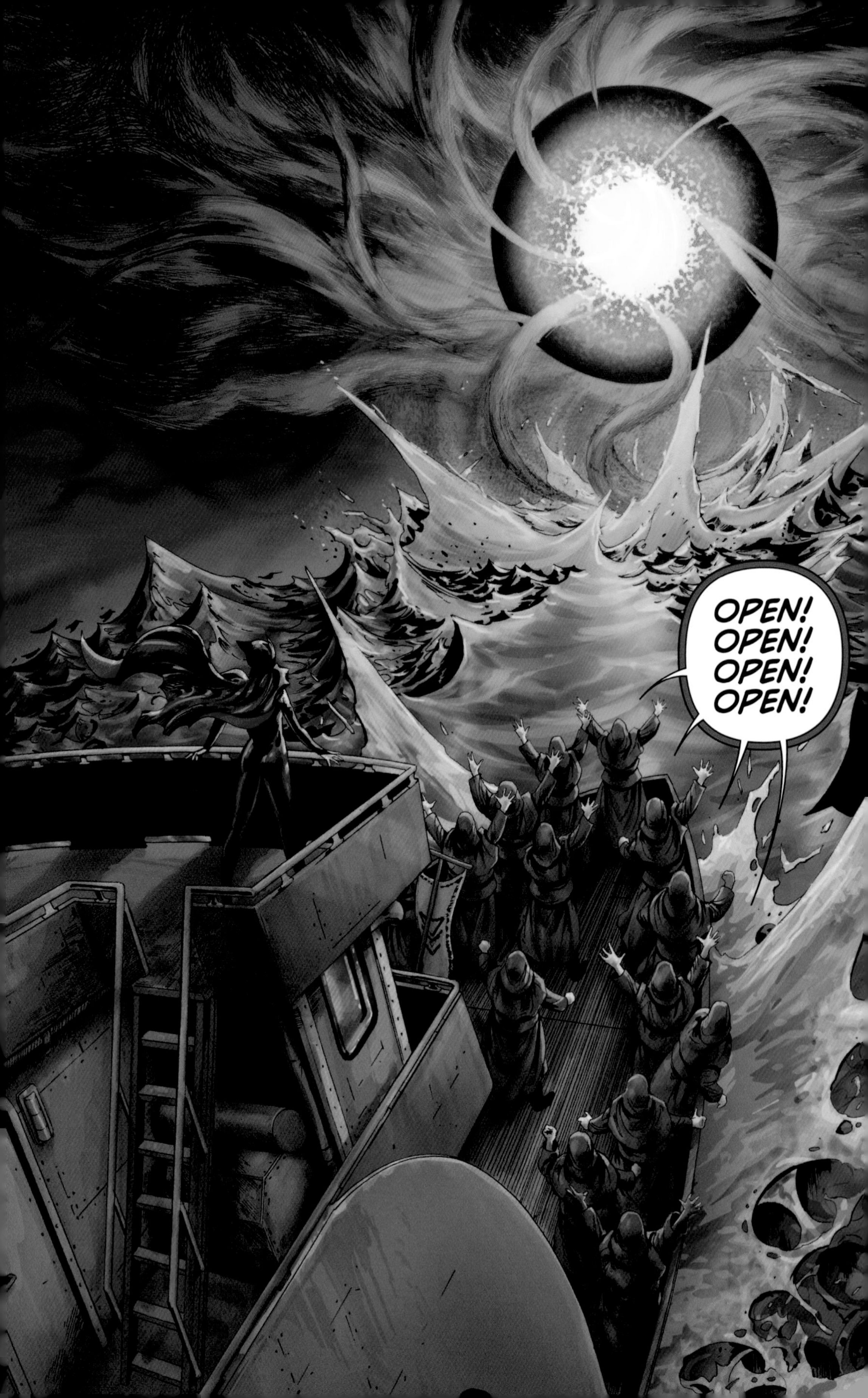
OPEN! OPEN! OPEN! OPEN!

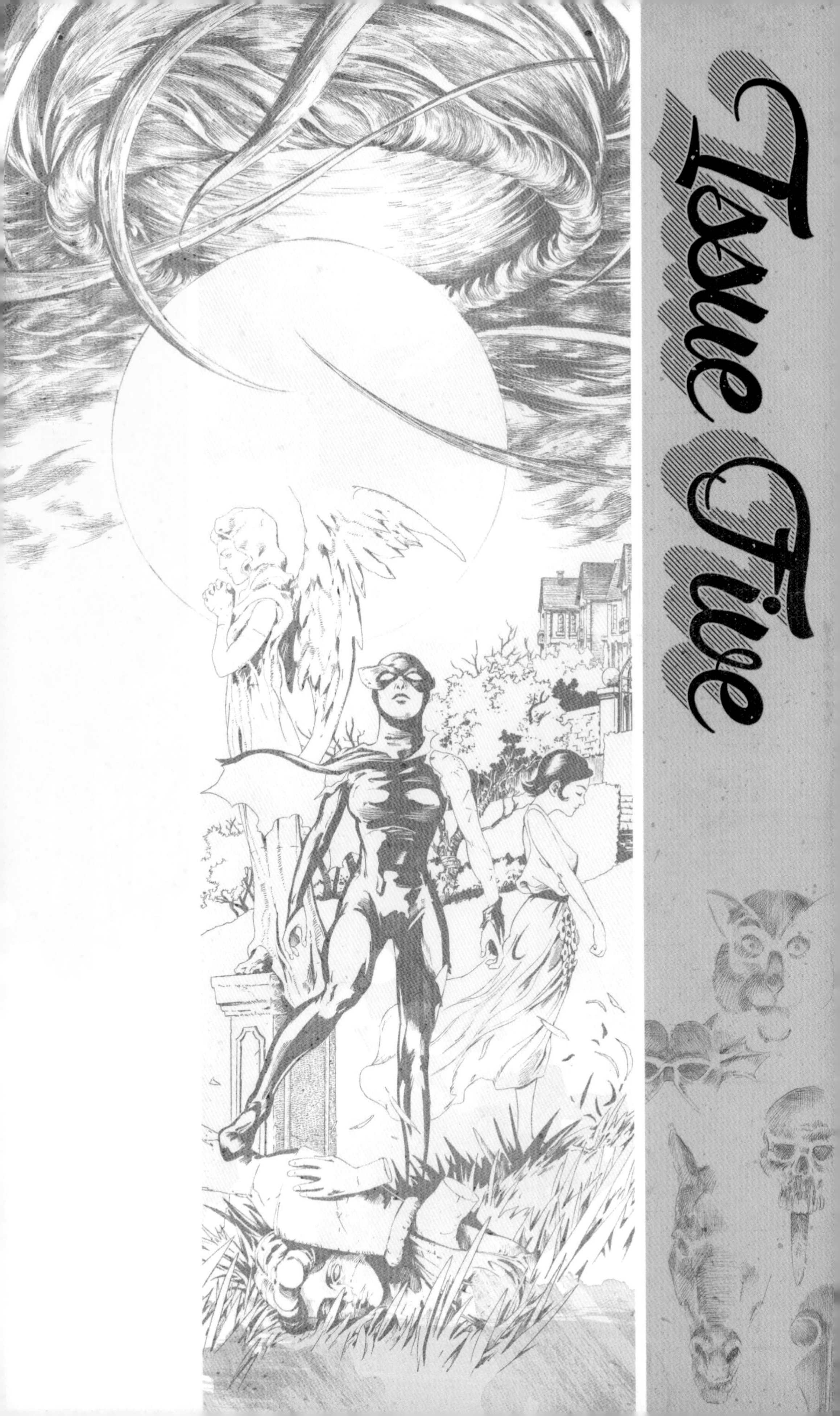
Issue Five

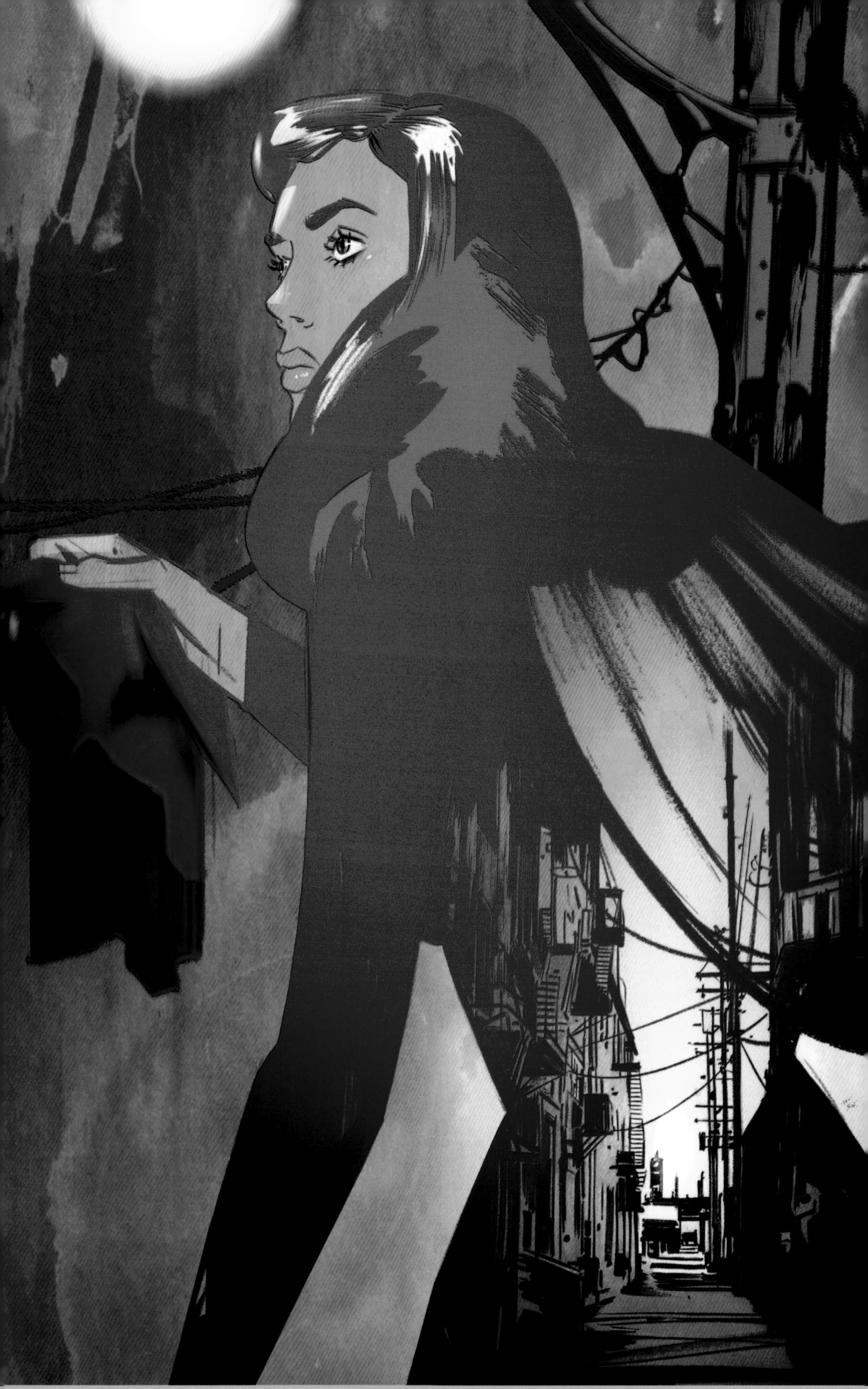

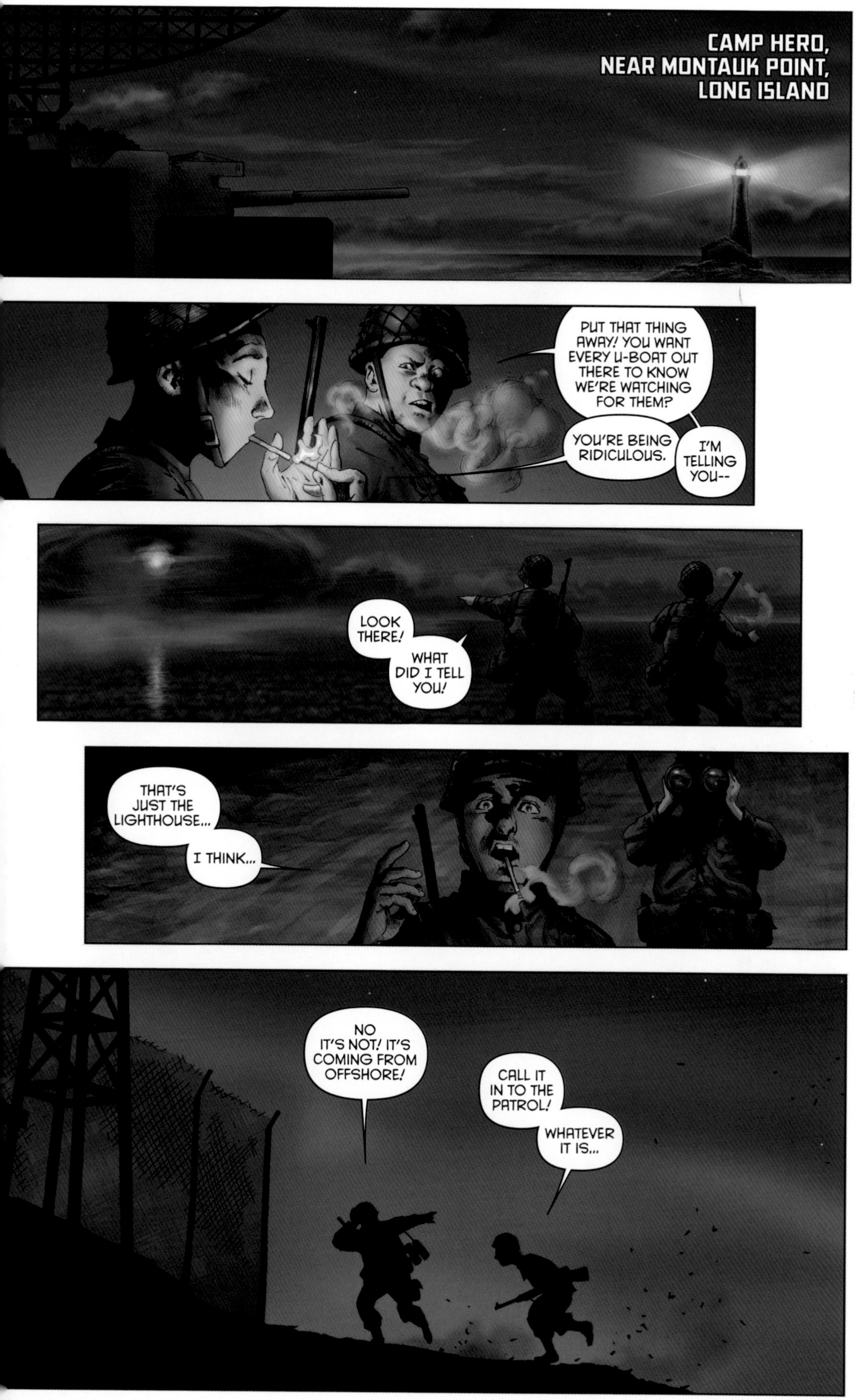
CAMP HERO,
NEAR MONTAUK POINT,
LONG ISLAND
PUT THAT THING AWAY! YOU WANT EVERY U-BOAT OUT THERE TO KNOW WE'RE WATCHING FOR THEM?
YOU'RE BEING RIDICULOUS.
I'M TELLING YOU--
LOOK THERE!
WHAT DID I TELL YOU!
THAT'S JUST THE LIGHTHOUSE...
I THINK...
NO IT'S NOT! IT'S COMING FROM OFFSHORE!
CALL IT IN TO THE PATROL!
WHATEVER IT IS...

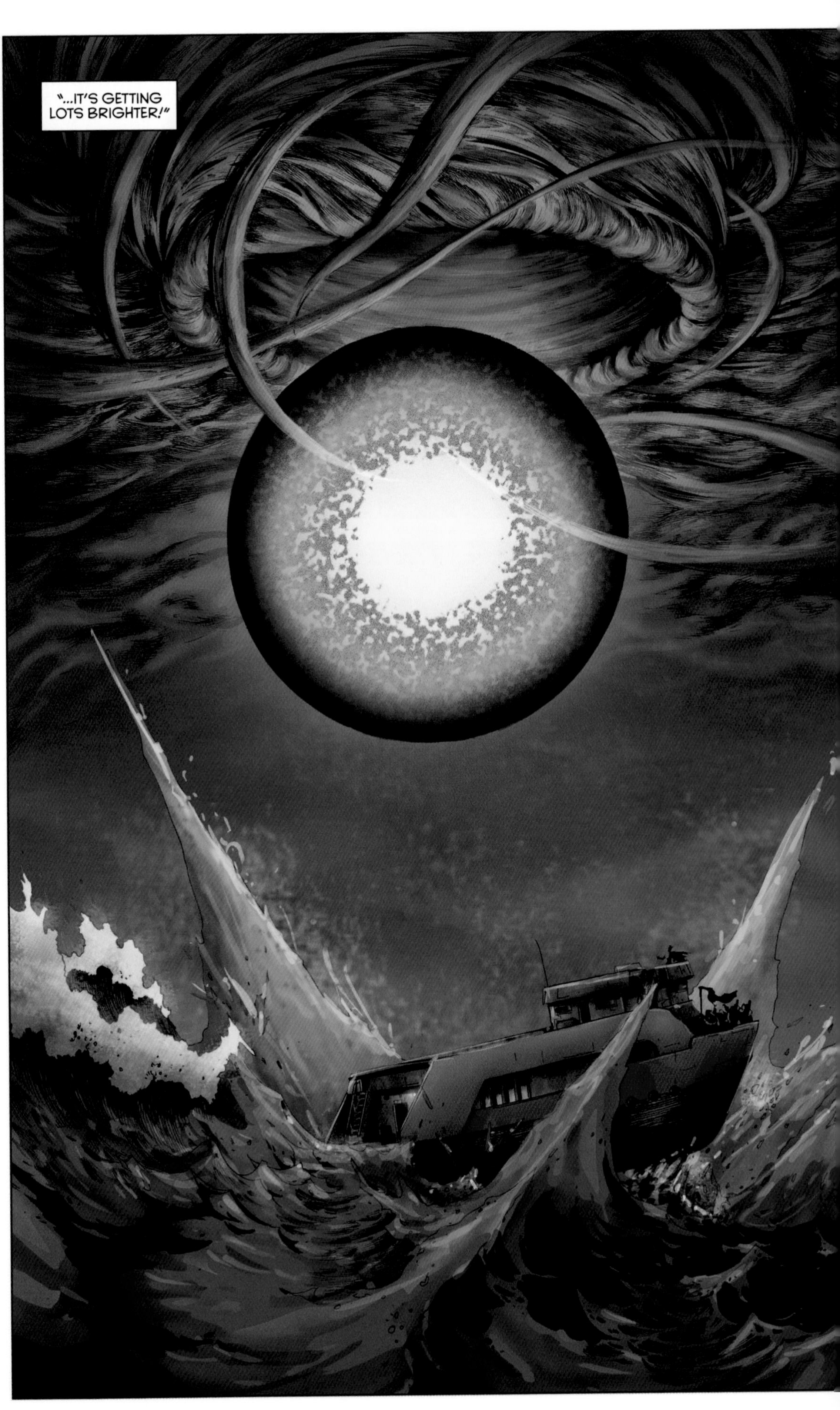
"...IT'S GETTING LOTS BRIGHTER!"

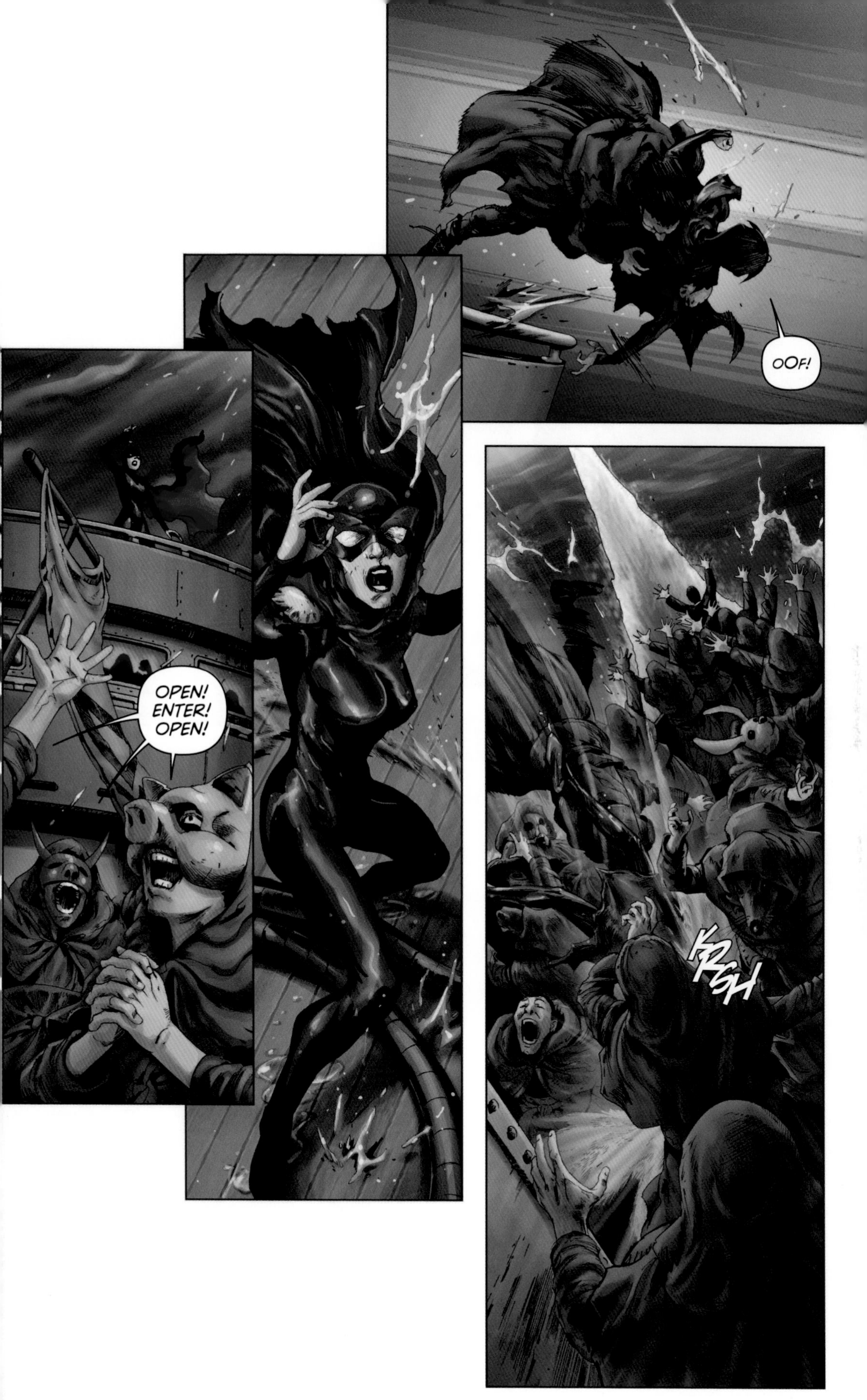
OOF!
OPEN!
ENTER!
OPEN!
KRSH

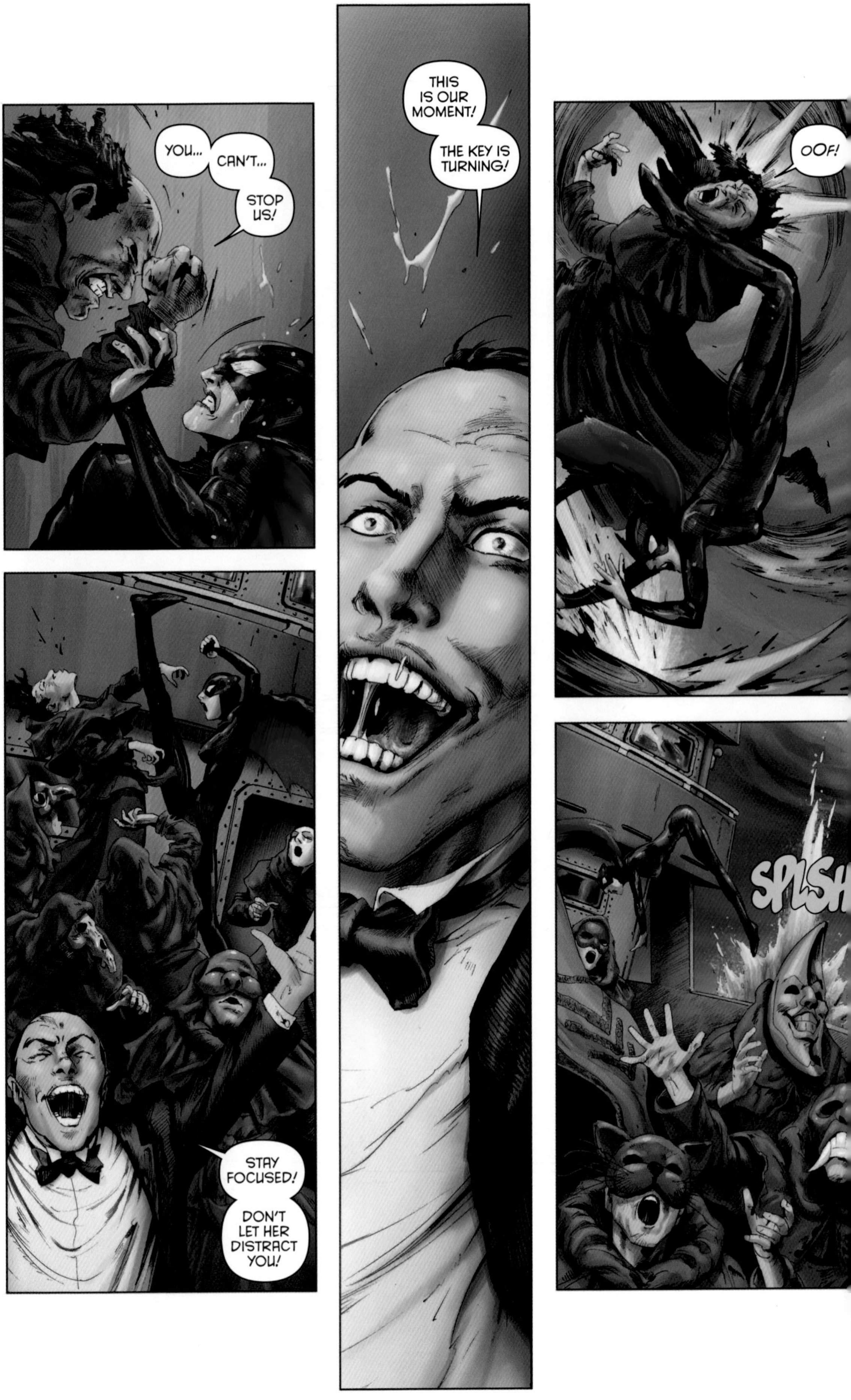
YOU...
CAN'T...
STOP US!
THIS IS OUR MOMENT!
THE KEY IS TURNING!
OOF!
STAY FOCUSED!
DON'T LET HER DISTRACT YOU!
SPLSH

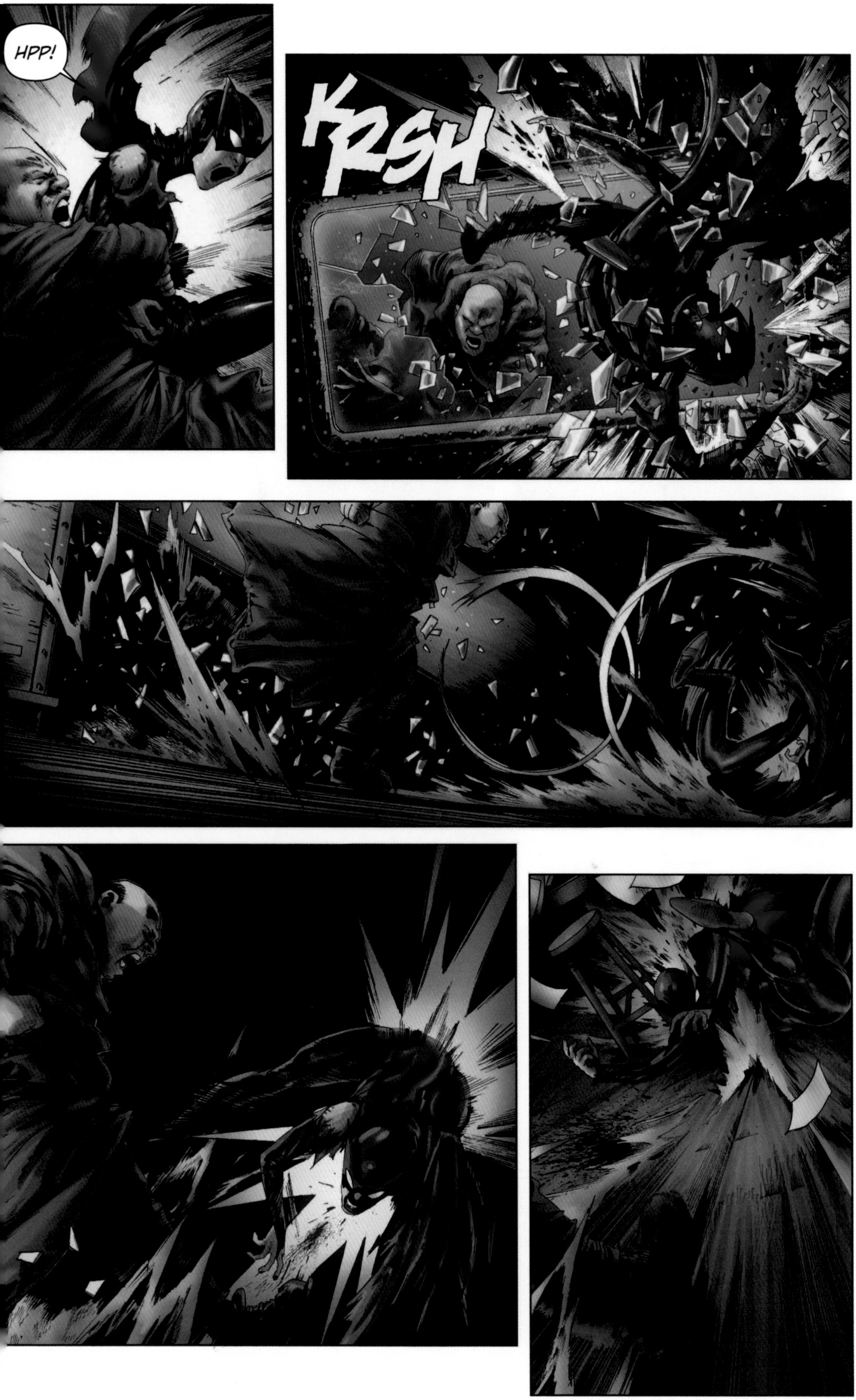
HPP!
KRSH

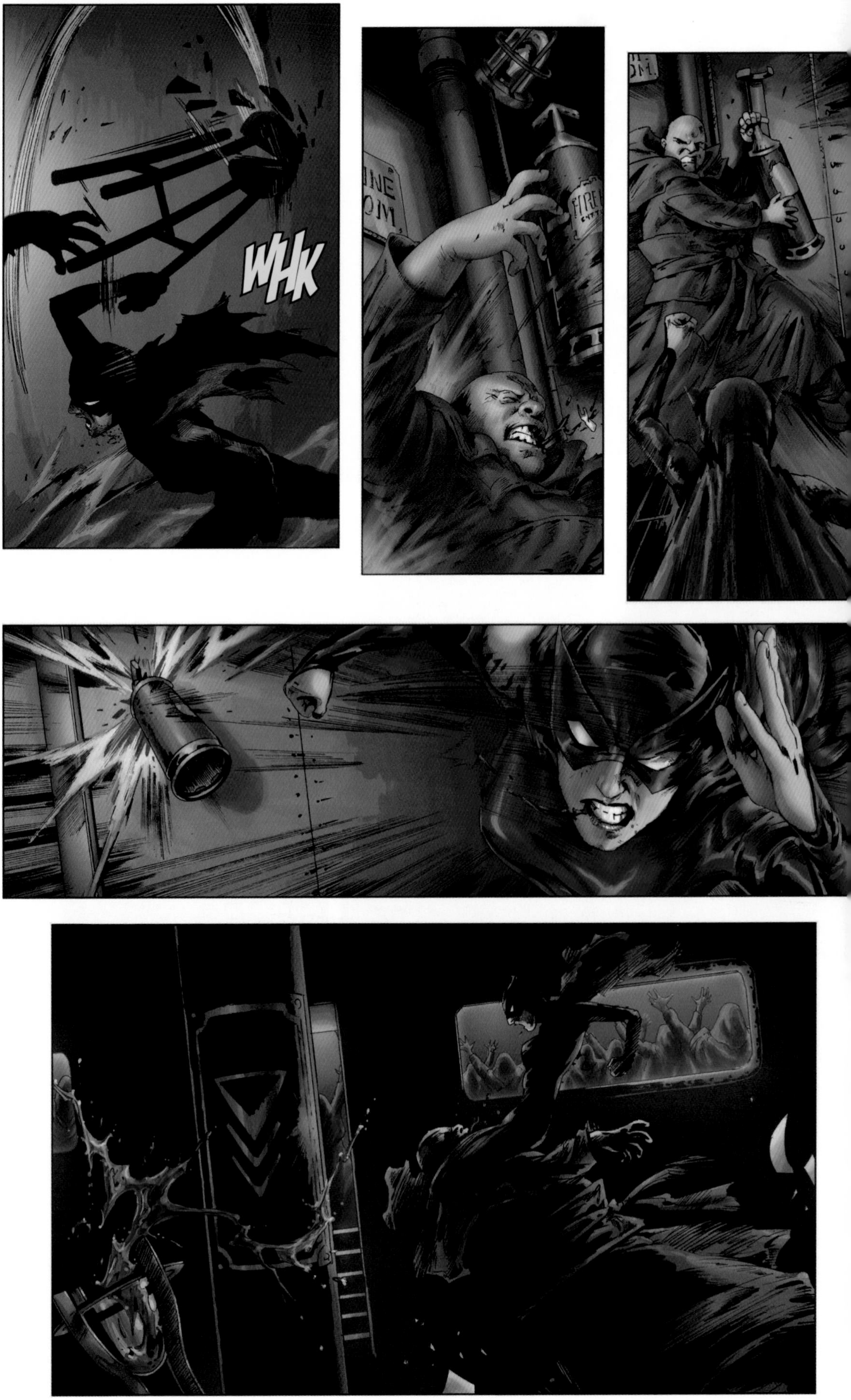
WHK

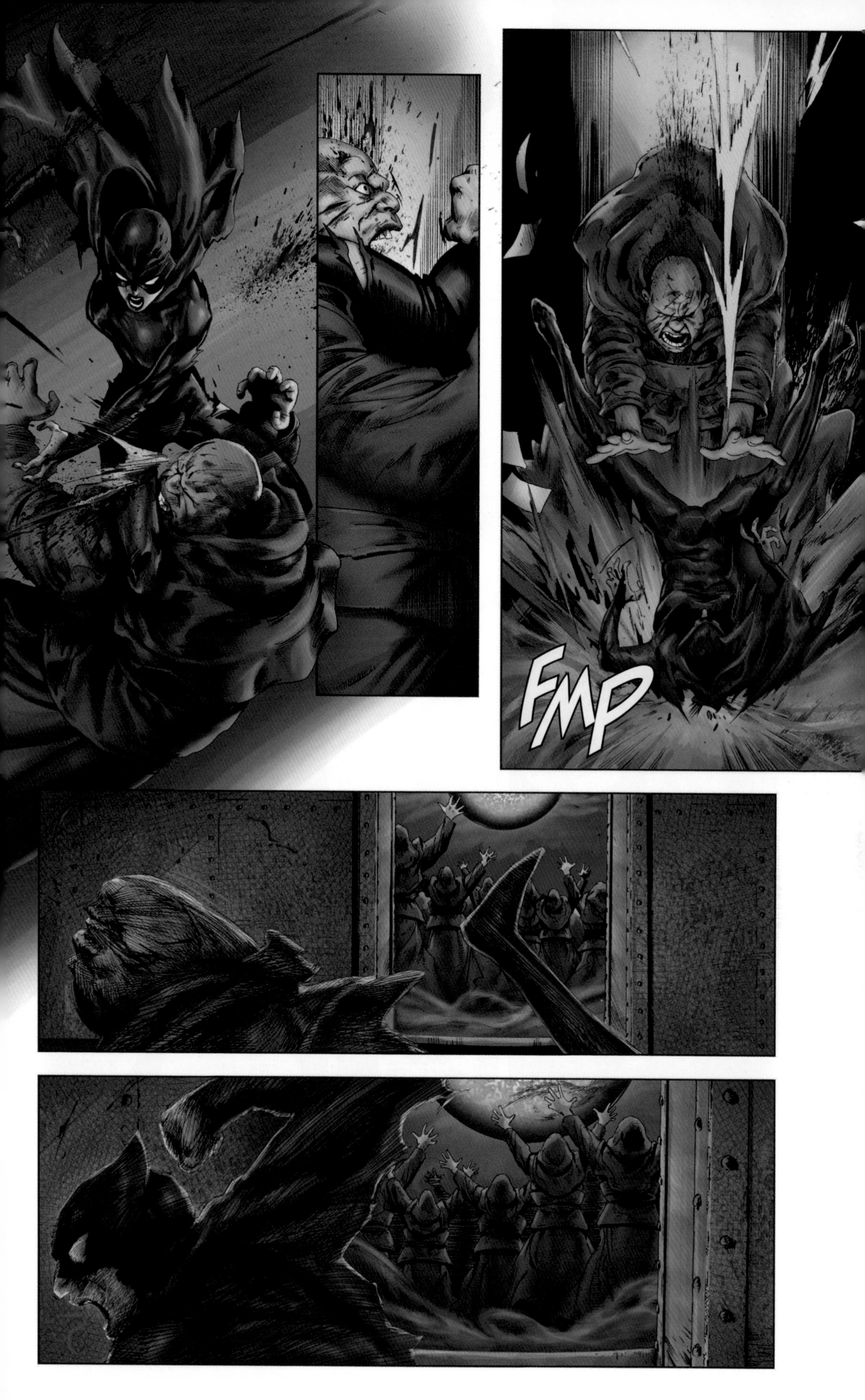
FMP

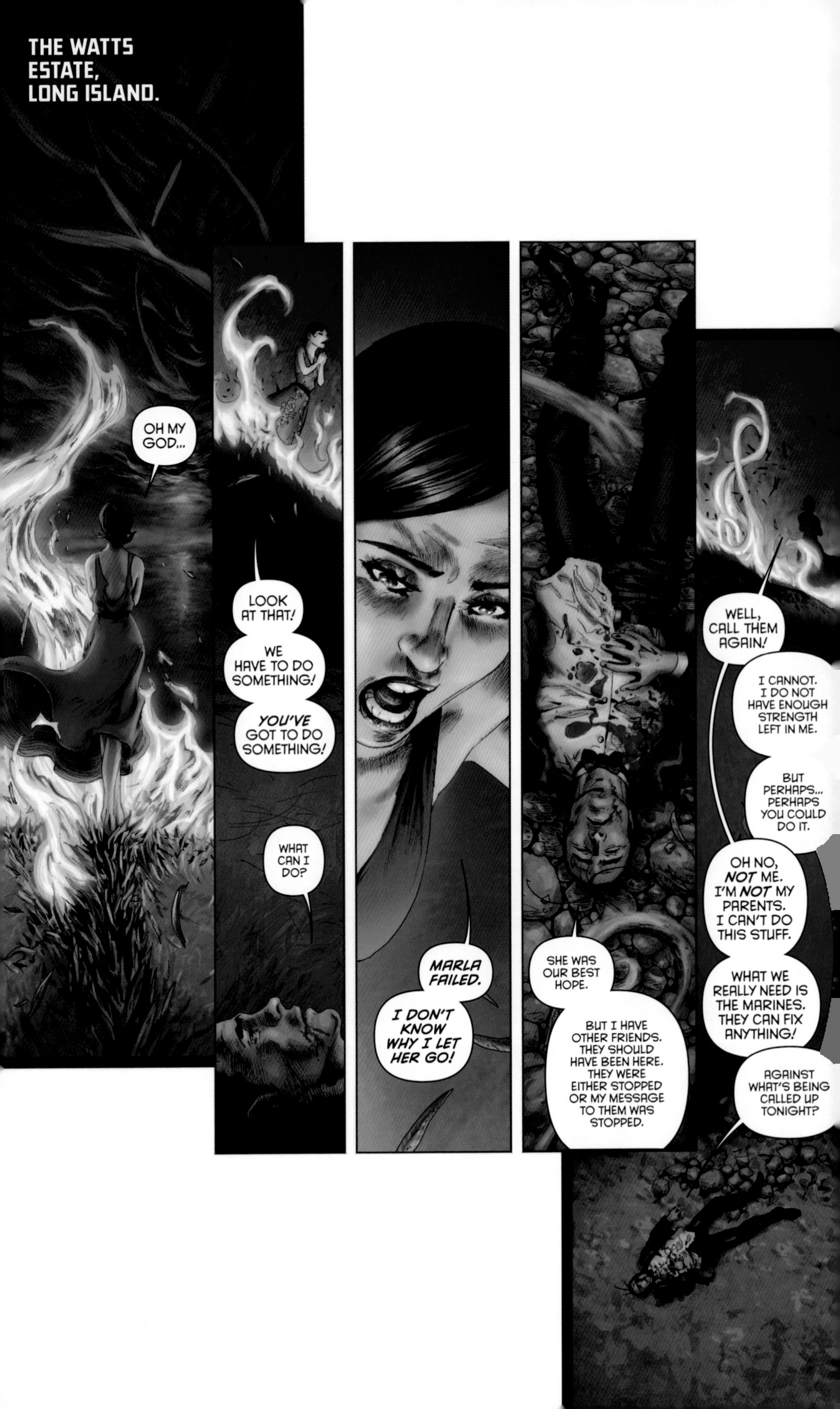
THE WATTS ESTATE, LONG ISLAND.
OH MY GOD...
LOOK AT THAT!
WE HAVE TO DO SOMETHING!
YOU'VE GOT TO DO SOMETHING!
WHAT CAN I DO?
MARLA FAILED.
I DON'T KNOW WHY I LET HER GO!
SHE WAS OUR BEST HOPE.
BUT I HAVE OTHER FRIENDS. THEY SHOULD HAVE BEEN HERE. THEY WERE EITHER STOPPED OR MY MESSAGE TO THEM WAS STOPPED.
WELL, CALL THEM AGAIN!
I CANNOT. I DO NOT HAVE ENOUGH STRENGTH LEFT IN ME.
BUT PERHAPS... PERHAPS YOU COULD DO IT.
OH NO, NOT ME. I'M NOT MY PARENTS. I CAN'T DO THIS STUFF.
WHAT WE REALLY NEED IS THE MARINES. THEY CAN FIX ANYTHING!
AGAINST WHAT'S BEING CALLED UP TONIGHT?

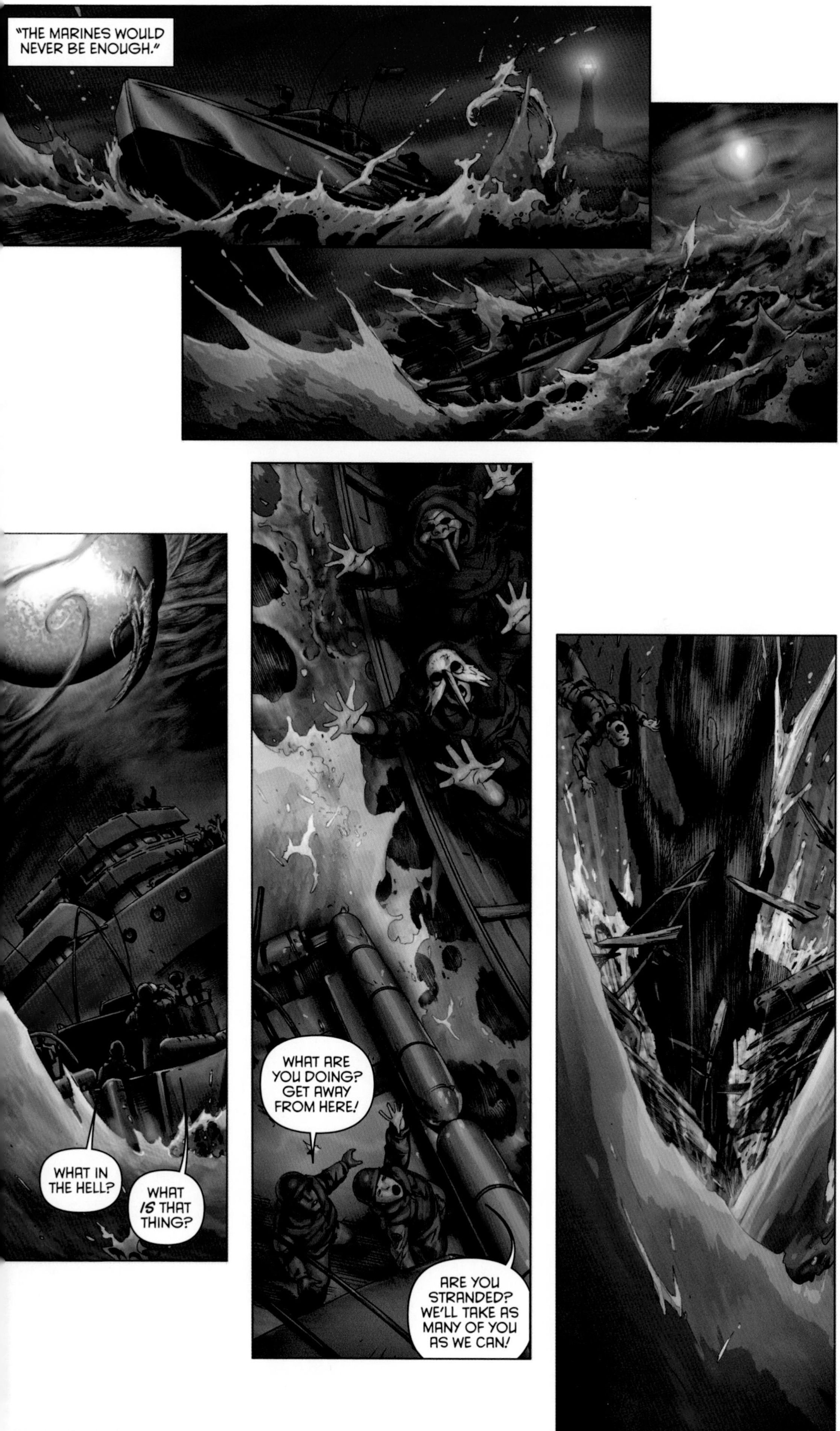
"THE MARINES WOULD NEVER BE ENOUGH."
WHAT IN THE HELL?
WHAT *IS* THAT THING?
WHAT ARE YOU DOING? GET AWAY FROM HERE!
ARE YOU STRANDED? WE'LL TAKE AS MANY OF YOU AS WE CAN!

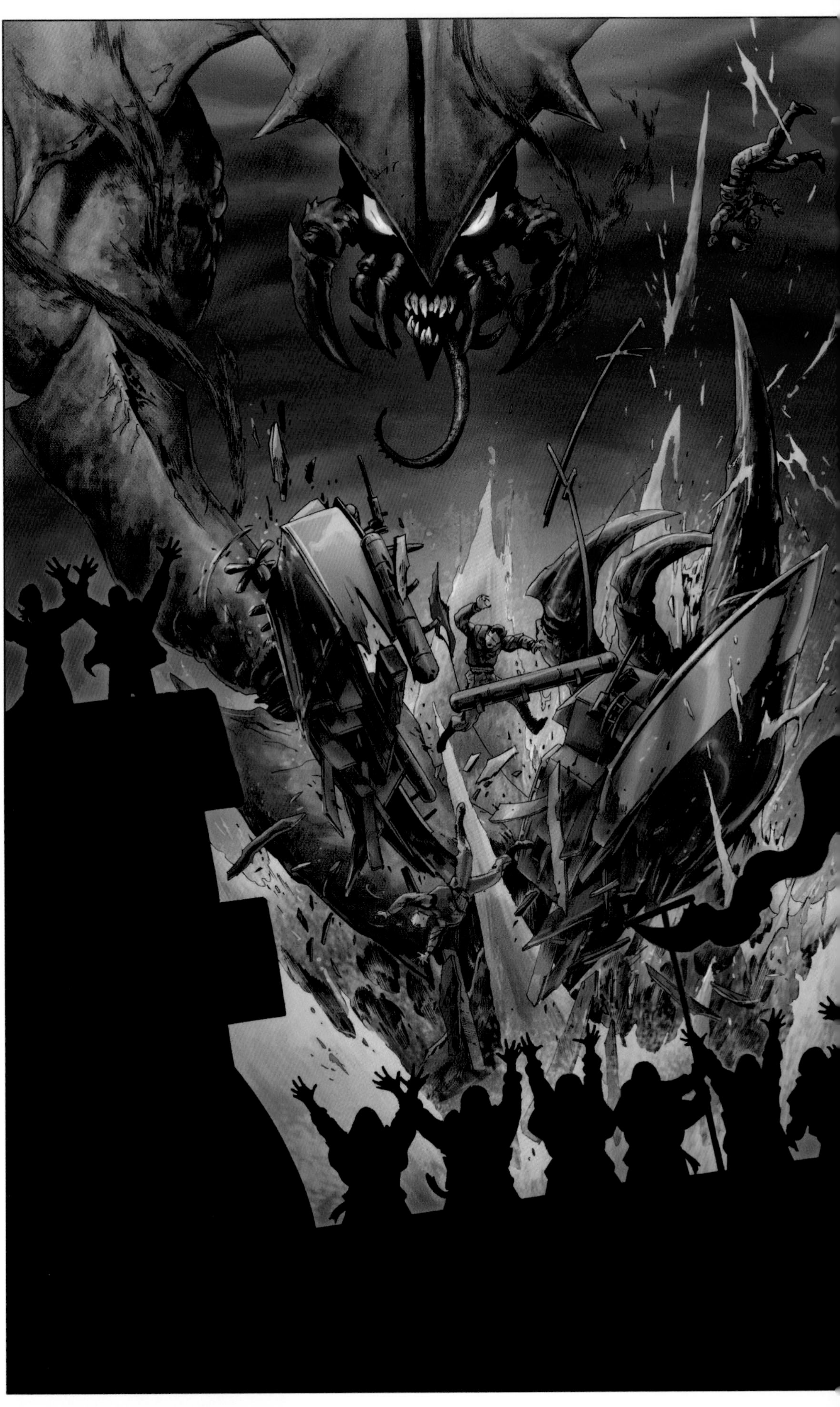

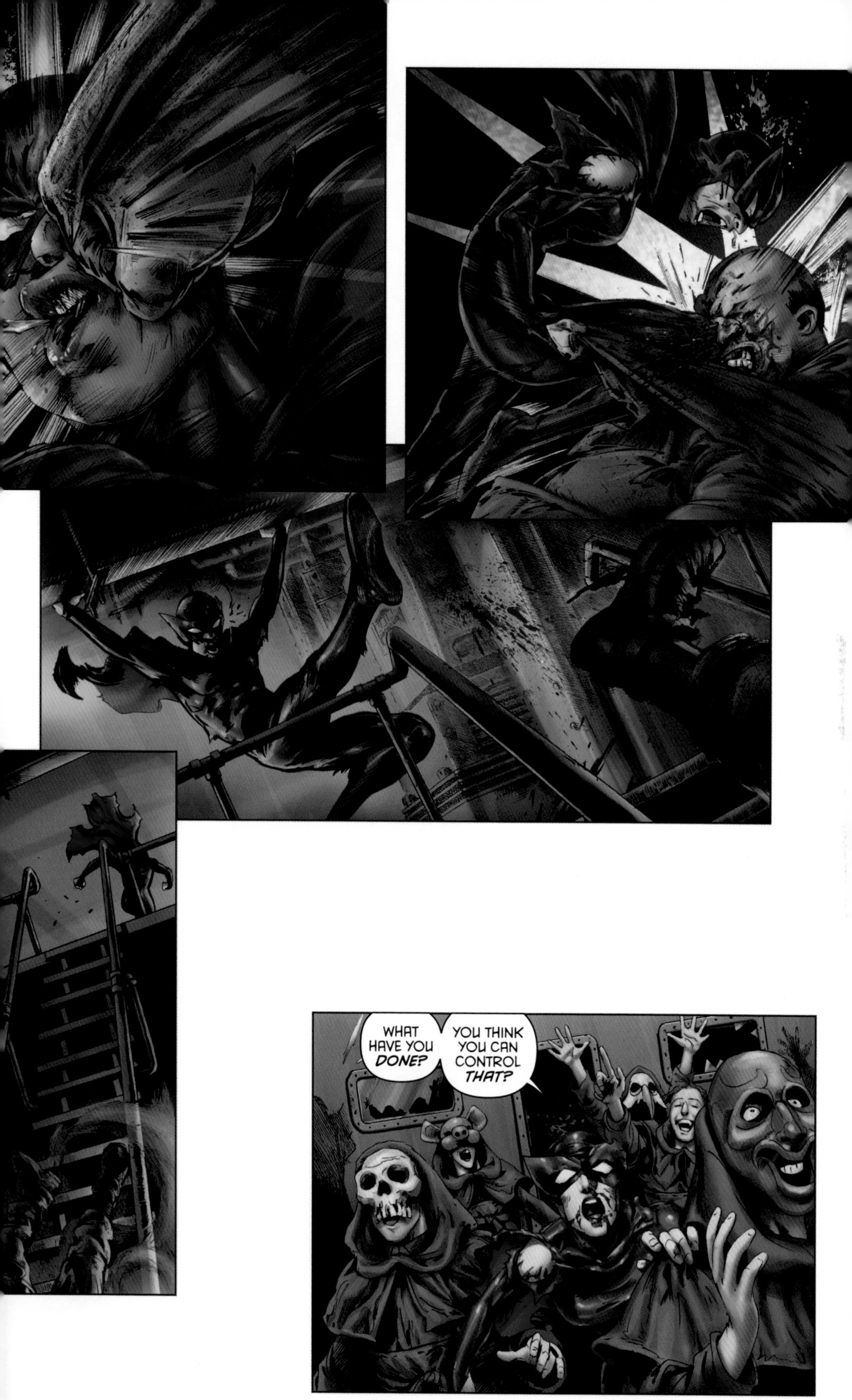
WHAT HAVE YOU DONE?
YOU THINK YOU CAN CONTROL THAT?

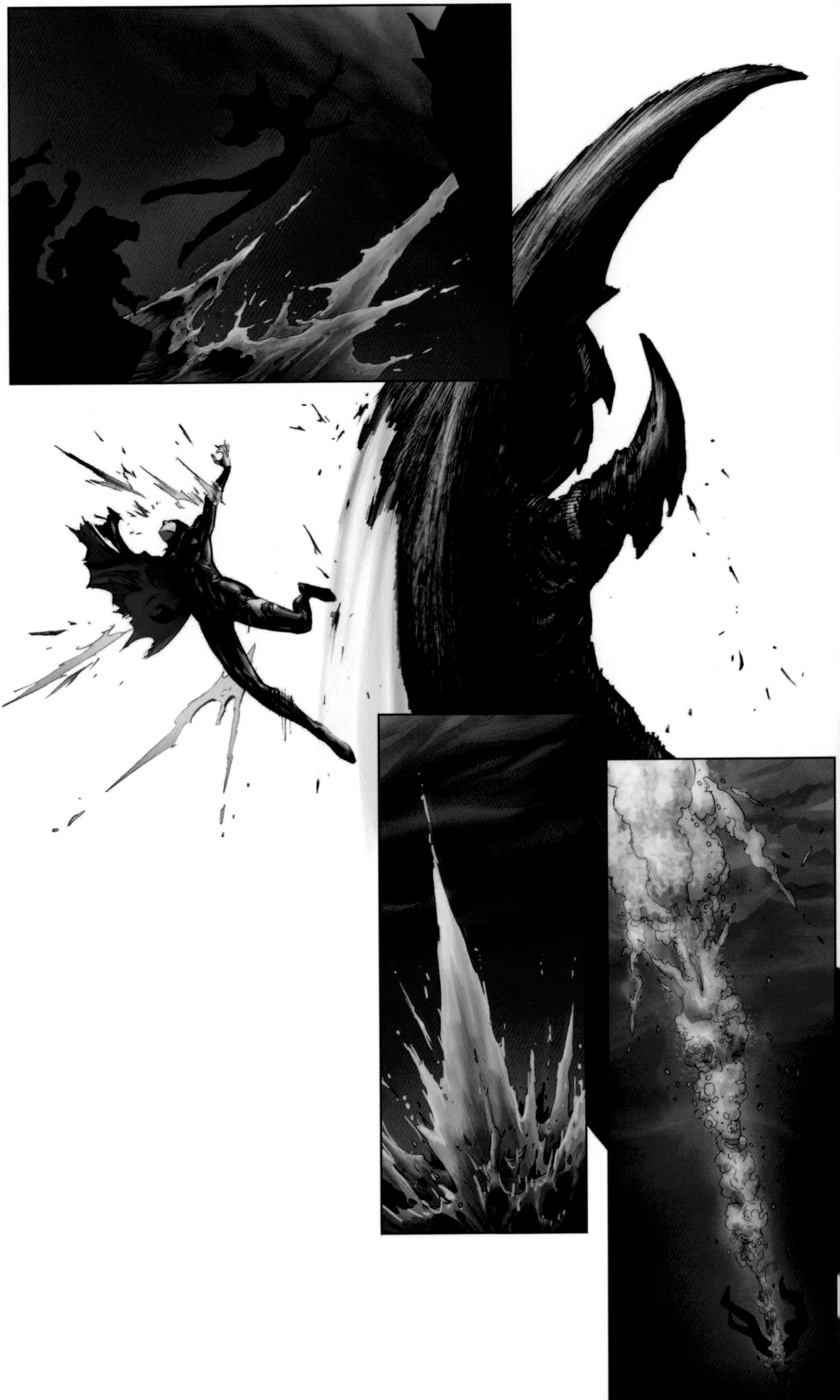

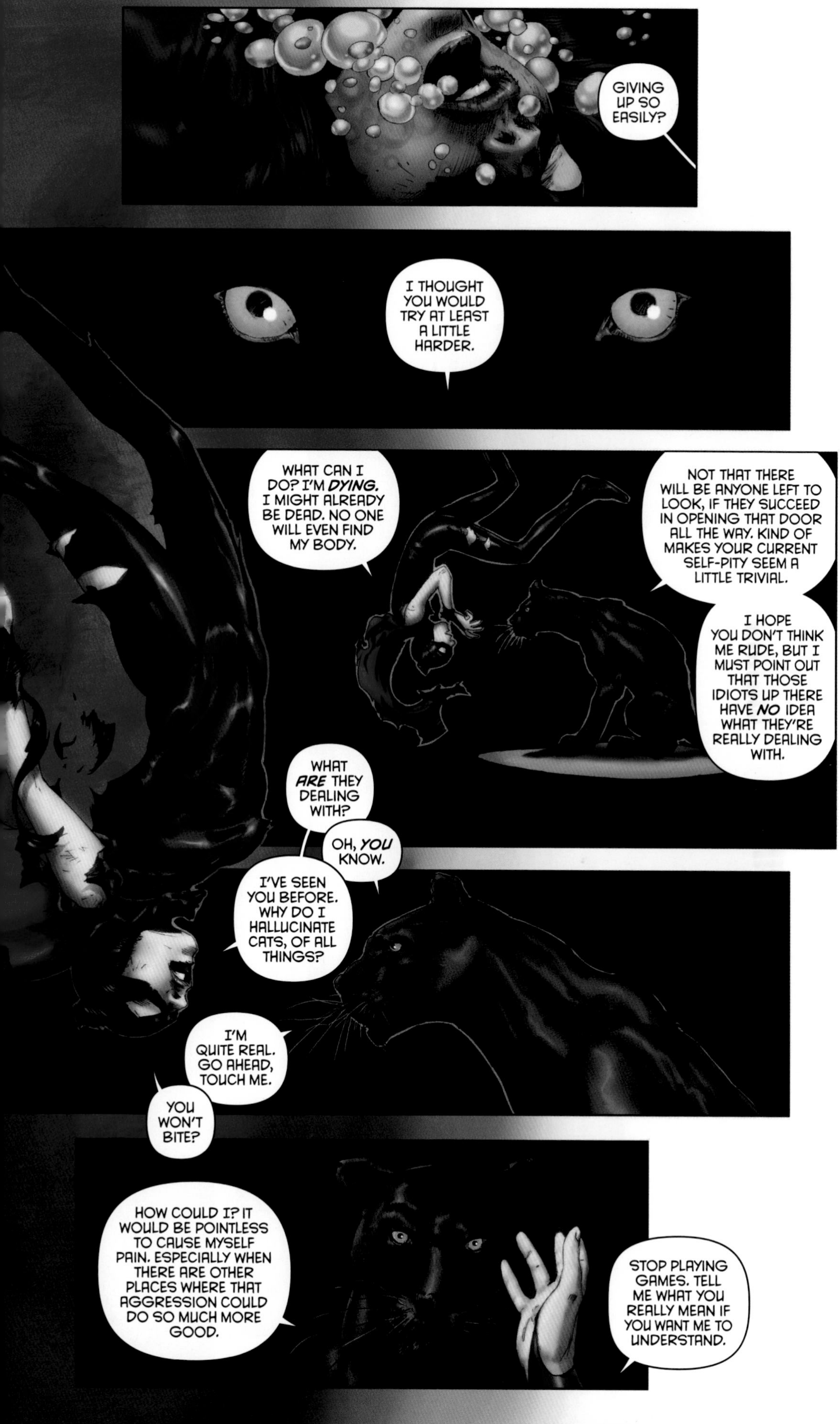
GIVING UP SO EASILY?
I THOUGHT YOU WOULD TRY AT LEAST A LITTLE HARDER.
WHAT CAN I DO? I'M *DYING.* I MIGHT ALREADY BE DEAD. NO ONE WILL EVEN FIND MY BODY.
NOT THAT THERE WILL BE ANYONE LEFT TO LOOK, IF THEY SUCCEED IN OPENING THAT DOOR ALL THE WAY. KIND OF MAKES YOUR CURRENT SELF-PITY SEEM A LITTLE TRIVIAL.
I HOPE YOU DON'T THINK ME RUDE, BUT I MUST POINT OUT THAT THOSE IDIOTS UP THERE HAVE *NO* IDEA WHAT THEY'RE REALLY DEALING WITH.
WHAT *ARE* THEY DEALING WITH?
OH, *YOU* KNOW.
I'VE SEEN YOU BEFORE. WHY DO I HALLUCINATE CATS, OF ALL THINGS?
I'M QUITE REAL. GO AHEAD, TOUCH ME.
YOU WON'T BITE?
HOW COULD I? IT WOULD BE POINTLESS TO CAUSE MYSELF PAIN. ESPECIALLY WHEN THERE ARE OTHER PLACES WHERE THAT AGGRESSION COULD DO SO MUCH MORE GOOD.
STOP PLAYING GAMES. TELL ME WHAT YOU REALLY MEAN IF YOU WANT ME TO UNDERSTAND.

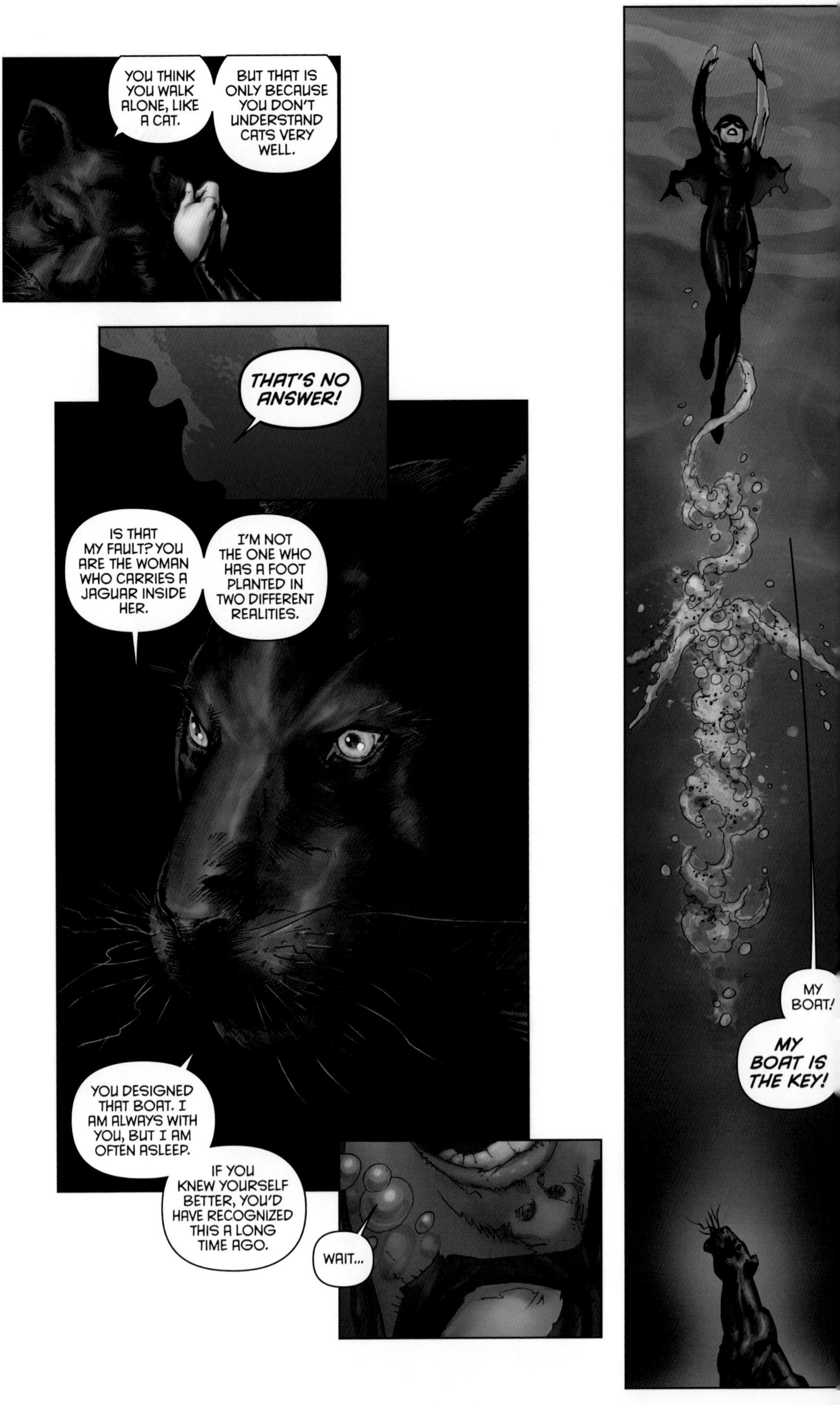
YOU THINK YOU WALK ALONE, LIKE A CAT.
BUT THAT IS ONLY BECAUSE YOU DON'T UNDERSTAND CATS VERY WELL.
THAT'S NO ANSWER!
IS THAT MY FAULT? YOU ARE THE WOMAN WHO CARRIES A JAGUAR INSIDE HER.
I'M NOT THE ONE WHO HAS A FOOT PLANTED IN TWO DIFFERENT REALITIES.
YOU DESIGNED THAT BOAT. I AM ALWAYS WITH YOU, BUT I AM OFTEN ASLEEP.
IF YOU KNEW YOURSELF BETTER, YOU'D HAVE RECOGNIZED THIS A LONG TIME AGO.
WAIT...
MY BOAT!
MY BOAT IS THE KEY!

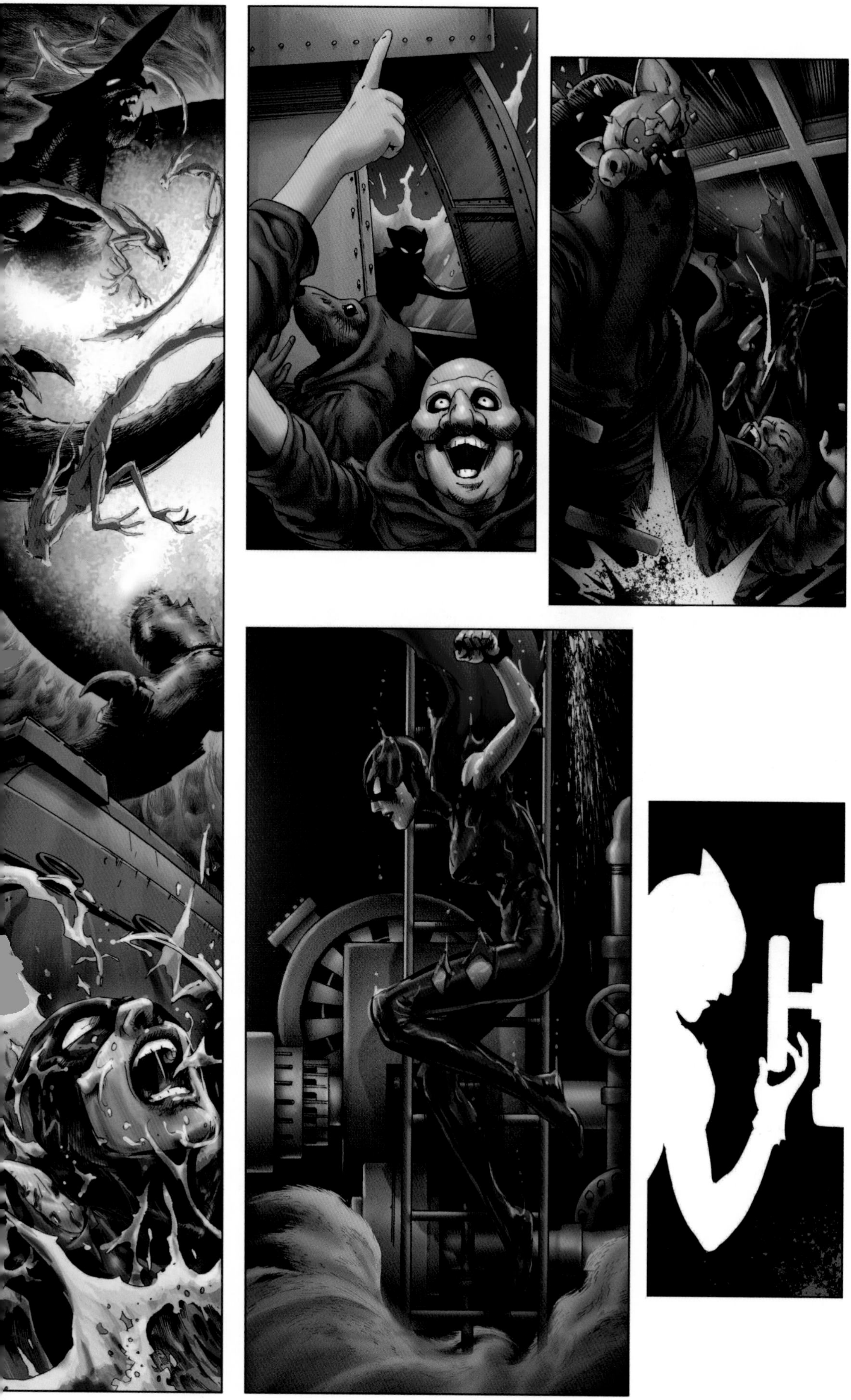

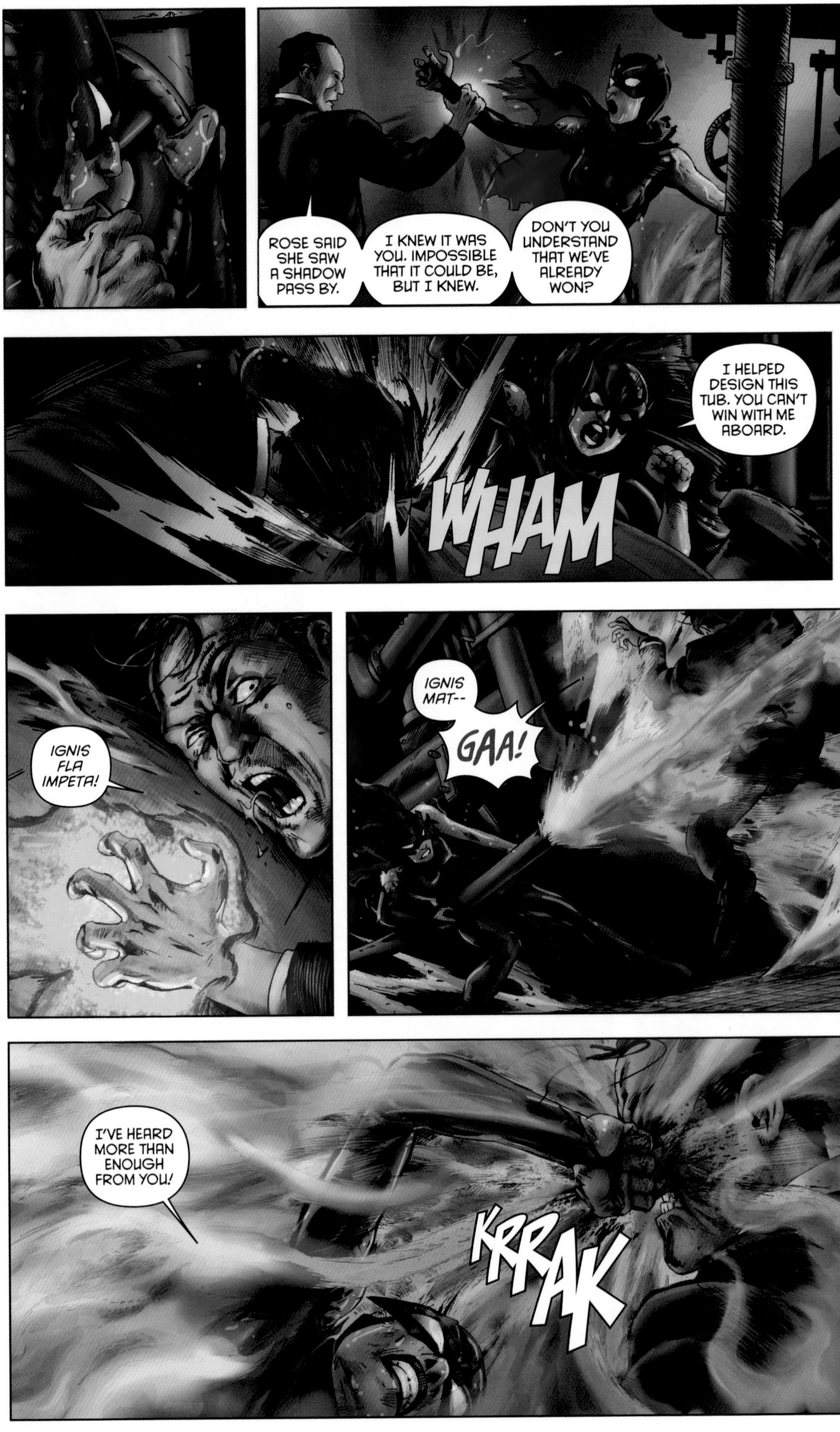
ROSE SAID SHE SAW A SHADOW PASS BY.
I KNEW IT WAS YOU. IMPOSSIBLE THAT IT COULD BE, BUT I KNEW.
DON'T YOU UNDERSTAND THAT WE'VE ALREADY WON?
I HELPED DESIGN THIS TUB. YOU CAN'T WIN WITH ME ABOARD.
WHAM
IGNIS FLA IMPETA!
IGNIS MAT--
GAA!
I'VE HEARD MORE THAN ENOUGH FROM YOU!
KRRAK

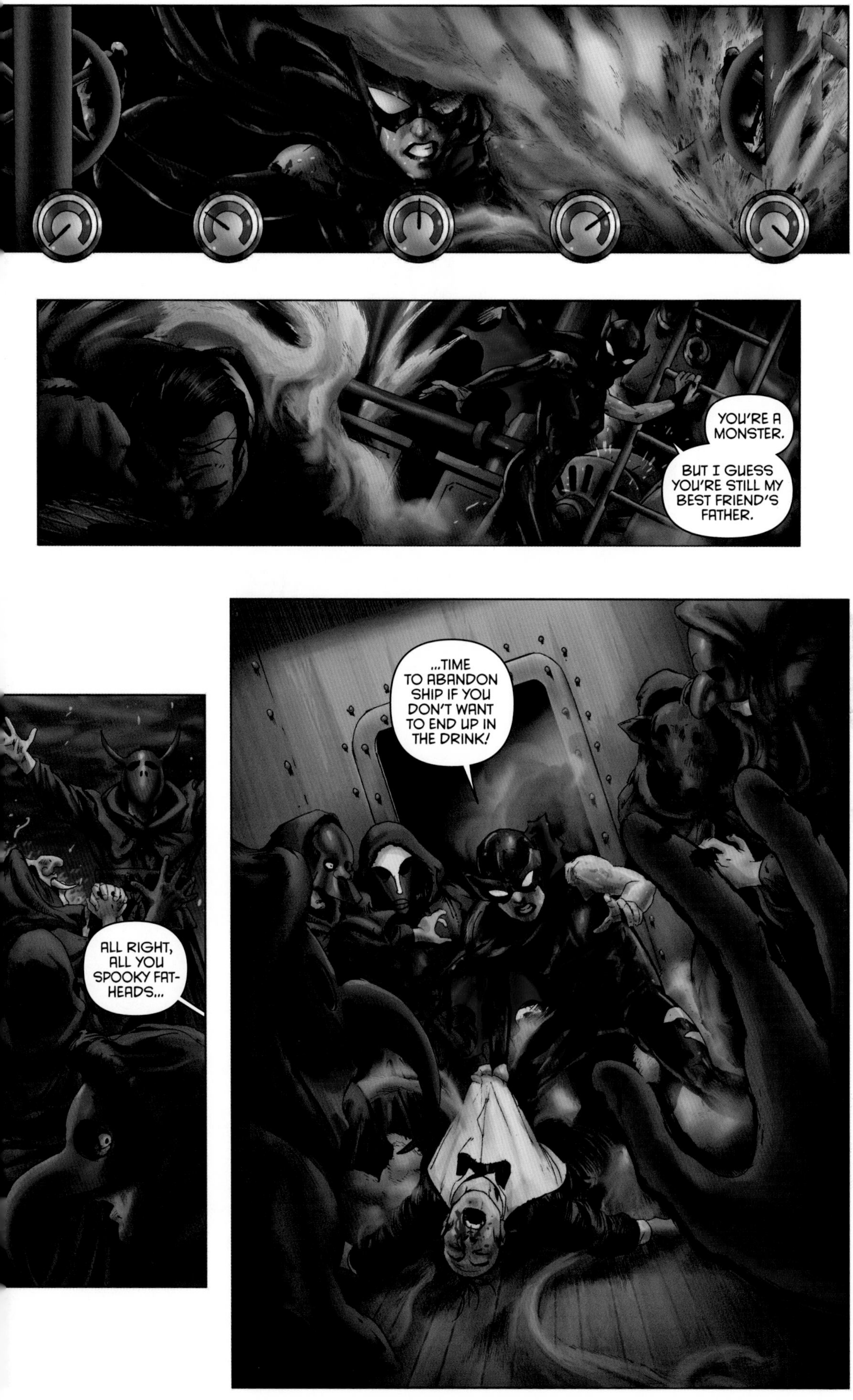
YOU'RE A MONSTER.
BUT I GUESS YOU'RE STILL MY BEST FRIEND'S FATHER.
ALL RIGHT, ALL YOU SPOOKY FAT-HEADS...
...TIME TO ABANDON SHIP IF YOU DON'T WANT TO END UP IN THE DRINK!

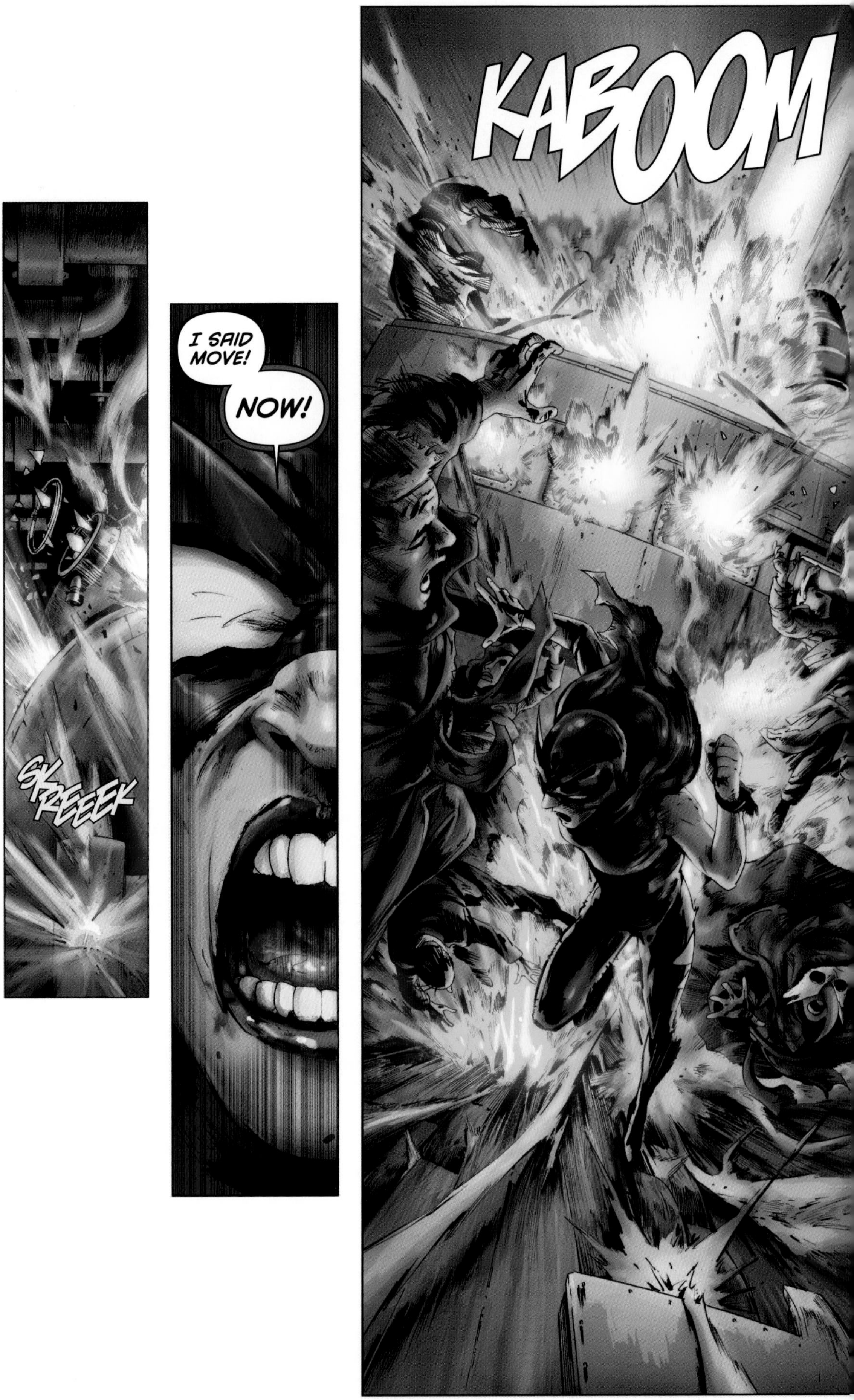

SKREEEK
I SAID MOVE!
NOW!
KABOOM

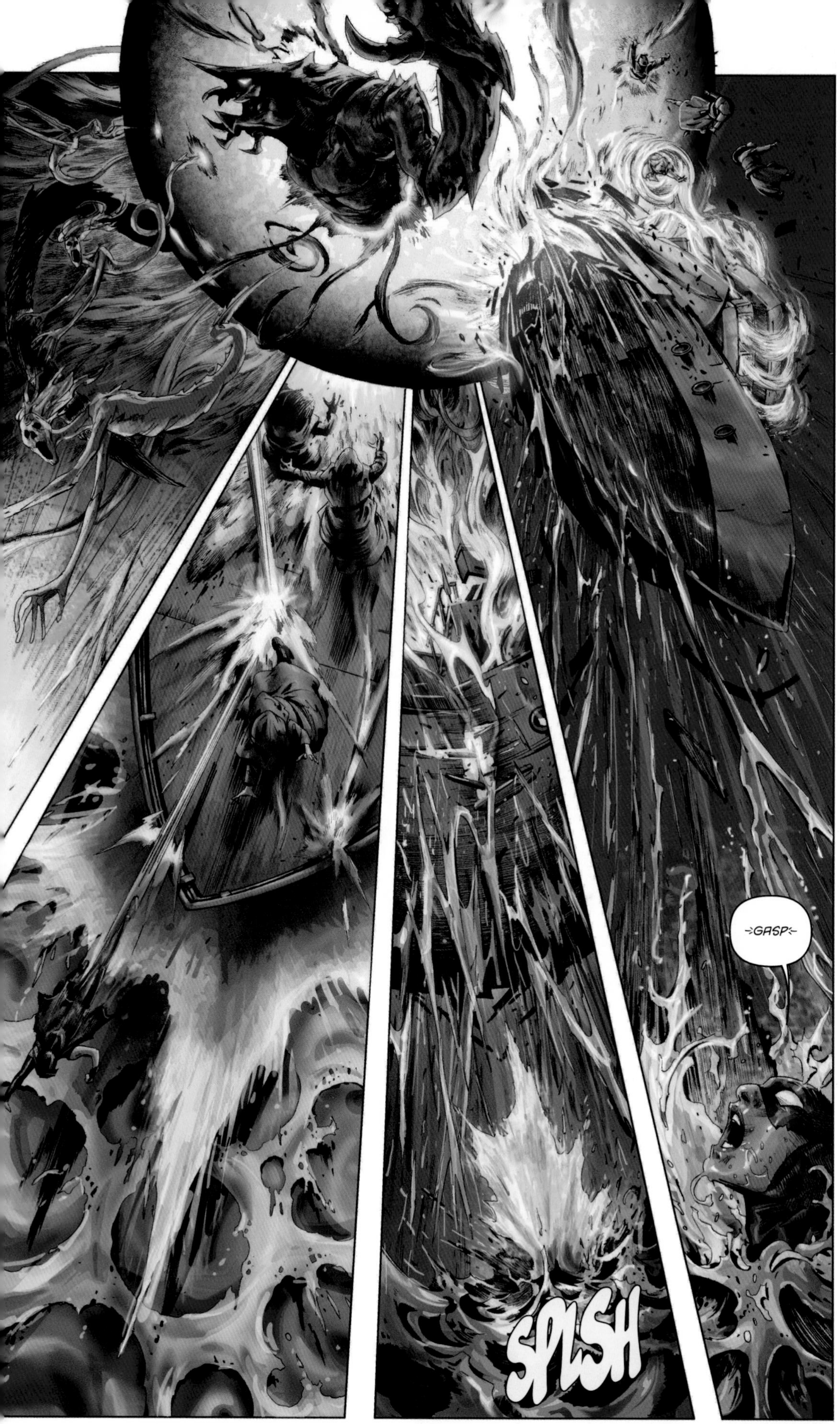

GASP
SPLSH

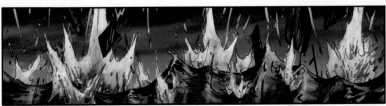

MAYBE I *AM* PART CAT...

BECAUSE I'M REALLY STARTING TO *HATE* BEING IN THE WATER.

AND WHAT THE HELL AM I SUPPOSED TO DO NOW?

WHUP WHUP WHUP WHUP

MARLA?

JOAO SAID YOU MIGHT NEED SOME ASSISTANCE?

WE'VE ALREADY RADIOED THE COAST GUARD TO PICK UP ANY OTHER SURVIVORS.

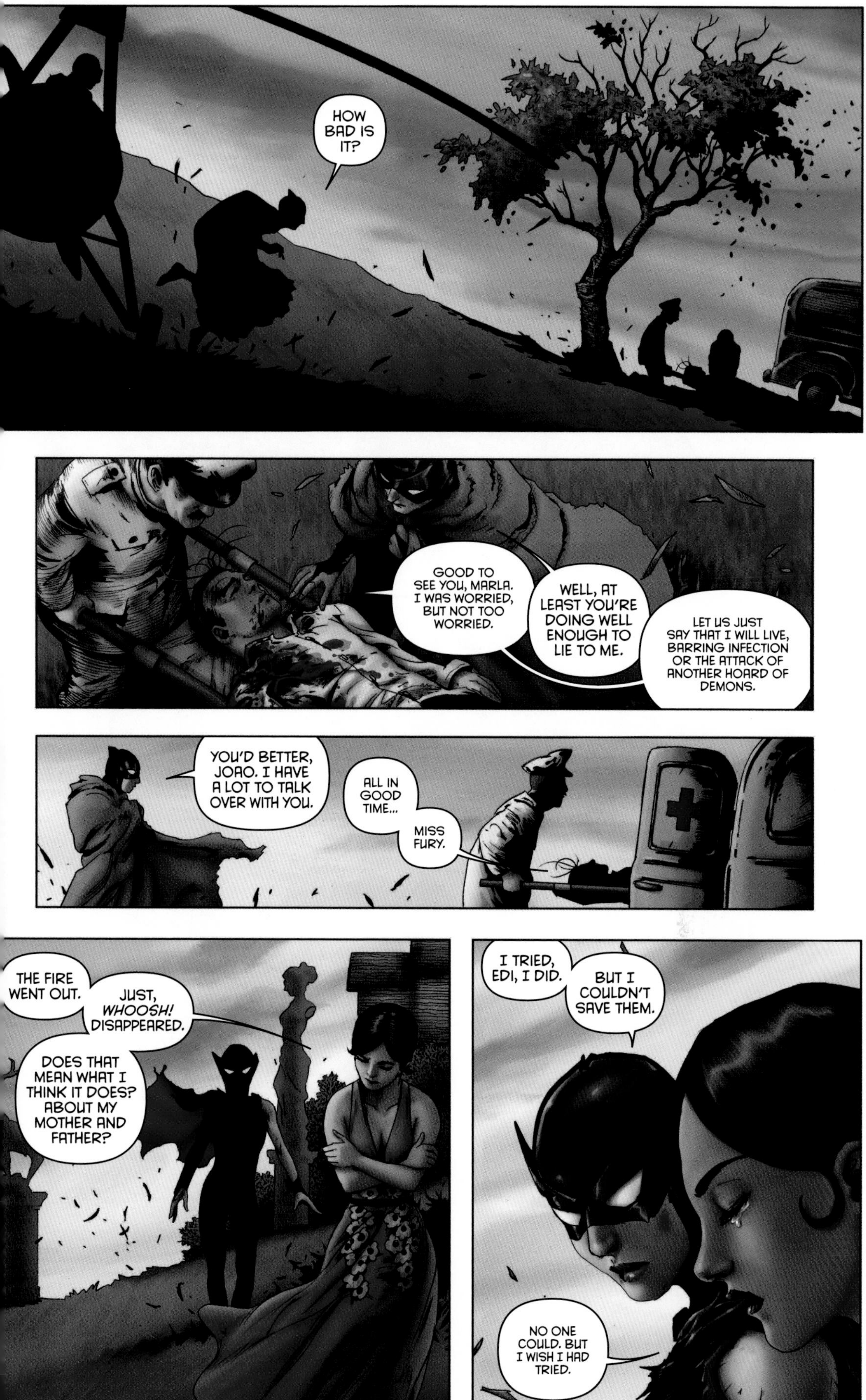

HOW BAD IS IT?
GOOD TO SEE YOU, MARLA. I WAS WORRIED, BUT NOT TOO WORRIED.
WELL, AT LEAST YOU'RE DOING WELL ENOUGH TO LIE TO ME.
LET US JUST SAY THAT I WILL LIVE, BARRING INFECTION OR THE ATTACK OF ANOTHER HOARD OF DEMONS.
YOU'D BETTER, JOAO. I HAVE A LOT TO TALK OVER WITH YOU.
ALL IN GOOD TIME...
MISS FURY.
THE FIRE WENT OUT.
JUST, *WHOOSH!* DISAPPEARED.
DOES THAT MEAN WHAT I THINK IT DOES? ABOUT MY MOTHER AND FATHER?
I TRIED, EDI, I DID.
BUT I COULDN'T SAVE THEM.
NO ONE COULD. BUT I WISH I HAD TRIED.

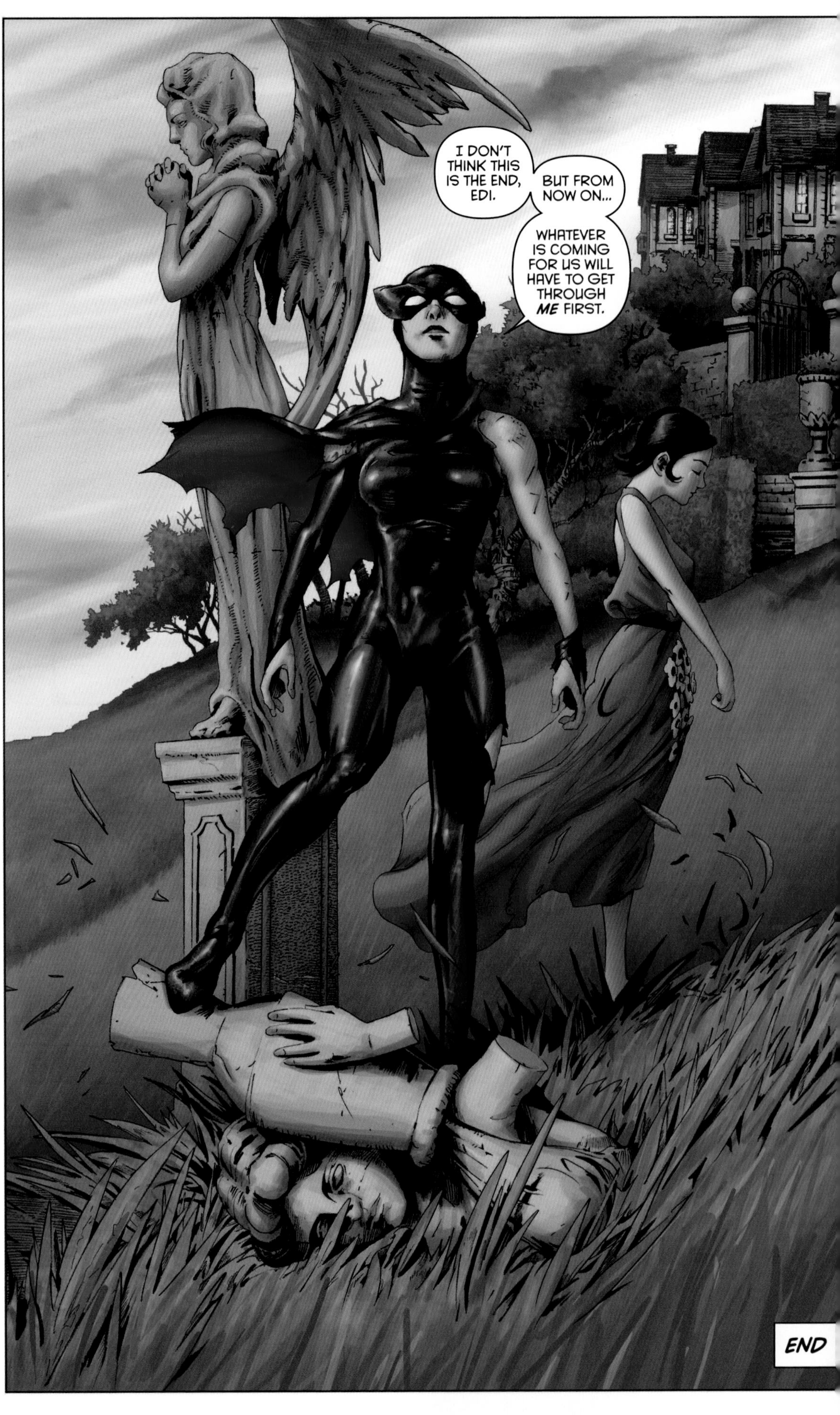
I DON'T THINK THIS IS THE END, EDI.
BUT FROM NOW ON...
WHATEVER IS COMING FOR US WILL HAVE TO GET THROUGH *ME* FIRST.
END

Bonus Materials

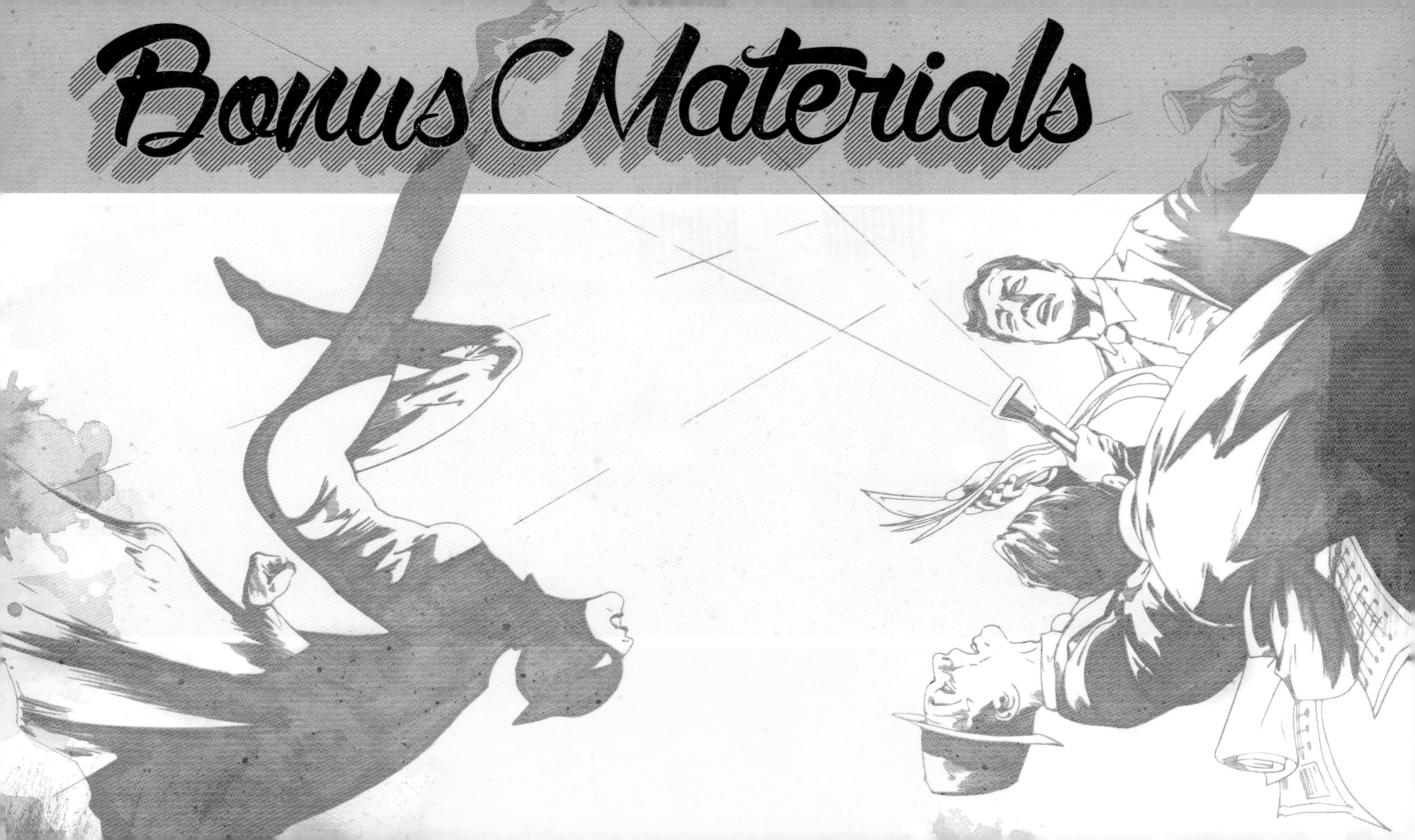

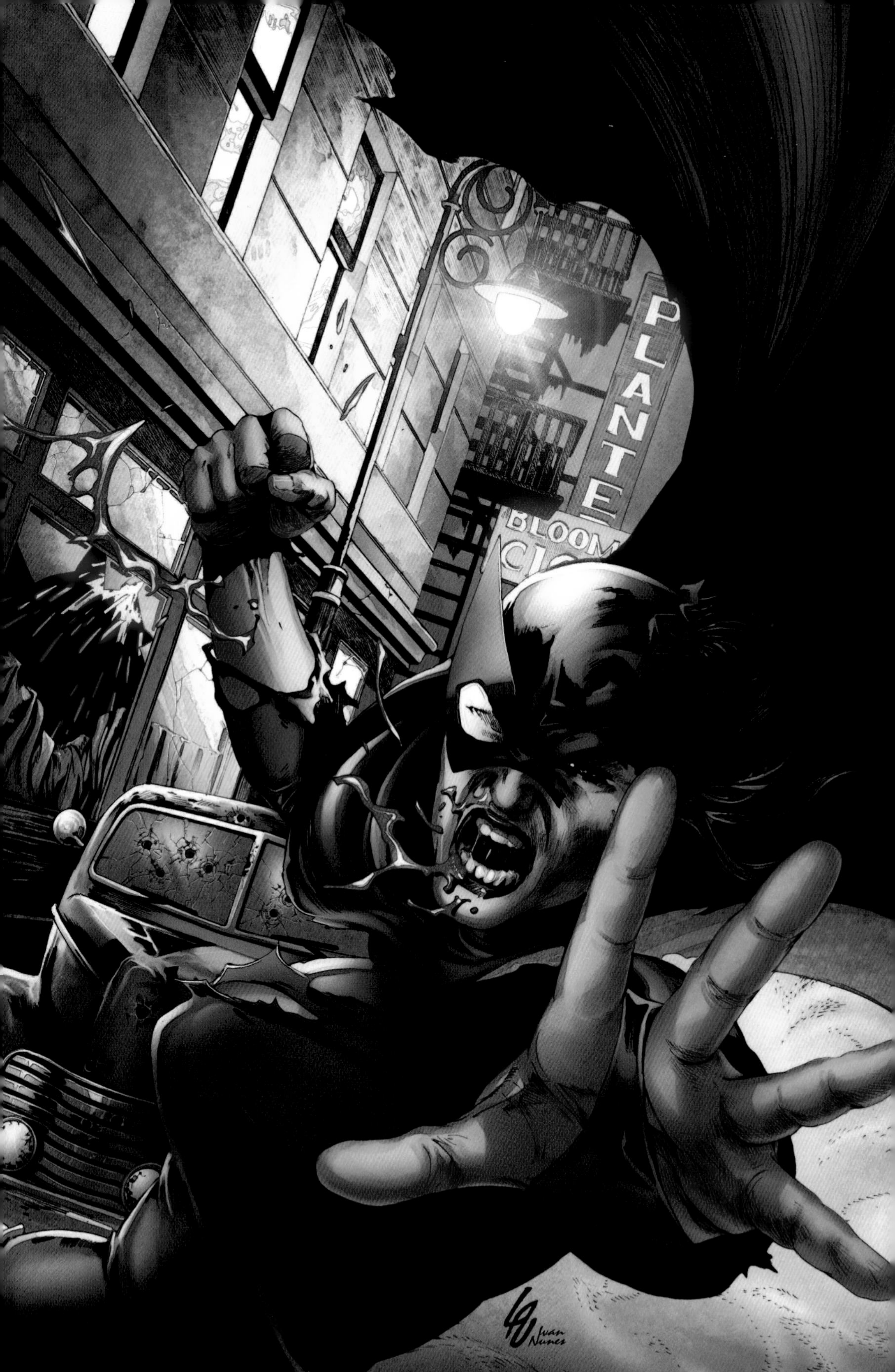
PLANTE
BLOOM
Ivan Nunes

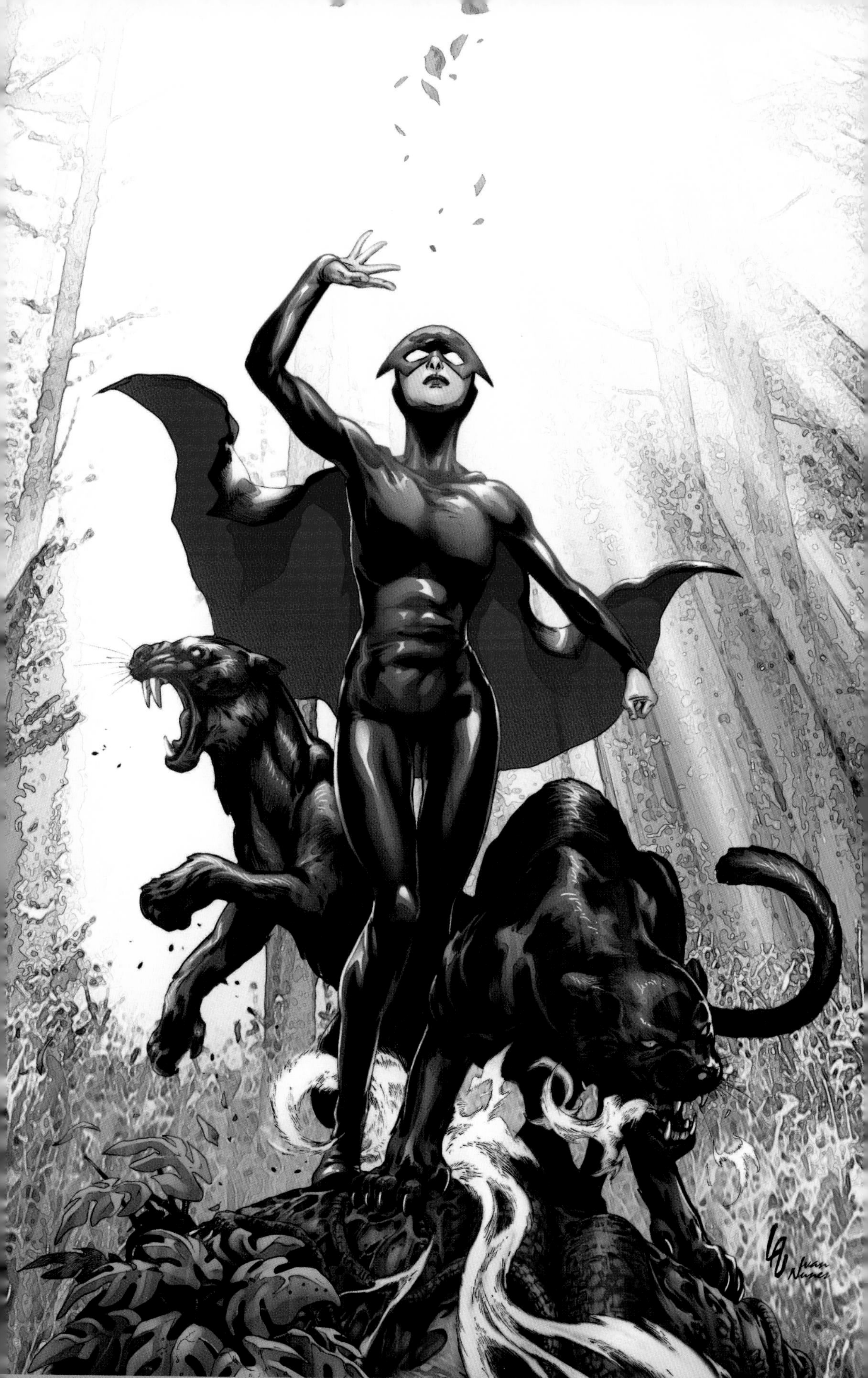
Ivan Nunes

Issue 2, Alternate Cover: Art by Jonathan Lau with Ivan Nunes

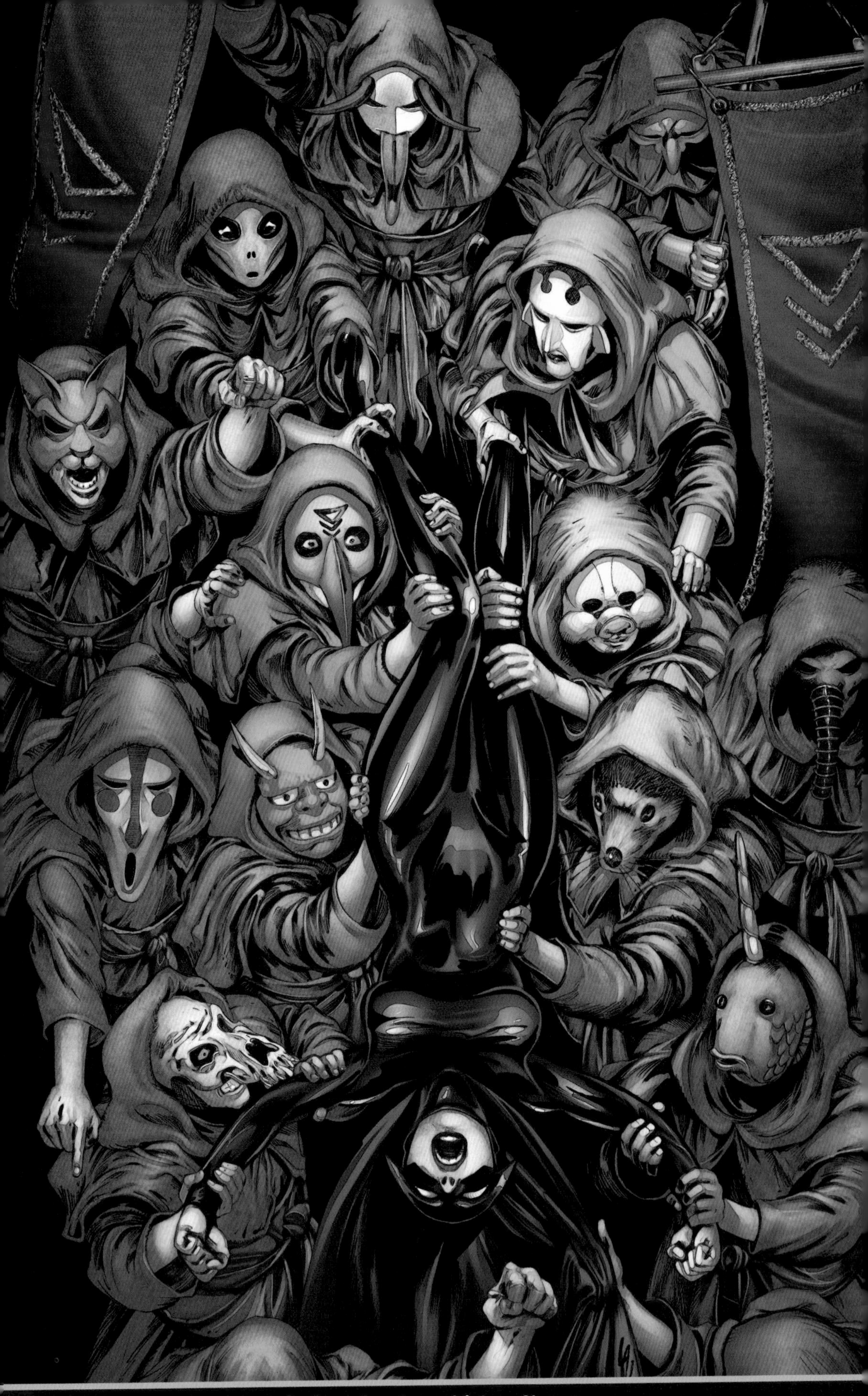

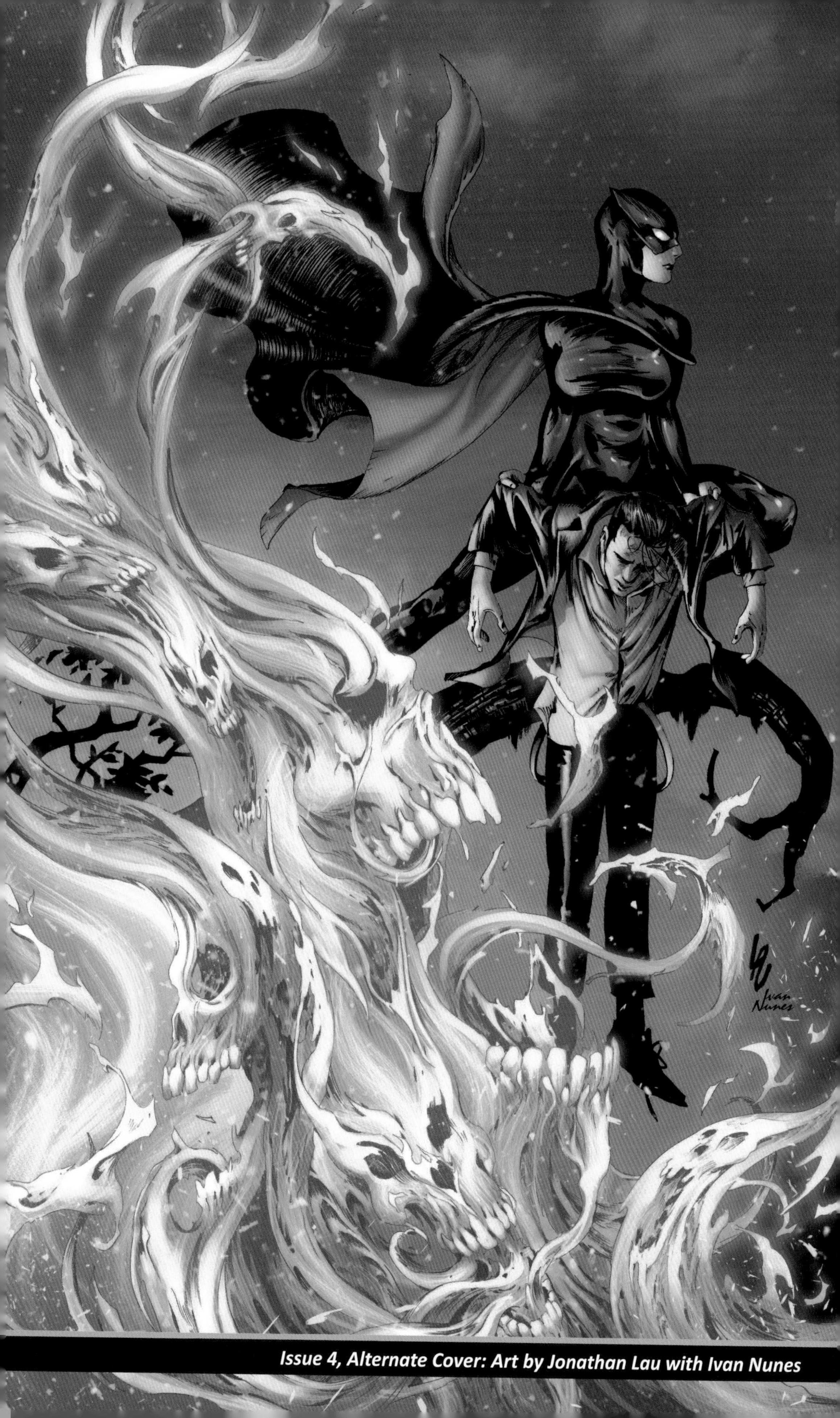
Ivan
Nunes

Issue 4, Alternate Cover: Art by Jonathan Lau with Ivan Nunes

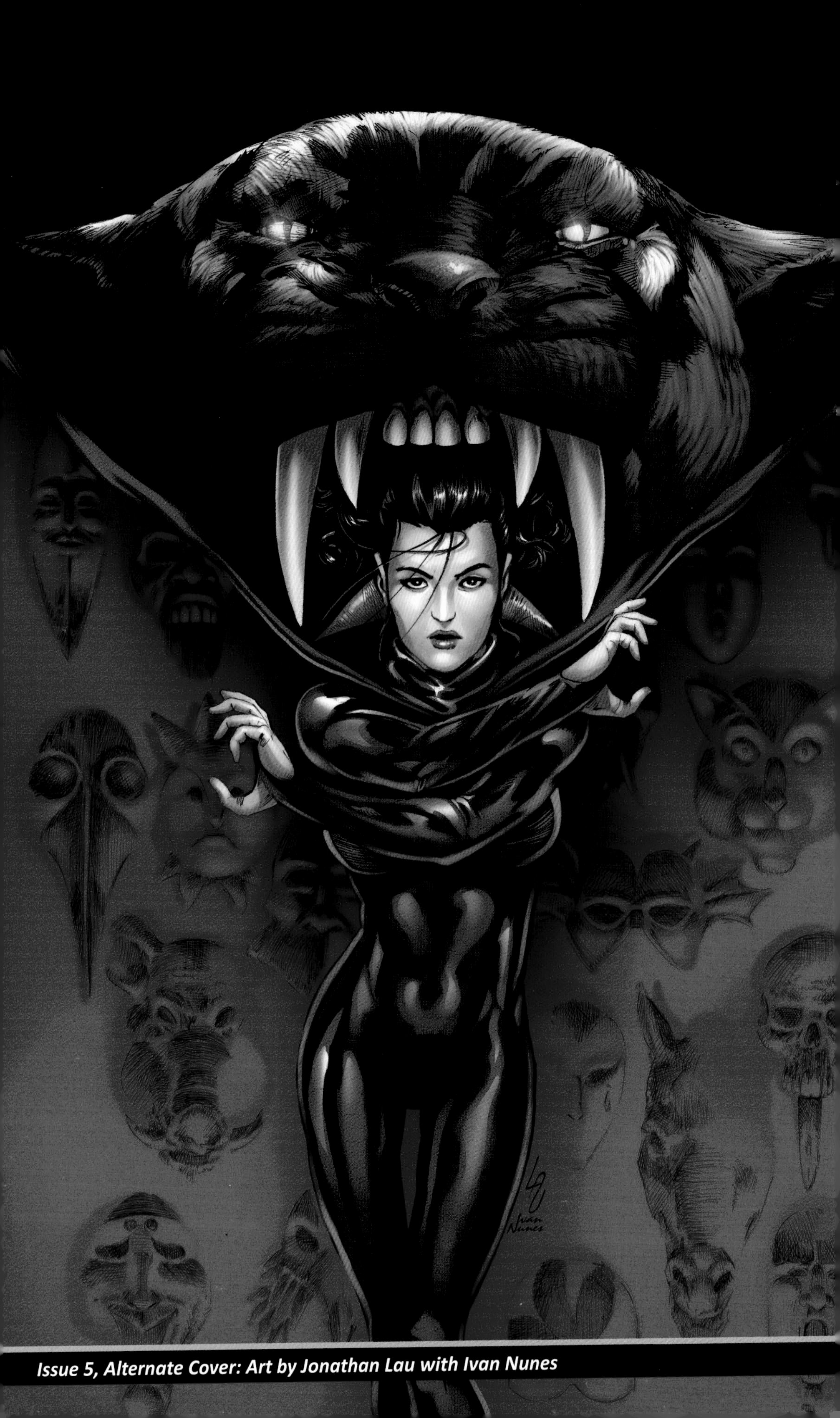
Lau
Ivan Nunes

Issue 5, Alternate Cover: Art by Jonathan Lau with Ivan Nunes